JESUS H̶̶̶

This Book has been Written,
Produced and Dedicated
To
The Glory of God

Jesus

Helps

me

Over one hundred Christian Testimonies written by ordinary people telling of God's extraordinary work in their lives

Published by
Christopher Stirling
2013

I am very grateful to all our contributors who have
helped to make this a very inspiring book, and
especially Peter and Yvonne Creasy who together with
Fred Maynard have persuaded some of their friends to
give their Testimonies for these worthwhile causes.

This Book is published by :
Christopher Stirling
15 Chapel Street, Steeple Bumpstead, Haverhill, Suffolk, CB9 7DQ
Email: yewtreehouse@btinternet.com

Printed & Bound by Berforts Information Press Limited,
Stevenage, Hertfordshire

Foreword

On 12th September, 2011, I heard the "small voice of calm" giving me the task of compiling and producing this book, He also gave me the title. Since then I have been appealing for Testimonies, as I was also told it had to be a big fat book!! Later, I was told there had to be at least 100 Testimonies.

The aim of this book is to show that it has been written by ordinary people. It shows how Jesus has helped us in the past, and how He continues to help us daily.

You will note that the title is in the present tense, as Jesus *really* does help people every day.

The Testimonies are placed in the book in no particular order. It is hoped this book will be a source of inspiration to all who read it.

The profits from the sale of this book will be shared equally between Steeple Bumpstead Congregational Church and the charities the Church supports:
> Samaritan's Purse
> The House of Joshua in the Philippines
> Bethesda Gospel Missions – India
> REACH – Haverhill, Suffolk

Christopher Stirling
June, 2013

Don't worry about anything; instead, pray about everything. Tell God what you need, and thank Him for all He has done. [7] Then you will experience God's peace, which exceeds anything we can understand. His peace will guard your hearts and minds as you live in Christ Jesus.

[8] And now, dear brothers and sisters, one final thing. Fix your thoughts on what is true, and honorable, and right, and pure, and lovely, and admirable. Think about things that are excellent and worthy of praise. [9] Keep putting into practice all you learned and received from me—everything you heard from me and saw me doing. Then the God of peace will be with you.

Philippians 4: 6 – 9
(NLT)

List of Authors and Their Testimonies

Many Testimonies were given without a title, so the following pages are here to assist the authors to find their Testimonies!

Contents

I

Am

Never

Alone

Because

JESUS

Is

Always

With

me

Addicted

"Addicted," there was no other word to better describe me. One particular sin, I knew it was wrong, but I just could not stop my self committing this sin every single day. I tried many times – the enemy (satan) kept telling me, "God won't mind, its only a little sin, nothing major!" But try as I could, I couldn't stop sinning.

Paul summed up my condition perfectly in his Letter to the Romans, Chapter 7, v. 25 as follows:

"So you see how it is: In my mind I really want to obey God's law, but because of my sinful nature I am a slave to sin."

One night I had a dream in that I was offered anything I wanted, it didn't matter whether it was right or wrong – I could have it. I agreed to accept a sinful act and was taken to a warehouse escorted by three men, I was led into an industrial lift, it was so big it was like a medium sized room! The lift gates closed behind me and the lift went very slowly down, down past the first floor.... then the second.... then the third floor and the fourth, before coming to a stop at the 5th floor down. It suddenly occurred to me that I was in the bowels of the earth and none of my friends, knew where I was. But then it didn't matter because I was going to get what I wanted, what I needed and that was the most important thing to me at that time. I was led into a room filled with every temptation I could possibly want and I was told, "what ever you want, you can have – anything goes here!"

Suddenly, I was coming round. I felt as if I had been drugged and not in complete charge of my senses and I was coming round. I realized I was in a bad situation, but how could I escape when I was five floors down?

I did then, what I should have done right from the beginning of my dream, I prayed in my mind "Jesus, help me." In a flash, even quicker than it takes to read these few lines, I was above ground and safe.

I truly believe that Jesus was showing me with this dream how I could escape from my addiction, how I could escape from my sin. Life was good for the next week or so and the dream began to fade.... And my addiction started again......

On 2nd November 2009, I realised my addiction was a sin which I couldn't stop, and I prayed, yes I got down on my knees and I prayed as I never had before, "Oh Jesus, please help me, please help me never to commit this sin again." Jesus heard my prayer and I am no longer addicted to that sin, I am free!

In the hymn "What a friend we have in Jesus", are these words at the end of the second verse:

"Jesus knows our every weakness,

take it to the Lord in prayer."

I can't think how many years I have been singing those words, but it is a lot! I had the answer to my problem all the time, but didn't put it into practice until after I had prayed so fervently! The years have now passed since I prayed that prayer and I am still free from that sin! All thanks to Jesus, He helped me, when I couldn't help myself, and He continues to help me every day!!

Chris Stirling

A Do It Yourself Problem Solved

One day I was doing some DIY at home, and I just could not work out how to do something. I prayed "Jesus, you were a carpenter, how do I do this?" Within a minute I had the answer come to me!! When I tell people this, they are really surprised!!

But why when we pray for answers should we be surprised? Jesus really does answer prayers!

Chris Stirling
Steeple Bumpstead

When I get 'Overdone' and It Is All Too Much,

He helps me to keep it simple. 'Temper with tranquility my manifold activity that I may do my work for you with utmost simplicity'.

I am just back from a break, and fortunate to visit the Loire Valley and just sit on her banks with a book & baguette. Looking up, a little daisy caught my eye & I watched it for a few minutes & this little ditty popped up:

Memories of my Holiday in the Loire Valley
September 2011

Hey little daisy on such a long stalk
How you reach up to the sky and long to talk, talk, talk.

On the banks of La Belle Loire you nod all day
Giving pleasure to this tourist and reveal all you have to say.

You open your face to the sun when it comes into view,

And smile as she 'gets' Pilgrim's * message about life's
stew, stew, stew.

Such are the glories of resting on the bank!
Our tired old tourist unwinds with so much thank,
thank, thank.

Your joys are so simple; who could perfect such an art?
Our Father in Heaven sends this message as straight as
a dart.

So go home, refreshed little punter and let it remain in
your heart
To take it gently, keep it simple; and hop in God's cart.

    * Reading Pilgrim's Progress beside the River Loire

'Lessons from Little Things'

I've come to realise that the most important events in
my life have been given to me by little things.
e.g. This one is about my 'Grace Grower'.
God's nature speaks to me through Nature. I'd planted
some tiny daffodil bulbs which flowered a bit early which
gladdened my heart. Then, wham! Hard frost & snow for
ten days. When they thawed, I could hardly believe the
beauty of the tender bright and smiley daffs, their
delight and joy completely unaffected by the frost &
snow. I think of the daffs as God's example of grace
when things get rough.

The other one, above, "Loire Little Daisy", is the joys of
simplicity.
God gives us peace when we ask for his wisdom.
One of my favourite verses in the Bible is when
Jesus grieves over Jerusalem :-
'O Jerusalem .... how often I have wanted to gather your
children together as a hen protects her chicks beneath

her wings...' The picture is of God's protection for us all. Apart from the obvious image of being warm under a down duvet, its not fun being on the receiving end of a broody hen's beak. And as for the hard primary feathers, they are like armour!

A person wandering through the ash after a forest fire found a charred shell of the mother bird. He investigated it and was astonished to find live chicks sheltering beneath.

That is how much God loves and protects us! I thank God for the way Jesus uses nature in his teachings.

Rosemary Watkins
Tilbury juxta Clare, Essex

"...I Listened to The Small But Insistent Voice.."

I could not have got through the greater part of my life without learning to trust Jesus and let him direct and protect me through many difficult times, especially with serious and life-changing illness and surgery. When I had to accept early retirement from teaching, a vocation which I loved, I asked through much prayer, how I could serve God: this led to me looking into several Christian charities, The one which impressed me most was Samaritan's Purse. I found out that one way I could get involved was by helping with Operation Christmas Child, and I did this for several years at the Chelmsford warehouse. The passion growing in my spirit gave me a real desire to be more involved, and in 2003 the area managers asked me to start something in the Sudbury area, and I found myself called "District Coordinator".

I prayed with a friend about the idea of starting our own little Satellite processing centre, and I really felt directed and supported by Jesus when there was so much to learn, and much to organise. God really never wastes anything, so my experiences of staff leadership, training and teaching helped to create a small team and some school contacts to run our first local campaign. God grew the work till in 2007 we were just so squashed, things were really difficult, and I said "That's it, no more shoebox campaigns .... unless Jesus finds somewhere bigger".

In 2008, my faith began to really rise, knowing that if God the Father wanted our local work to continue, His Spirit would help me find the perfect place, and His Son would give me the strength to move forward into a whole new plan. Late in July 2008, the small but insistent voice I had learnt to recognise as one I had to obey, directed me to go and have a coffee in a little cafe nearby. I went not understanding why, and God's master plan unfolded and Jesus steered me through such a lesson in faith. With only 1 customer in the cafe, the owner asked what I had been doing lately, so I mentioned about looking for empty premises in Sudbury, The other customer asked "Why?" and when I said "For the Shoebox Campaign" he jumped up and said "Oh, wow, shoeboxes, I was on the very first trip out to Romania with Dave Cooke in 1990" Now how could it happen that out of the whole county, the one person in Suffolk who really knew about the Shoebox Campaign was visiting this cafe at exactly the same time when I was too!

He swept me outside saying "You need to speak to Bob" as we met a man just walking past. "This lady needs a warehouse" he said (this wasn't the way my manual had told me to do things) and Bob gave me a card, asking me to ring later. I did, and was asked to go and see him next day at 9am. I went, not knowing who he was, and showed him the Christian Mission Statement for Samaritan's Purse, talked a bit about shoeboxes, and then was mystified when he suggested having a look round. We toured the Business Park, and as I rode along on my scooter listening to Bob offering cages, pallets, racking, parking, toilets, chairs .... and a WAREHOUSE, my jaw kept dropping. It transpired that Bob owned the whole business park! Despite feeling this couldn't be really happening, deep inside I just knew this was God at work, big time.

With all the paper-work completed, I had a phone-call from Head Office ... "ringing about the warehouse". "Oh, dear, what have I done wrong" I mumbled. "Nothing, we thought we would tell you that you are the first to register for the 2008 Campaign and as you have absolutely everything there, so you are now an *export* warehouse" Wow, that meant upping things from 3,000 to 10,000+ shoeboxes – yet the steadfast love of Jesus kept me steady and calm (mostly!) as we doubled the team from 50 to over 100, we organised vast amounts of forms, school visits, fillers, collections and team training, the very first of which was at this church in Steeple Bumpstead. It was so exciting to launch that huge campaign, praying that as we gave it all into Jesus' hands, everything we did would honour Him and that His love would be tangible. It would take a whole book to describe even some of the ways where people were touched by that love that flowed. His grace and enabling have allowed the Sudbury Shoebox campaign to continue to grow, with more schools visiting, more shoeboxes and fillers and more wonderful helpers joining the team. As I tackle each new challenge in being Coordinator for Samaritan's Purse, the passion for the work does not diminish – indeed I get more excited at seeing what God is doing through the various projects that the charity run, and I am thrilled to still be involved. I often fall far short of where I should be spiritually, but the fact is that I am Jesus' friend (John 15 v 15) and through Jesus Christ I have been given a spirit not of fear but of power and love (1Tim. 1 v 7) so I need to "always trust, always hope, always persevere".

Nena M Harding,
Samaritan's Purse

I Called Out "Jesus!"

Shortly after dusk on a fine summer's evening last year, I was driving my car along a road which was only wide enough for one car in each direction. As I rounded a corner I saw a car coming straight at me as it overtook three others. I called out "Jesus!" There was no crash, just the miracle of being and feeling safe. All thanks to Jesus!

Chris Blyth

An Answer to Prayer!

I'm a country girl at heart. My childhood home was situated on an unmade road in an area of coppiced bluebell woods & pasture land. We roamed the fields & woods, climbed trees & dipped in the local pond for frog spawn & newts.

Since becoming a Christian, in my early thirties, the world around me has taken on a new significance. I'd always known it is God's creation – but now I *really* know. I feel as though God reassures me of His presence through the skylark, the family of buzzards which soar over the house every day, a fox crossing the road late at night, the first snowdrop after the winter, a beautiful sunset & - of course - a rainbow.

Recently, my friend Pam & I were travelling to a meeting first thing in the morning. It was a few days after we'd had heavy snow, & it was still too cold for the snow to melt. The temperature overnight had fallen to -15C or so & it was still about -10C. There was a heavy rime frost covering every tree & even blade of grass, but the sky was blue & the sun was shining.

These factors combined together to give an effect I've never seen before. The deep snow covering the field sparkled like diamonds, as did the trees. Our journey was amazing, as was the meeting when we arrived. We certainly weren't the only ones to have experienced God through His creation that day!
My answer to prayer account is an example of how the Lord uses His creation to speak to us.

Rosie & I had arranged to meet to chat over the early stages of planning an "Alive@5" service. The group of clergy & lay people who organise Alive@5 had agreed with my suggestion of venue, & I felt quite passionate about it being at that particular church.

However, I was now having doubts. Was this what God wanted or was I somehow pushing my agenda through? The initial reaction from the church concerned had been lukewarm, rather than enthusiastic & I was worried I was forging ahead without approval.
We were combining our time together with her dog walking duties, so we donned our boots & set off. It was a grey, cool day, with no sun in view & the walk was unfamiliar to me. We talked about the forthcoming

service & I shared my misgivings with Rosie & said I needed to pray about it.

We'd been walking along footpaths until then, but had just started across a meadow. Rosie suggested we sit on a (convenient!) fallen tree to have a time of prayer. I expressed my fears & misgivings & asked the Lord to help me know His will on the matter.

No sooner were the words out of my mouth, but a small patch of cloud above us rolled back & the sun shone on directly on our faces. It was an amazing moment & we both felt that God had given us a firm sign of approval & a swift answer to prayer.

Wouldn't it be great if I could say that a profound response had burst forth from my lips? Alas not. What I actually said was "That'll be a yes, then!"
The Alive@5 service duly took place, with our own dear Ian & his family leading us in worship. The feedback afterward was very positive; with some saying it was the best Alive@5 since the very first at Tilbury juxta Clare. But only because God was in it.

Karen Hurrell

Jesus Saved me On The M. 25

On Friday 12th January, 2001, I was driving my van on the M.25 quietly minding my own business and concentrating on the road ahead, while I was overtaking a big lorry. Suddenly there was a loud **bang** quickly followed by another loud **bang.** I immediately looked in my wing-mirror to find that the lorry had hit the side of my van. Now, it was an enormous lorry – a six or eight wheeler with a trailer, huge in fact *(this sounds like a fisherman's story!).*

I expect you are wondering what the damage was? Well, apart from a couple of small dents on the van, there was hardly any damage at all. Due to the fact that the lorry had hit the van exactly in the centre, I was able to keep it on a straight course. If the lorry had hit the van at either the front or the rear, the van would have spun into the 3rd lane where the traffic was speeding well in excess of 70 mph, and I shudder to think what would have happened to me!

I did not suffer any injuries and the van had so little damage, I was able to drive it back the 40 miles or so to Saffron Walden. Later in the day, one of the ladies in my office said **"Someone *was* looking after you today!"** But when I think what could of happened, and it doesn't bear thinking about............... I just want to say **Thank You JESUS, Thank You Lord** .""" and to slightly alter the words of a fine hymn:

*Thank you JESUS, thank you JESUS, for **saving** me.*

Chris Stirling

How The Lord Helped me

The year was 1957. If I remember correctly it was the Sunday night of 16th August. when the Lord answered my cry for help.

In those days I was a very keen follower of traditional jazz, especially the English bands like Humphrey Littleton, Chris Barber and Sandy Brown. I used to travel up to Soho in London quite often to hear these and other groups playing. At that time I played, or should I say tried to play, the clarinet and my best friend Ben played the trumpet, his brother the drums, and another friend, Alan, played guitar.

One weekend most of us were very keen on going down to a well known Pub in Lee Green, South East London to listen to a jam session where lots of musician from the area would get together and "jam" for a couple of hours.

We were about to go in when Ben said, "I'm not going in". on being asked why he replied, "I've just become a Christian and don't feel its right to go in there."

We were quite taken aback and asked him what had happened. He explained that for some weeks on a Friday evening he had been going to Westminster Chapel in London to listen to a very famous Christian preacher, Dr. Martin Lloyd Jones.

On the last Friday night he felt he had to talk to the Doctor. (as he was known) and it was he that led Ben to Christ.

A few days later, I was with Ben and chatting to him about his new found faith. By the end of the evening in his front room, I knelt down to ask Christ into my life. When I got up again I felt that nothing seemed to have changed, not realising how the Lord works. The next two weeks after this prayer, in myself I became wretched, and seemed to deteriorate in my behaviour and language. I couldn't understand what was happening to me.

On a Saturday, a couple of weeks later, Ben invited me to a Christian youth rally at Welling in Kent. When we arrived the place was packed with young people. The evangelist tried to speak above the hubbub. I wanted to hear what he was saying and had a bit of an altercation with someone behind me. What I remember him saying was that if you really wanted to know God, challenge him to show Himself to you. To an 18 year old that seemed reasonable. That night on three occasions, I challenged God to do just that. (Can't we be arrogant!)

The next day I woke up feeling absolutely awful. It was like a hangover. As soon as I could I went to see Ben and when he opened the door something unforgivable for an 18 year old happened – I began to sob uncontrollably. I gave up trying to speak and had to go back home again. In the afternoon my parents saw something was wrong and asked me about it. I broke down again in front of my parents and started confessing to them some of the things I had been getting up to. Normally I would have expected them to be horrified by what I was saying, but they saw I was extremely distressed and were kind and even tried to encourage me, which didn't help.

Finally, that evening while I was laying down at about half past six, the dreadful blackness and horror came over me again. This was the third time. I wanted to pray but did not know how so in utter desperation I called out at the top of my voice **"Jesus"** Immediately the blackness went and I had peace. Such a wonderful peace.

A couple of weeks later I was reading the Bible (that in it self was a miracle) and read in the book of Acts 2:21, "Whosoever will call on the name of the Lord shall be saved". I didn't know that promise, but God honours all His Promises.

I was in a moment of time transformed and became a follower of Jesus Christ. The Evangelist was right, I had challenged God to reveal Himself and His Presence and He had made me aware of my spiritual state and the ugliness of my sin. He forgave me all my sins. Thank God for Jesus and His saving power.

Fred Maynard

There is Power in The Name of Jesus!

On this particular day I was busy in the kitchen – tidying up the way you do. I opened the fridge door and, while there, decided to pick at a piece of cooked chicken which looked really appetising. I popped it into my mouth and chewed, then swallowed. Suddenly the food, which was a little dry, got stuck in my throat and I couldn't breathe. I knew what I needed was the "Heimlich Manoeuvre" but, of course, you cannot apply it to yourself. Within seconds my thought patterns had worked through the fact that I couldn't phone anyone or rush out to a neighbour as they were at work. There was no time and I realised that I could suffocate! As I couldn't speak, I couldn't even pray! So I raised my hands and in my heart said the word 'Jesus' and immediately the meat flew out of my throat and mouth and pinged across the room. *There is power in the name of Jesus!* And I am alive to tell the tale.

Jennie Papa

Prayer Mends a Broken Tooth

Some church members will remember that while on holiday early in 2011 I had an accident and came home with a very colourful face and a very swollen eye. Whilst in Abu Dhabi I decided to do a 'hop on / hop off' bus tour. I left my seat at the back of the bus and moved forward to speak with the driver while we were stationary when I stepped out onto nothing (there was a step in the middle of the bus which was not particularly visible) and I went flying down the bus. I managed to hit my head and face on the way down and caused quite a stir among the passengers! My eye came up almost immediately, finally closing up by that evening, and the colours of my face over the next few weeks went through

34

the rainbow spectrum. Amazingly I felt no pain, not even a headache, either at the time or during the days and weeks that followed – surely a miracle!

About 3 months after this incident I was due for a routine dental check up, and during this I was x-rayed. Afterwards the dentist rang me up at work; asked me if I had received a blow to the head recently, and asked me to come in to see her. She showed me the x-ray displaying one of my teeth clearly fractured and separated below the gum line. I was told the tooth had to come out. Well, I came away quite horrified as you can imagine, but decided to believe God's Word rather than what the dentist had proclaimed over me. I stirred up my faith and took the authority I have in Jesus and spoke to my tooth, telling it that it was perfect and that the next time it had an x-ray it would show itself to be so, being fully restored. Time passed and I changed dentists, and during the initial consultation yes, you've guessed it, I was x-rayed. Once these were developed, my new dentist announced that the x-ray had shown nothing at all wrong. Now that really is a miracle!

Jennie Papa

Call upon Me in the Day of Trouble
Psalm 50 v.15

The year was 1978. It was a very cold March outside our home situated on the western end of the picturesque market town of Pickering, North Yorkshire. How we came to be living there instead of our familiar surroundings in South East Essex is a long and involved story.

My son, who had just celebrated his fourth birthday in February, was gravely ill but I was unaware of the seriousness of his condition. He was lying, propped up

35

with cushions, on the couch in our living room and his breathing was very shallow and erratic. Was he breathing? Yes, but only just; his condition was deteriorating and his body temperature was sky-high. I suddenly felt an urgency to call for help as by now I realised we were at the point of losing him. In desperation, I called out to God from my heart.

His condition had been of concern since January and my wife had wearied the doctors with requests to do something about his breathing which was laboured and erratic at nights. They assured her that his cough was a result of whooping cough and after a brief course of medication left the condition to clear in its own time.

In March, my wife was admitted to hospital and to cheer my son up I had walked two or three miles along the high Bempton Cliffs, near Bridlington, with him on my shoulders, to visit the colonies of Puffins and particularly a rare nest of Gannets. The countless numbers of sea birds of all kinds was a never-to be-forgotten sight. Alex's condition did not improve, but worsened.

By now he was unable to walk the few steps to his grandmother's house and was only taking small quantities of water. My wife insisted I call a doctor immediately and late in the evening I called the duty doctor, who was none too pleased at being called out from Newton upon Rawcliffe to see a patient he had already seen several times. However, after asking a few questions, he came out immediately and after a brief examination decided my son was suffering from a life threatening chest infection and phoned Scarborough Hospital to book an urgent admission. He asked us to take him to hospital immediately rather than await an ambulance. We wrapped him in a warm blanket and set out on the twenty mile journey to Scarborough General where we were met by a small team of hospital staff who took him to a prepared private room. His fluctuating high temperature prevented any immediate attempt to clear his lungs which were filling with fluid, despite our attempts to clear them. It was crucial to stabilise his body temperature which was eventually achieved after 7-8 hours with the help of nebulisers and other equipment. Finally, his condition was diagnosed as bronchiectasis, the first case they had had in thirty years. The hospital staff were puzzled as to how this chest infection had been neglected and allowed to get out of control but accepted that we were not to blame as we had made many visits to the doctors.

A consultant chest surgeon from Castle Hill Hospital, Cottenham, North Humberside, Mr Moghissi, was called in to take charge of the situation as the staff were not confident enough to operate on such a young child. Tubes were passed down into both lungs and the fluid removed. 3-4 pints were drained and the surgeon was amazed that Alex had survived with that quantity of fluid and so little of his lungs able to function. X rays showed darkened areas which indicated permanent damage. Further drainage and possible removal of part of his lungs was thought necessary and after a few more days at Scarborough, he was moved to Castle Hill Hospital under close observation. Mr Moghissi even drove him around in his sports car. You can imagine Alex's reaction to that treatment!

Fortunately, the infection cleared up and no surgery was required other than further drainage of his lungs and after a couple of weeks he was allowed home. His respiratory system was much weakened and it was thought that his growth would be affected and he would be susceptible to infections throughout his life.

My wife and I had learned to call upon God for His help in time of great need and watch Him respond. The second half of Psalm 50 v.15 says, "I will deliver you, and you will glorify me".

Alex made a full recovery and enjoys good health and is (almost) as tall as his mother, at 5'10". His lungs are exceptionally good and show no sign of damage or weakness. He made medical history and the hospital records-if they have survived- would be the only evidence that there was ever a problem. But we can never forget God's faithfulness.....

Peter Creasy

The Only Prayer We Knew was The Lord's Prayer

My upbringing was not in any way religious as my mother had been compelled to attend church three times on a Sunday as a child (probably to keep her clean and out of mischief) and was far too busy scraping a living after World War II finished to spend time in church. Their car, like all others on coastal areas, had been impounded to prevent it falling into enemy hands and left in an open compound for years, causing it to rust beyond repair. My father bought a pony and trap and used it to convey his building materials and family about, or we travelled by bike. Tragedy struck when I was about two when he first contracted pneumonia, then later cancer, dying when I was four. We were left with nothing and moved to a 'holiday home', a timber shack with no proper foundations at Lakeside, on Canvey Island in the Thames Estuary. I attended the local school and dull assemblies which were led by the headmistress who sang in the robed choir at the local

Anglican church. Mum worked first in a factory making Army great coats, then later, very long hours in a seaside amusement arcade during the summer. Once the season ended, we depended on 'National Assistance' which was not granted if you had more furniture than beds, chairs and a table in the home. My great-aunt Evalyne, still the pearl stringer for The Goldsmiths Company at 82 years of age, occasionally sent bags of drab, crepe materials from Finchley, for mum to cut down and make fresh dresses for us and lamb stew was our main food. If I am ever served with it again, I shall probably be very sick, even before I eat it!

You would have thought the situation could not deteriorate but on the night of 31st January, 1953 we were aware that something unusual was happening. The normally strong winds seemed exceptionally so and there were reports of extremely high, rough seas. I was awakened at about 1 am by my mother shaking me and telling me to get out of bed quickly. I stepped out of bed into freezing cold salt water and drew my breath sharply in shock. Mum grabbed a blanket and we went into our small front room and sat on the couch arms, but not for long, as the water crept higher. Everything was straining and mum, worried that the door would be smashed in, opened the front and back doors to let the water pass through. It was a horrible sight. By the pale light of the moon we could just make out fish boxes, dead chickens and other debris being swept along in the water in the eerie stillness and darkness. I had suggested trying to walk to a neighbour's taller house but now we realised that to attempt this would only mean us joining the mass of debris being swept along by the tide.

Mum asked me to stand on the dining table and try to open the trapdoor leading to the loft, so we could climb clear of the water but as I banged frantically at the bolts, it became obvious that they had been painted up and were not going to move and I was not going to be able to smash my way through the ceiling. Mum was barely 5' 2" tall and she was standing on the couch arm, whilst I realized that the dining room table was now floating and I needed to keep my balance. By this time it must have been about 3am and we knew that unless something drastic happened we were going to be drowned. When we returned to the house, 3 months later, the silt mark on our walls was at 4 foot.

For some reason, I suggested to mum that it might be a good idea to pray and she agreed. The only prayer either of us knew was the Lord's Prayer, so we decided that might connect us to the Almighty and we prayed sincerely and desperately. Then we waited....and waited....and eventually realised that the water had not come any higher since we prayed. At about 8am we heard police with megaphones urging anyone in earshot to gather a few belongings and make their way to the nearby Haystack bus stop, where there were buses to carry us to reception centres on the mainland. Fortunately, the tide had turned and we were able to paddle there unaided and it was not until a few weeks later that we found out that at least 10 people living about 100 yards away had been drowned in 10' of water.

Another strange fact we discovered was that mum's former employer, a devout Jew, hadn't had a drop of water in either his nearby shop or his house. All this made a very real impression on me and was probably instrumental in my decision, as a bitter, frustrated teenager, to commit my life to Christ; a decision I have never regretted. Through listening to God and taking his advice, I now live in a 4 bedroomed house, have an intact marriage, am surrounded by children and grandchildren and have enough to share with others and I can only thank Him for this privilege.

Anon

Before you call, I will answer

Are you one of those people who think of God as living in a far-away heaven and as totally disinterested in the problems and struggles we face on earth? I grew up like that and I must admit that although at times my experience of God has been very real and I know that Jesus came to earth, lived a perfect life and died in an excruciatingly painful way to reconcile me and others to God, sometimes I feel God is far away. I should have learned by now as He has done some really amazing things for us over the years, such as providing affordable potatoes for all our family and friends in the midst of a drought; running trains where they would not normally run, on the one day we needed them, at a ridiculously low price; providing a management job for me at the age of 60 after my son had told me to accept that my working days were over as people half my age and double my experience couldn't get work......need I go on? The 'coincidences' are far too many and too improbable to have happened by chance. However, I have had a few unexpected health problems in the last couple of years and I haven't been so conscious of the nearness of God as I was. Then I was given a timely reminder of His care for me.

We were recently in a position to replace my husband's elderly car which was proving a problem as it was needing rust repairs and I wasn't fit enough to climb in the passenger door and over the steering column every time I needed to borrow it, as he did. We part-exchanged it for a similar, low-mileage Ford and he was very happy with his newer model which was proving very reliable and economical. Our driveway is very narrow, so one evening, rather than calling him away from his hobbies, I borrowed his Ford and set off for singing practice. That over, I offered one of the singers a lift home, jumped into the car and set off...but not for long as loud 'bumps' alerted me to the fact that I had a 'flattie'. Pulling in to the side of the road, I discovered that both nearside tyres were flat, in fact pancake flat! Slashed tyres? Fortunately, one of the musicians was just pulling away, so I asked if he could take my passenger home and headed for the boot to find the spare tyre and a foot pump. No foot pump was to be found, no wheel brace and worse still, no spare tyre. Why on earth had that silly man removed them from his car? (I apologized later!) I had come to a stop in a very dangerous position, right by the Moot Hall junction and it was a pitch dark night which was very worrying. Even if I could borrow a foot pump, it looked as though I needed at least one new tyre, late at night. Worse still, I didn't know his breakdown company and had no mobile phone with me.

Before I got round to thinking of praying about the situation (I can be really slow sometimes), I heard a cheery voice say, " I know that face. Do you need a hand, Yvonne"? Surprised, I looked up and recognized an old friend from our Methodist church days. "Two flat tyres", I muttered, and with that she was out of her car, not only holding up her foot pump but offering to pump up the tyres for me. "Need to lose some weight as I don't get much exercise these days", she said as she happily pumped away. "Lucky I came this way", she continued. "I got held up at school by a late meeting, met traffic and decided to come home by a different route, or I would have come home my usual way"

Wow! One of those 'coincidences' again. To say I was relieved was an understatement as I really wasn't feeling up to that much exertion. One tyre was fine but the other was definitely 'past its sell-by date', so she followed me all the way home and drove of with a cheerful wave.

A brief discussion with my husband revealed that he was not the 'silly man who had removed the essential items' but that the garage hadn't returned them to the car after valeting. We replaced the bad tyre and a quick call to the garage sorted out the lack of foot pump and wheelbrace. In Isaiah 65, verse 24 God promises His people that *"Before you call, I will answer"* and that was exactly my experience. Before my brain had time to switch in, He had provided the solution to my problem, for which I was so thankful.

Yvonne Creasy.

I Called Out for a Miracle and One Came

Just over 10 years ago, before I became a Christian, I was at a very low ebb and feeling extremely vulnerable, not knowing where to turn. I had many sleepless nights and as I lay in bed one night I called out in earnest, "God, I need a miracle!."

I don't recall after all this time whether it was the next day or a day or two later, but a letter dropped on my doormat which was to be the turning point in my situation. That letter was never intended for my eyes but, suffice to say, it came to me and it was a revelation.

It made me realise that out of adversity, good can come and that God really does do miracles. The realisation that God had answered my prayer was the catalyst which led me to begin my walk with Jesus.

Chris Blyth

A Great Big Answer to All Our Prayers!

Our Church has been donating money through our tithes scheme for several years now, to fulfill Mary's dream of buying the land and then building a Care Home for abandoned street children and finally the news we have been waiting all these years has come – On 9th January, 2013, The House of Joshua in the Philippines took in its first 2 residents, as shown in the following email:

Dear Friends,
I thought I would just forward this email received from Mary this morning as I know so many of you have contributed to making this happen

I have seen the deprivation and squalor of Tahanan myself on many occasions and as I type this with tears in my eyes I really can't imagine how these boys must be feeling right now.

Thank you for your prayers, love and support that have brought us to this day – we now have an ongoing commitment to provide for the needs of these children going forward. It is a huge challenge – when the house is up to capacity at least £1000 a month will be needed to pay the bills as well as feed and clothe up to 75 hungry boys but, with God's help, I know we can do it.

Andy Conroy

From: Mary Louise Rendon.   Sent: 09 January 2013

Subject: First boys arrived

Just a quick note to let you know WE ARE OPEN!!!

Our first two boys arrived this morning transferring from Tahanan boys jail - Miko is 12 with some learning difficulties and Benjamin is 16. Both have just been there for a long time without any criminal case but nowhere else to go. Its great because Ramil, Jay, and Gerson all know these two young lads from the boys jail ministry and Benjamin has been asking to 'go home' for a few weeks.....

It is truly wonderful to finally welcome them HOME!....they arrived dirty, ragged - only with the clothes on their backs (over sized and grubby), skin allergies from the dirty cramped jail conditions but GIANT SMILES....so happy to be 'free'......Miko loves cars and was so happy to have a box of toys....you can see they haven't held toys for years....even Benjamin, who is older just dived right in - eager to show me all the english words he knows and that he can do 20 press-ups....He said he had been working out as the other guys there had been beating him up at night....Both boys are apparently on medication for not being able to sleep - couldn't imagine how they could sleep there anyway.....am praying that their first night will be a restful one without feelings of threat, fear but instead knowing God's peace, presence and rest.....They ate a lot at lunchtime! Jay and our social worker Charis are taking them out shopping this afternoon (after they take a shower) to go and buy their own clothes (they haven't had anything that was their own)....they aren't wearing any underwear...bless them.....They will also take them out for ice-cream.....

45

Can't really express how great this feels - but its truly wonderful.....I left them after lunch sat on their beds with Gerson and Jay being 'big brothers' sat with them.....

There are a bunch of other kids that they are ready to refer - we have agreed to take a few over the next few weeks - have been praying for 2 each week for the next month - so that each one has the chance to settle and we can give them the right attention and support the transitions properly.....

Lots of prayer appreciated!!!   Love always,

Mary
House of Joshua,
Phillipines

Will you be my friend...?

I had been happily married for over twenty years, brought up two children and served for many years in a key role in my local church. My husband was not a Christian although he would accompany me to church on special occasions and tolerated my involvement and commitment to something he didn't understand but could see meant a great deal to me. I prayed for him daily and knew in my heart that one day he would come to the Lord.

He had started his own business a few years earlier and initially things went well, but then we hit the recession of the late '80s. The business floundered and we were facing bankruptcy and losing our home. My husband's pride couldn't take that. He felt he had let me and the children (now both in their late teens) down and we would be better off without him. That's when he first attempted suicide. I say attempted, by all earthly wisdom he should have died from the huge amount of alcohol and drugs he had taken, but God had other plans. After being unconscious for a while, my husband came to, regretted his actions and called me for help. I called an ambulance which got lost en route and took nearly forty five minutes to reach us. I could have driven to the hospital myself in a little over ten minutes.

I don't know what happened to my husband while he was unconscious, suffice to say that during that long agonising wait for the ambulance I was able to talk and pray with him and, for the first time we read the Bible together. He suddenly said, "Do you know, all that stuff you've been going on about all these years is really true!" He made a full commitment to Christ and I thought, "Wonderful. Things will get better now."

But my husband had lost all his self confidence and had not found real God confidence. Several more attempts at suicide followed in the course of the year and I didn't like to let him out of my sight for more than a few hours, just in case! But again and again God rescued him, often leaving it until the very last moment before sending help. My husband's depression grew deeper and deeper as did our financial problems. He refused to seek medical help or even acknowledge he was unwell. He was living in denial and very few people had any idea of his real state of health. Then he managed to get a job and I thought things would improve. I also got job in a local office and it looked as if we might be able to come to some arrangements with our creditors.

Having become a Christian and been confirmed into the Anglican church, my husband continued to come to church with me and found a measure of peace and some new friends. He even agreed to go on a Men's Weekend to a Christian Conference Centre on the coast. I warned the leaders of his real state of mind and prayed hard that this would be the turning point. Surely God would answer my prayers and restore my husband's mental health. I was convinced he would come back from the conference a changed person. But no, as soon as I saw him I could tell that, if anything, he was in a worse place. Five days later he made another attempt at taking his life and this time was successful.

The years that followed were tough. But God was there for me and I knew His loving care in so many ways, but somehow I could not face that Christian Conference Centre. Over the years I was invited several times to join a group there but I always managed to find a reason (excuse) not to go. That was until this year when I was at last persuaded. I went with fear and trepidation, determined not to enjoy it. I was angry and hurt and realised I had been so for over twenty years since my husband's death.

The weekend went well and I got to know some people better, deepened some friendships and began some new ones. Gradually I began to relax. On the final morning I was praying and reading my Bible in bed, waiting for the bathroom to be free, when I sensed God saying He wanted to meet me on the beach. Yes, before breakfast, in fact right NOW!

I duly got up and headed out into the cold, blustery October morning. The beach was deserted and I found myself shouting at God and pouring out all the anger, frustration and hurt I had carried around all those years without even realising it. Gradually I calmed down and my rantings started to turn to praise as I saw the loveliness all around me with the sea washing in over the millions of pebbles that made up the beach.

I felt God responding, "It's time to stop blaming this place for what happened. It was my decision not to heal your husband or to rescue him that last time. I wanted him here with me. It's time for you to forgive this place and enjoy it."

Even as I took all this on board my mind went to John 21 and the barbecue on the beach. I knew Jesus was asking me as he had asked Peter, "Do you really love me?" But I felt He was saying "Come on, let's be friends." He was asking me to love Him as a friend. I don't know Greek and I didn't understand the different meanings of the Greek words used in the Bible but when I returned to the Centre and the first seminar of the morning I was amazed to hear the speaker talking about John 21 and explaining that Jesus was asking Peter, "Do you truly love me more than these? (Greek agape love) Do you truly love me? (again the Greek is agape) Do you love me?" (Apparently this time the Greek is phileos or love as a friend).

When I had been walking along the water's edge earlier I had stopped to look at the waves rolling in to the shore. I looked down and there at my feet amongst the millions and millions of stones and pebbles on that beach was a particular dark red stone in the shape of a heart. I felt it was God's gift to me and represented all he had taken out of my heart.

I found a special peace there. The great burden of hurt and anger I had carried unknowingly all those years has gone and I am walking closer with my friend, Jesus. That red heart shaped stone will always serve as a reminder of our meeting that morning on the beach when Jesus asked me, "Will you be my friend?"

GMS Jan 2013

Church Growth an Answer to Prayer

The years of 2003 to 2011 has been described as Steeple Bumpstead Congregational Church being under an open heaven, the growth during that time was first and foremost an answer to prayer, seeing people saved and added to the church..... It was all God's work and the church's obedience.

Anon

Then Call on Me When You are in Trouble, and I will rescue you, and you will give me glory.
Ps. 50: 15

It was near midnight on a very dark winter's night and my (not-yet Christian) husband was driving us home from a family event. Suddenly, instead of going straight on which would have been the shortest way home, he turned right down a narrow country lane. When I queried this he replied that he just felt it was the way we should go on this particular occasion. At the next crossroads, instead of turning left as I had expected, he went straight on down an even more remote, narrow lane. It was very dark and beginning to rain and I seriously wondered where he thought he was going at this time of night.

After about two or three miles we came across a car parked on the verge of the road. My husband stopped our car, and much to my consternation got out and went to see if there was anyone in the other car. Indeed there was. Sitting there alone in the dark was the wife of one of our friends. She was a nurse and had been on her way home after a late shift at the local hospital when the car had died on her. She had managed to get it off the road but she was stuck. This was in the days before mobile phones. We transferred this lady and her bags from her car and drove her the seven or eight miles to her home where her husband was waiting for her.

I asked her if she had been frightened finding herself stranded all alone in the dark on a very lonely narrow country lane. She replied that no, she had not been at all worried. She had prayed to her heavenly Father to send her someone to help and then passed the time singing a few hymns while she waited for rescue. She had been there about ten minutes when we pulled up. I realised it had been just about ten minutes since my husband had turned off the main road!

G.S.

A Testimony of Destinations; A Faith Journey

It's the early 60s. The Beatles were the new kids on the Mersey-sound block, I had just started an engineering apprenticeship and had met my first Christian. I didn't know he was a Christian. As far as I was concerned he was a religious nut who blathered on and on about God and Jesus.

However, although I didn't realise it at the time, meeting him put my feet firmly on the faith path, and my first destination was just over the horizon.

Two years later he had nagged me into submission and I went along with him, and a whole coach load of young people, to hear Billy Graham at Earls Court, London. It is 1966, and reluctantly I find myself standing in front of the charismatic American saying the sinner's prayer. The Holy Spirit had fished another one from the waves.

Going to the small Brethren hall for the first time was a cultural shock. I managed a few weeks, but I didn't own a suit, and I felt uncomfortable in this weird environment. I left and joined the young conservatives (not such a cultural shock!) learned guitar, formed a folk duo and managed to avoid God stuff for a year. But the Holy Spirit still had his fish-hook in me and began reeling me in.

The folk duo split and the attraction of the Young Conservatives faded. So after a year of invites to a young people Bible study, I RSVP'd a "yes", and got back on the faith-track. It was at that Bible study I began to learn what being a Christian was about. It was also the place where I met my future wife. At the time of writing (2013) we have been married 40 years! Nice one God!

The next few years saw me involved in a coffee-bar evangelistic team, a couple of local churches, getting engaged, an outreach rock band, getting married, buying a house and then.....

..... all our furniture is stacked around us. We're sleeping on the floor of an old house in Birmingham. Our house is sold, the bridge is burnt and we're at Bible College. How did we get here? Another destination along the path and this path is straight up a really steep learning curve. The journey along this bit of the path was, and remains, 30 years later, a priceless spiritual experience at the feet of men and women of God who led us to places we would never have visited in a local church situation.

Faith in God is easier when things are going well. Real faith grows when you have nowhere to turn, except toward God. Many times at College we find ourselves praying that our Father will meet our different needs. Money to buy food (we never go hungry), healings, guidance, spiritual insight, courage, battles.

The water of a number of different jobs and different churches flows under the bridges over the next few years. We now have a Son. We work together at a Christian outdoor centre and we move to the North-West, to the Wirral, and I work for a few different Christian charities. In the local church we belong to, we are involved in home-group leadership, diaconate, worship group, preaching, teaching, Sunday School. The steep learning curve in Birmingham pays dividends.

Then the local church falls on hard times. There are three huge leadership splits and traumas. We wonder should we stay. God says stay. We stay, but often find ourselves caught in the middle as people take sides. But from the middle, sometimes, the view is clearer. We are able to see things others don't, but it doesn't prevent the traumas, but God does reveal the spiritual truth behind what is happening.

At the end of it all, God says it is time to go. We join with the ex-Pastor building a new fellowship; a fellowship which will do things differently. The difference lasts a few months. It isn't working. We leave. But now our pathway starts to lead in a strange and very unexpected direction. For the first time in decades we realise our path is leading away from the institutionalised church we have been used to, have been an integral part of, and could never imagine being outside of.

And this is where we find ourselves now, still continuing along the path of faith, still following Jesus, still fellowshipping with other Christians, but not aligned to a building, denomination or institution. We are openly involved with the body of Christ - which is what 'Church' really is - but not behind brick walls, not under some man-made idea of 'church'.

The journey continues. Already there have been new and interesting destinations, but the ultimate destination is still over the horizon. But in the dark sky of this fallen world, its glow is now brighter as each day passes, and we keep our eyes fixed on that one final destination; The New Jerusalem!

Dave Peddie

The Live Cannon Shells

After working a few years in the metal trade I was now in the position where I could have my own furnace built. The Good Lord has been very good to us as a family. At this particular point in time I was working at West Hanningfield, near Chelmsford. Working with me was my brother Brian, my father and my son Stephen. We were anxious to be used by the Lord in a full time ministry or whatever the Good Lord had planned for our lives, but a living had to be earned, and if we could only realise the fact we were in full time ministry, letting our light shine before all men. That is all we are called to be, lights shining for Jesus. I found out, that this is ministry, and a great privilege. Our furnace was for melting aluminium contaminated with steel or other metals or foreign materials. We bought in this type of metal from far and wide as we had the only furnace in the area.

One particular customer we had was a large museum, they used to locate aircraft that had been shot down or crashed during the war years. They would go on what we called a "dig", after locating the aircraft. Many had crashed into the Thames in the war years, and parts were recorded in different parts of the Thames, some above the low-water line.

One of these digs was in progress, a Messerschmitt 109 had been located. It was quite a formidable aircraft in its time. All the parts were to be taken back to the museum and sifted through for parts to be cleaned and then exhibited. The rest of the well-damaged airframe was sent to our yard for us to melt down into ingots. One day, a lorry arrived with the remains of the Me. 109 that could not be salvaged for display purposes.

The next day we started to feed it into our furnace manually. One particular piece was so heavy, my son Steve and I lifted it onto the hearth of the furnace, but with burners on full and door wide open we struggled to push the heavy lump into our furnace and then close the door. It was then that a voice spoke gently from behind saying "take it out", no loud voice, no panic, just a calm voice said "take it out". I turned to my son and said "let's take it out", and we both pulled the piece of airframe from the furnace.

On closer examination, I noticed a quantity of hard mud packed down tight in the hollow part of the airframe. It was then that I stood up in horror, as under the mud, we pulled a belt of 20mm cannon shells from the airframe packed tight under the mud. I will never cease to thank God for the voice of the angel who said "take it out". The impact of these live shells would have been equal to a WW2 bomb landing down our furnace chimney. They would have blown our furnace to pieces and my son Steve and me with it. It was the closest I have ever been to death. No wonder my voice shouts the praises of Him who loved us and saved us. **God is good, and I am in full-time Ministry serving our Saviour day by day.**

Graham Turnidge

God's Protection

The Bible says that God chooses those people who have faith to believe. He certainly chose me.

When I was aged about 4, so my mother told me, I contracted pneumonia very seriously and that at the suggestion of our GP I was treated with a very new drug called a sulfonamide. It worked, as I am still here.

When I was 19 I was cycling in France, staying at Youth Hostels, where they have 2 or even 3 level bunks. One night I fell off the top bunk onto a hard stone floor. I suffered neither broken bones nor even a bruise. At the age of 22 I was cycling down Barnet Hill and at full speed, I hit a van illegally crossing the road in front of me. I suffered serious chest injuries but miraculously I was back at university within 3 weeks.

In 1962, I was married to Shirley, who is now my wife. That was after God saved me from what would have been a disastrous marriage to a Danish girl. Two sons were born to us, Chris and Dan. We felt that our two sons should attend a local Sunday School, so we started to go to services at a local Baptist Church. One Sunday, the church news included an offer to go on a coach to a Christian Tent Campaign on the South Coast run by Dick Saunders. It was at this meeting that the invitation was given for all those who wanted to give their life to Jesus to get up from their seats and come forward. Instinctively I grabbed Shirley's hand and we walked to the front to start a new life in Christ.

In 1980 my wife and I with our two sons were walking in the Peak District, when we saw some nearby climbers dislodge a very large boulder, which bounced towards us. We were transfixed to the spot while the boulder travelled ever closer to us; suddenly it stopped in mid air and dropped harmlessly to the ground right in front of us.

On another occasion my wife and I were driving on a very windy day towards Horsham, when a large tree blew down right in front of us missing us by only a few feet. God saves those who trust him.

Michael
Eastbourne

Is This How a Christian Behaves, I Thought?

My journey to Christ was fairly slow and I was fooled for a long time into thinking that I was truly a Christian when I wasn't. One day an event happened which changed everything.

My parents in law were staying with us at the time. During dinner, one of the children knocked over a glass of water and I dealt with it in a very angry and impatient way. My father-in-law leant back in his chair and said, sarcastically . . .

"The trouble with you Christians is that you spend half your life at church, but it doesn't make a bit of difference to the way you behave."

I was stung. I was already ashamed of the way I had behaved and that remark was the final straw. I heard the unpalatable truth, which I did not like at all.

Since the day I had spoken to the curate, Richard Buck, in distress about my life, I had attended church faithfully; I had been baptised and confirmed. In Isleham, I was secretary of the Parochial Church Council. I sang in the choir, cleaned the church, did the flowers, made the rolls for the parish breakfast, and we helped people whenever we could: all good Christian stuff!

In addition, I was busy with many good works, which ought to have given anybody assurance that I was a Christian. However, I knew that in my heart, in the very core of my being, despite all that I did, I had remained hard and unchanged. I was certainly a pillar of the church, but where was the love, joy, and peace in my life?

A great deal of the time, I was unhappy and dissatisfied on the inside; reactive and defensive, not usually in public, of course, but in my home. I was actually no different to those people I had criticised in church as a teenager; in fact, I was probably a lot worse!

After my bad behaviour, I escaped from the dining room as soon as I could and stomped upstairs to talk to Tony, who had disappeared earlier to do some GCE exam marking. Through gritted teeth I said, "Would you please ask your father to stop being so rude to me?" "Why?" he said. "What has he said to you?" I repeated the stinging remark that had convicted me so badly. "Well," he said, quite calmly and not very unkindly . . . "but it's true, isn't it?" At that moment, I was furious, and I lost all control. I took off my high-heeled shoe and hit him over the head. As the blood ran down his temple, momentarily, I froze in horror before running, as fast as I could, down the length of our upstairs corridor to get away from what I feared would be certain retribution. Tony followed hotfoot and caught me at the top of the stairs. He put his arms round me and held me firmly in a secure embrace. We sat down together on the top step.

The realisation that murder was in my heart, and that I could have killed him, was utterly horrifying. I could only say meekly, "I am so sorry. I am so, so sorry" I was indeed so sorry. Is this how a Christian behaves, I thought? I was so confused.

Two very unpalatable thoughts came:
The first was that Christianity was not the truth at all, and the second was even more unthinkable: that maybe I was not really a Christian.
I was quite desperate to know the truth. I knew that my children were suffering from a dissatisfied and often ill-tempered mother. I knew that Tony was totally committed to me and really loved me, but that maybe if I continued to treat him badly, I could be on my way to a second divorce.
Rescue came in an unsuspected (unexpected, maybe?) way.

The Isleham vicar had announced in 1972 that we were going to have a parish mission the following year. I had no idea what that might be, and at the time it sounded very scary indeed. It sounded even worse when I discovered that the expectation was that we would go through Isleham, two by two, house-to-house, telling people about Jesus. At the time, I thought . . . mmm . . . . I know a few Bible stories but that is my limit! I could not imagine what I, personally, could tell people about Jesus.

The plan was that a Reverend Tom Rees would come to take the mission. The whole event was centred on understanding the Book of Common Prayer, which Father Goodchild, the vicar, valued greatly, but it did not sound too exciting to me!

The Missioner eventually came to meet the PCC and explained what we had to do to prepare for that week. He was a lovely, elderly man, and I warmed to him straight away, but I was absolutely flummoxed when he announced:

"A Christian is not someone who prays.
A Christian is not someone who reads the Bible.
A Christian is not someone who does good works.
A Christian is not someone who goes to church.
A Christian is not someone who believes in God."

At this point, I thought, 'come on . . . what on earth are you are on about?' He was bit by bit whittling away all the things that I had assumed qualified me to be a Christian.

He then said, "A Christian is someone who has a personal relationship with Jesus Christ." This was an uncomfortable bombshell. Immediately I thought, "A personal relationship with Jesus? Crumbs! I don't have one of those, and I have no idea how to get one." I had a hasty look around the room to check if anyone might have noticed the shock that my face must have registered. I do not think anyone had noticed, at least I hoped not. Everyone was looking studiedly into the mid-distance with stony faces. We were not a very responsive bunch of people. I went home that night reeling. Was there any hope at all.

I had made a decision earlier, on that fateful day when I had hurt Tony that I needed to find out how I could change. I knew that I believed in God absolutely.

I had heard his voice, and I had felt his presence. I had seemed to receive his guidance. There was no doubt in my mind that He was a total reality, but I decided that I would make a disciplined search to find out if Christianity was true or false. If it were false, I would find something more productive to do with my Sundays.

If I found Christianity to be true, but I was not a Christian, I would find out how to become one!

The mission preparation spurred me on further and increased my determination, especially now that I knew what a Christian was supposed to be! So, having thought about it a good deal, I made a decision . . . I would go to my bedroom at nine o'clock every night. I would determinedly read the Bible, pray in the best way I knew, and sincerely ask God to show me the truth Himself.

I soon discovered that the task in hand was quite difficult. When faced with the silence of my bedroom, my mind was blank. I did not have much of a clue about what to say to God. Just saying a list of requests seemed utterly futile. Then I hit on the idea of getting a book of prayers out of the library and it worked a treat. It increased my prayer life from two minutes to at least ten! Ha ha ;)

At first reading, the Bible was hard going, and for some weeks it seemed that this particular activity was going to be a bit of a dead end. However, I was desperate enough to persist. I started with what seemed to be the easy end . . . the New Testament. Sometimes when I read it, I would finish and just close it with a sigh, but after a while I began to enjoy it. I felt drawn into the stories, and I saw many things about Jesus that I had never realised before. I found my heart strangely warmed towards Him because he actually seemed to be a real person. I began to see how remarkable He was, how human He was, and yet so supernatural. Could all of this about Him possibly be true?

One night, I recalled a revelation that I had had the time that I visited Greece as a student. During the trip, I had gone to Athens, and as we stood on Mars Hill,

overlooking the Acropolis, the guide said, "This is where St Paul stood and preached the gospel to the Greeks."
I remember thinking . . . Oh? . . . Maybe this means that the Bible is true. This was a completely new thought to me because all but a few people had told me that the Bible was just man-made stories, which could not possibly be true.

During the time of my search for the truth, the *New English Bible* was published. I was nonplussed to find that Tony picked it up and read it quite purposefully from cover to cover. It seemed rather odd for someone who confessed to be an unbeliever to want to do this, and it seemed rather like a bad joke. The supposed believer could not easily read the Bible, but the unbeliever could!

However, as weeks went by, I treasured these moments of time when I felt a growing intimacy with God. I began to linger in silence, feeling his presence and having a growing expectancy that I was about to discover something wonderful.

One night, I had just read the Bible and prayed from my heart. I was kneeling, quietly enjoying God's presence. Suddenly, I was startled by a sudden shaft of light that came streaming across the room, filling the whole room with the most glorious, amazing presence.

Amidst the dazzling light was the form of the most wonderful being I had ever seen.
Then slowly, it dawned on me just who this amazing person was . . . It was Jesus . . . It was Jesus in all His resurrection glory. I cannot tell you how I knew it was Jesus, but with my whole being, I knew it was He. Revelation tumbled into my heart. At that second, I knew . . . Jesus really was who the Bible said He was. I

knew that He was truly the Son of God, and that I was, at that very moment, in the presence of the very Son of God . . .

This was the Jesus of the Bible, who at that very moment was choosing to make himself real to me and showing me that He was actually a living being . . . absolutely alive today . . . truly risen from the dead . . . an awesome person.

The effect on me was electric . . . I was awestruck, transfixed, and very overwhelmed by the sheer holiness of His presence. His presence was so real, so beautiful and great, and so awesome that I thought that it would be better if I could just melt into the carpet and be unnoticed. A holy reverence filled my heart, and even my breathing seemed too noisy.

In an instant, I saw so clearly that He, and He alone, was the one who was worthy of my worship and my whole life. The famous hymn says it all:
'Love so amazing, so divine, demands my life, my soul, my all.'

I was acutely aware of my own uncleanness, and yet I did not feel condemned. I just felt His love. I managed to blurt out His name, "Jesus", and continued drinking in the glory of His presence. Speaking was difficult and even felt irreverent - unnecessary somehow. He was communicating loudly enough without words. How long I was there, in His wonderful and wholesome, healing presence, I do not know. I hardly moved; I hardly dared to breathe as I did not want that moment to ever end. Eventually, without even being consciously aware of the words forming in my mind, I said, "Jesus I love you. I am so sorry that I have tried to live my own life. I have made such a mess of it. I do not want to do that anymore. I just want to serve you and obey you. I want to do anything you want me to do.

Take my life; I give it all to you. From now on I don't want to live my own life. I want you to take hold of my life and live your life through me."

I buried my face in the bed and drank, and drank of a great river of life that flowed out of Him into me. I was so grateful; there were no words adequate to express my thanks. The struggle was over. Every question of faith that had been a problem to me was settled immediately, with finality, in one brief moment of time.

I lingered long after the light had gone from my room and His presence had left . . . trembling with excitement and holy fear.

It was thrilling. I had had a life-transforming encounter with the living God.

However, the experience did not end that night . . . something utterly amazing and wonderful had happened in my heart. A small glow of love and joy and peace had settled there, and I felt so different, so light and so clean. I felt totally clean and new on the inside! I was a bit afraid that when I awoke in the morning it would have all evaporated; that it would just turn out to have been a great experience with passing feelings.

I need not have worried because when I woke up the next day, I found, to my delight, that the warm feeling was still there. Somehow, I knew that I would never be the same. This 'feeling' began to influence my life and my behaviour; it did what no information, doctrine or philosophy had done . . . It changed me on the inside, which is how I know that only Jesus can change a heart.

For the first time ever, I felt an inner warmth and security . . . daily; I felt a lightness . . . I felt peace and a new love for everyone.

Margaret Cornell

Excerpt from, as yet unpublished book
'A Life Shared'

You Will Again Go to The Land....

We went to Bible College by faith, but didn't have much in the way of resources. I remember well the day when we had no food and the canteen which provided food for the singles had a lot of liver left over and they brought it to us. Elaine was pregnant, so it was just what she needed.

We ate it alternate days for the next week and were glad of it. When we finished at Bible College, the council eventually coughed up some money that they owed us. We then had the same amount of money in the bank that we had when we went.

We went to Nepal in obedience to God's call and were saddened when there was no more work for us after our first term. However God spoke to me upon our return through the scriptures. "You will again go to the land to which you went, and your seed will inherit the land."

We then spent our time in the UK doing whatever God gave us to do. Elaine worked as a teacher and took an Open University Degree, not realising that she would need that degree to get a visa when we returned. I worked as a Land Surveyor.

It was twenty-five years later that God's promise was fulfilled. We have been serving God here for two years and have until Christmas until we return to the UK. This time, our stay has been much more fruitful and we are so glad that we were obedient to the heavenly vision. Elaine's work has been mainly with expatriate children and I have been performing surveys for new buildings at a hospital run by the mission. However, it is in the church where we have been most blessed. I am in the worship team and am twice the age of the others in the team, but I have been made so welcome. The leadership saw my enthusiasm in worship and so asked me to join the team in the hope that my enthusiasm would be infectious.

I recently lost a fairly valuable item which I would have been most embarrassed about losing. It had my bank card inside it and it would have been exceedingly difficult to get another sent out to Nepal. However, when I prayed, I had a feeling inside that it would be returned to me. My faith was justified and both items were returned to me the next day. PTL. *(Praise The Lord)*

Dave and Elaine
Nepal, India

The Power of a Tract

I was fifteen years old and pregnant when I first had a desire to attend a church. I didn't go though, but every time I passed a church the desire was there because as you walk past the buildings, you hear the singing as you're going past and I always felt a longing to go in. But I reasoned to myself, "I will only ever enter a church when someone invites me." And I always thought that. Every time I walked past a church, I thought, "No, I'm fifteen; I'm pregnant. I'm not going to go in unless

66

someone invites me." That was my reasoning and that's the way I thought.

When my first child was born, my partner and I got married and we moved into a flat together and I remember how I was always afraid now, afraid of everything. That was my life. I was afraid of being alone. I clung to him so much, it was terrible. When he went to work I wanted to go with him, and I did go with him once to work and actually sat in the car all day. His boss said, "Is she all right?" but that's how I was gripped by fear.

So I was afraid of being alone; I was afraid of death. If anybody spoke of dying, I didn't want to hear it; I didn't want to hear anything about death. If there was a programme of a funeral I'd turn it off. I was terrified of death.

I was afraid about not knowing. Before you're a Christian you wonder what's out there, why we're here and things like that. What am I doing here; what is the meaning of life? And I was afraid of having pets at that time, because I was afraid they might die. I had a fear of everything. I didn't want to love. I didn't even want to hug my son properly; I didn't want to get close to anyone in case I lost them. Fear was my "buddy" and I was tormented by it. I lived in fear.

So within the next two years my second child was born and I decided to go to my aunt's. She lived where we lived in Dalston about ten minutes from us. So I thought I'd go to see her. When I visited her we had a nice time together. Now her partner was a Christian and he had those Gospel "Chick" tracts, which tell a little story in a magazine form. So she gave me one and I thought, "All right, I'll hold on to that." And when I returned home, I read the tract – I sat in my bedroom and I read the tract. I was gripped by what I read: how God loves me; there's somebody out there who cares; how Jesus died; how we were sinners; how lost we are without Jesus. And that little tract, it really got to me. So every night for that week, I sat in my room when my husband was out and the kids were down, and I read the 'sinner's prayer' and I kept on reading it. For one week I read out the sinner's prayer asking God for His forgiveness and Jesus into my heart. I'd still not attended church. I still had the reasoning, "I'll go when I'm invited." But God knows our hearts. He knows. After that week of confessing, my aunt visited me and guess what she said! She said, Kay, there's a Gospel Church downstairs about two minutes from where you live. Would you like to go? And I said, "Yes, of course I'll go. I'd love to go." It was only downstairs, because we lived on the third floor, five minutes, downstairs and across the road and there was the church and the women praising the Lord. I heard the Gospel explained again and I made a confession again. As I began attending the church – it was called Bible Path – and hearing God's Word being taught I felt a great desire for the Bible; I couldn't get enough. I was like a starving person. My questions were being answered. I found that I no longer had that feeling of fear. That was definitely getting replaced by love. I was learning and He was filling me with His Word. Instead of all the old anxiety and fear, I felt love; I felt joy. I was there all the time, praising the Lord, excited.

When you think of the gloom and doom of fear and terror and not knowing, and then having this light shine, well after that I started going and feeling the changes, I told my entire family about Jesus. I went and visited aunts and uncles to ask whether they'd heard of this. Some of them were a bit doubtful, "Oh, you've become on of them have you?" "Yes!" I took bundles of tracts and I was giving them out as I was walking along, giving them to people at bus stops. I attended conferences and crusades. God has become very real to me. Each day is a blessing and I love having the Lord in my life. It's wonderful. I've got someone I can talk to all the time. He's always there. I don't feel alone any more. I'm not afraid of death any more; I've got a home. Our citizenship is in heaven. He's even saved my children. He's not only touched my life. One by one they came to me. I think Irone came to me when he was about eleven and he said, "Mum, what's that sinners' prayer. I want to know that sinners' prayer. Then I talked to him and he gave his heart to the Lord, and then Leah and then Daniel. God is in the business of saving and changing people's lives.

I've been a Christian for fifteen years now and God has brought me through the good and the bad; He's always there, hallelujah. God so loved us that He gave us Jesus. He made it very easy for us to come to Him to have eternal life – whosoever believes. That's my testimony. Never underestimate the power of a tract.

Khardine Musisi
Pitsea, Essex

I put my Trust in Jesus

Firstly, my name is Stephen Hewitt and I am 19 years of age. I have been a born again Christian for three years – it has totally changed my life. Simply by putting my trust in Jesus and asking Him into my heart.

See, I find that your heart is like a room with a door and the door handle is on the inside and Jesus waits patiently on the outside, waiting for you to open the door and invite Him in. Because God is a gentleman, He won't barge into our lives. He gives us this little thing called free will and with it, we can do whatever we want.

Now there was a time in my life, at the age of fourteen and I was in a state of depression. I didn't know what to do with myself. I didn't care for anybody and I hated my parents. I couldn't even look at my father - we used to argue constantly. I wouldn't even have cared if he had left home and never came back again. I really hated him - from the depths of my heart. I couldn't bear the sight of him - and all he would ever do was love me and boast about me. But when he would try and talk to me - I would walk away in disgust.

Even with my mother, I used to take advantage of her by treating her like a piece of rubbish and calling her every name under the sun and for absolutely nothing. I even thought about hitting her a couple of times, and then I would walk away and cry someplace.

I didn't like who I was becoming. I was in my own little world and I knew that if I didn't do something about the situation I was in, I was going to do something that I would regret.

Anyway, as time passed by, I got older and even more stubborn. I was never a violent person, but if I had to fight, I would. That was just the way I had been brought up. But I was very 'mouthy' and I didn't care what I said to anyone because I was never frightened. Plus, I never thought of the consequences.

I couldn't talk to anyone without having an argument. But there was one person I really loved - and that was my old grandfather, Charlie. I could talk about absolutely anything with him and he would never tell anyone about what I had told him. That to me was everything. He was a person I could trust and he wasn't just an old grandad to me - he was my best mate.

At the age of fifteen I started going to night clubs and pubs - drinking and smoking. I thought I was a little man – with a fag on my lip and a pint in my hand. And I thought I had everything going for me. But little did I know it was going to get worse.

A little later down the line I got in with some boys that dealt with drugs. Even though I was totally against taking drugs I didn't let it get to me that my mates were, because I thought 'What they do is their business and what I do is mine.' But each time I'd go out with them they would always be out of their heads – stoned and paralytic and I'd always feel left out. So I thought 'If you can't beat them, join them'. So I did.

Going out all through the week and every weekend was my life. I used to love getting drunk, stoned and going out womanising. I couldn't get enough of it. But as time went on I was drinking every night and the drugs were taking hold of me.

I'd come in every night about three o'clock in the morning and roll through the front door. I used to be so drunk and stoned that I didn't know how I got home. And when I got in, my mum and dad used to argue and go mad. I could see that if I kept on doing what I was doing, that it was going to break my parents and my home up. I knew I needed a change but I never had the power to do it. I knew I need something but I didn't know what it was.

Every time I had a problem, at home or somewhere else, I turned to the drink and the drugs. I knew it wasn't helping but it was the only thing that took my mind off everything. Well, for a little while at least.

At home at this time, things were miserable, especially with my mum and dad arguing all the time over me. But with my grandparents living next door if anything happened I would go over there and lie low for a couple of hours.

With everything going on as it was, the thing that used to 'get right up my nose' the most, was my granny would always come over and keep on and on and on about God and Jesus to me. And it really drove me mental. Every time she mentioned it I would swear and go mad at her and tell her to get off out of it. And I would pretend and say it was a load of rubbish. But deep inside I knew it was true.

Anyway, a couple of weeks later my granny came to me and she asked me if I wanted to go to church. Normally I'd laugh and tell her to go away but something inside of me was telling me that I should go, so I did.

When I got there I thought 'Whatever am I doing here with these idiots?' Everywhere I looked people had a big smile on their face, and I thought this is no church – this is an asylum.

So anyway I sat down and watched them all lift their hands and close their eyes and sing while I was in the corner laughing my head off at them. But little did I know that something was going to happen to me.

After all the singing was finished they all settled down and the preacher got on the stage and he preached about what Jesus had done for me. That He died on an old rugged cross for my sin, and that if I didn't ask Him into my heart, I was eternally condemned. I was going to a place called hell, where there is eternal darkness. A place where there is eternal pain, sorrow, wickedness, suffering - a place of depression and loneliness. But then he said that I don't have to go there - I didn't have to go to this terrible place. He said it says in John 14 v 6 (Jesus said) "I am the Way the Truth and the Life. No one comes to the Father except through me." And he said that through your putting your faith in Jesus Christ, asking Him into your heart to take over your life, but you've got to mean it, he said and if you do, Jesus will perform a miraculous change in your life. He would deal with the things that you can't deal with. He'll mend the broken heart. He will deliver - He will heal.

After it was all finished I went home, and all that night I couldn't sleep because I kept remembering what the preacher said about hell and about what Jesus had done for me. And I knew that deep in my heart, that this was what I was looking for all along. So that night I decided in my heart, that I was going to give my life to Jesus and give Him a try. I thought I have got nothing – so I have got nothing to lose.

And since I decided and I asked the Lord into my heart – immediately He took the desire away from me to drink and smoke. He took the smoking away. I even stopped swearing. He took the drugs away, He took the womanising away. And He has replaced all that with goodness. You know, God has given me a love for my parents that I have never had before. I have become a better son; I have become a better person altogether. He has cleaned me up.

And what Jesus has done for me, He can do for you.

Stephen Hewitt
Essex

Light and Life

Hi, my name is Ann and I have been saved since 7th May 1992. I came to know the Lord in a tent Mission run by 'Light and Life' - Gypsy travellers. The meetings were on the Orsett show ground. It was a Thursday evening - my daughter Lisa's 16th birthday. Lisa gave her heart to the Lord two years before and she kept asking me to go to her local meetings. I use to say "No, that's okay. You go."

Friends had been testifying about Jesus and His love all the week before. I asked some questions but thought no more about it. On the Monday my daughter was working, she wanted me to take her to the meeting. So, along we went and chatted to friends on the field. Then an announcement over the loud speaker said "Come to the tent and meet the Lord."

So I went to the tent and when I walked in it was full of people praising the Lord. I found it all interesting and the music was nice. Well, my daughter wanted to go every night (and so did I). By Wednesday, we were arriving even earlier than previous nights and I was asking questions of Jeanie, a pastor's wife. I went into the meeting that night and I felt fine. By the time I came out - I felt weak. I know now, that I was fighting against the Lord.

The next evening we arrived even earlier at the show ground. During the evening a man called Graham Jones got up and gave a testimony about his son dying in France - only 21 years old. He talked about how the

Lord had strengthened him and his family. And then he played the accordion and sang a song called 'Heaven is better than this'.

Later, the sermon was given, and the Pastor called for anyone who would like to give his or her life to the Lord or who wanted prayer for healing to come forward. My Lisa and friends kept coming up to me saying "Do you want to go to the front?" "No", I kept saying - but I kept looking around the tent seeing men and women praising the Lord unashamedly - hands in the air - men praying out loud. I had never seen a Gypsy man sing unless he had a pint (or several pints) in a pub. But these people loved Jesus and praised Him freely. Then the Pastor said, "If the Lord is speaking to your heart tonight, come to the front!" Jeanie looked at me again, and she just walked with me to the front where I gave my life to the Lord. I cried and cried - tears of Joy. I felt so full. I had butterflies in my stomach. Then we sang some more songs of praise to the Lord. I was over-awed.

Two sisters in the Lord came and sat with me and told me that when the week was over, I needed to find an evangelical church where there were born-again believers in the Lord. So I went to every meeting until the Saturday.

At that time I worked in Pitsea Council Offices and I told all the girls I worked with, how I had met with the Lord. I was amazed how I could testify to people and I gave my testimony of how I gave my heart to Jesus. But one thing bothered me. Where would I find a Church? I didn't know any locally.

The following Saturday I went shopping with my family to Pitsea and I could hear a song being sung in the Market place. It was 'My shackles are gone'. So we

75

followed the sound of the music. And there, to my amazement, was a group of people singing to the Lord and with them was the man who was at the tent meeting, who had given his testimony and sang 'Heaven is better than this.' I sat on a wall humming along. The children wanted to carry on shopping, so I said "You go, and leave the baby with me". When they came back to find me, I was standing with the group singing to the Lord! The Lord had found me my Church (which is not a building, but the people of God.) I still go to that church – the Church at Gun Hill.

Jesus has done so much for me I do not know how I managed without him. The Lord doesn't say it's easy to be a Christian - we still have trials. But He does say – 'come as you are - problems and all!' He gave His life for me - a sinner. He shed His precious blood for me - and for you as well. I thank Jesus every day for His grace and Mercy.

Accept the Lord today! You have nothing to lose, but so much to gain. I trust in the Lord to guide me daily. I have a granddaughter and she is a miracle from the Lord (but that's another testimony, for another day) and I pray every day for the rest of my family and for people who know something is missing in their life. Don't let pride or family stand in your way. Jesus is a wonderful friend. He is our Saviour and our King.

'Come unto me, all ye that labour and are heavy laden, and I will give you rest.' *(Matthew 11 v 28)*

Ann Lee
Essex

He Knew Where He was Going

Saturday, 17th August 1991 looked as though it would be the same as any other Summer Saturday. In the morning, I put the finishing touches to the decorating of my youngest daughter's bedroom. I then cycled the four miles to our church and back to spend a short time in prayer. After lunch, my wife and I went shopping. Life was going on much the same as usual, with so many things to do and so much to enjoy.

Then, at about six-o-clock, came the stunning blow - a telephone call to advise us that our 21 year old son, Daniel, who was on holiday in France with a Christian group, had drowned earlier that afternoon. How could we believe such a fine Christian young man, a son to be proud of, was dead? How? Why? If only....! The thoughts and questions raced through our minds. Even now the situation is difficult to grasp.

When Daniel was buried nearly three weeks later, the church was packed to hear the reassuring testimony that here was a young man who, although he did not expect die, was prepared for death. He knew where he was going. (Phil. 1:21-23) As a youngster, he had committed his life to the Lord Jesus Christ. (Matt 16:24) At 17 years of age he declared that publicly by being baptised. (Mark 16:16)

As I was later sorting out his affairs, I found a letter which he had written which contained the following testimony:

"I write to you pleased to have a testimony that the Lord Jesus Christ has come into my life and forgiven my sins. (Eph. 1:7) This has saved me from everlasting destruction and separation from Him in hell. (2 Thes. 1:8-9) I thank God for the obedience of His Son Jesus who willingly was mocked and persecuted and then crucified for my sins. God so loved me and He so loved you that He sent His Son to die for our sins in our place. (John 3:16) Praise the Lord that Jesus, on the third day rose again (Luke 24 :46 -47) and later ascended in heaven. (Acts 1:9) One day I shall see Him in Glory. (John 17:24)

"There was nothing I could have done to earn this great gift of salvation. (Titus 3:5) It was only through humbling myself to the place of repentance that Jesus, through His grace and mercy, could forgive me. (1 John 1:9) The Lord has regenerated me and made me a new person in Him. (2 Cor. 5:17) In other words, I have been born again by His Spirit's power." (John 3:3-8)

Although sad at being separated from one we loved so much, my wife and I have found great comfort from the knowledge and assurance that our Daniel is with the Lord and that one day, when we all see Jesus, we shall be reunited. This has been the Christian faith and certain hope for nearly two thousand years - not a dead religion of form and ceremony. but a living relationship with a living Saviour, the Lord Jesus Christ.

Maybe you too are going through all the usual routines of day-to-day living, just as I was on that Saturday in August; just as my son was in France. But are you ready for death? Do you know where you will go then? Perhaps you have experienced a devastating situation which is crushing you more than you can bear. Let me say to you that in the Lord Jesus Christ there is salvation for YOU.

Graham and Penny Jones,
Hadleigh.

The Lord Jesus Christ is Very Real to me

I hail from India and whilst a little lad, I recall travelling with my mother to several places as she sought 'peace of mind'. Mother visited Seventh Day Adventist, Methodist and various other churches but she did not find her answer.

Around this time I was sent to boarding school in the Darjeeling area, better known for its tea. I was about 500 miles away from home and up in the hills where the air was pure and fresh. On my return home at the end of term, I was to find that she had joined a fellowship where she found what she had been searching for, 'a body of believers' who knew about the 'deeper life with the Lord Jesus Christ.' At that tender age I did not take this seriously nor did I give it much thought. Back in school and perhaps a year or two later during an evening service at the cottage I was in, along with another 30 boys or so, I recall putting my hand up to accept the Lord Jesus Christ into my heart as my personal Saviour when the appeal was made.

Leaving school shortly after my 16th birthday, I went straight into the Armed Forces voluntarily and served in the Navy for the next 11 years. After my initial training of 9 months and a further 9 months period specialising in the Communication Branch of the Service, I was drafted to service on board a ship. I was transferred to a shore establishment in Calcutta a year later. I found my way to the 'Assemblies of God' Church and attended there regularly where I met and made many friends who were born again. Calcutta being so situated, we had many visiting preachers and evangelists who shared with us their experiences in the work of the Lord as well as His love and compassion for all mankind. It was during these visits by an evangelist from New Zealand and at an Open-Air Crusade that I made a firm commitment and re-dedicated my life to the Lord Jesus Christ and shortly after followed His example and was baptised in water.

After a two year stay in Calcutta, I was again sent back to sea aboard a ship and continued my life with the Lord and fellowship whenever possible at any port of call. I might add that for all of my naval career, wherever I served and amongst thousands of men, I was often the only born again believer among them. Life at times was very hard what with all manner of ungodliness around me. During my privilege leave I would return to beloved Calcutta where I always rejoiced along with fellow Christians. Life in the Navy did not permit one to remain for more than two years at any one ship or shore establishment. I was often on the move and returned to Calcutta on a posting where I now got married and a year later our son was born. Not too long after, I left the Navy.

My wife and I emigrated to England in June 1975, and shortly after arriving here, our daughter was born. I was at first very disappointed at not being able to find fellow believers and to worship. Being new in the country, the feeling was awful and on many occasions I felt like taking the first flight back. We moved to Basildon from Billericay and began worshipping at Church Road and then later my family and I joined the fellowship here at Gun Hill.

The Lord Jesus Christ is very real to me and I realise that without Him I would be "of all men most miserable." I have never for a moment regretted that day in my life when I put my trust in God. Even in the past, when for six months I had no permanent job, the Lord in His love and mercy provided at all times. I was temporarily employed and then finally commenced full-time work again. Praise His Name! Through the years He has never left me nor forsaken me. He is always there and is someone I would recommend to you.

Norman Freeman, Basildon

I Came to Jesus at a
Billy Graham Crusade

Hi! I come from Donegal in Ireland. I am one of eight. My family life was a sheltered one. I was brought up a strict Catholic, going to church every Sunday and confession regularly. I came to England when I was nineteen and got married shortly after.

After having six children I found my marriage on the rocks. My husband was violent towards me when he had a drink, which was most weekends. In the end we divorced.

The first few years I sat indoors and looked after my children. Eventually I started going to the pubs with friends. I was lonely and unloved, yet I never did find love. After all, what man would want a woman with six little ones?

Years after (I was working in a home for the elderly at the time), ladies I worked with were talking about an American preacher who was coming to West Ham Stadium. I wondered what all the fuss was about this Billy Graham, so I went along to see for myself, taking my friend Sue with me. Billy Graham preached on the forgiveness of sin and the death of Jesus on the cross. He asked us to come forward and surrender our lives to Jesus.

I knew I needed forgiveness, I felt a wicked sinner, so I went forward. I no longer need the pubs and men. I have found the love of God in Jesus. Thanks to Billy Graham's message and the grace of God, I am born again.*   God bless you all

Peggy Byrne

God had His Hand on Us

I was born and raised in North London, five minutes from Harringay dog track. I often lay listening to the dogs barking when I was supposed to be asleep. My mother and father were both Christians and went three times on a Sunday to the chapel in Wood Green. Of course, I always went with them. I had an older brother who was the bane of my life and I must admit to playing horrible and painful tricks on him. School I hated and, therefore, did all I could to make life "interesting" for me, and my teachers.

Now, one day, when I was 14 years old, two evangelists hired Harringay Town Hall, the place where some world class boxers used to fight, for a crusade. My brother, by this time, was doing his National Service, but I was taken along to hear the evangelists preach. The first night, as I listened, the invitation was given for all who wanted to accept Jesus as Saviour to come and kneel at the front. I felt I should go, but didn't. However, the next night, Jesus touched my heart and I responded and accepted Him as my Saviour. But being a precocious young lad, I was sometimes in trouble with the elders of my church for speaking my mind.

Then, when I was 16, I was baptised by immersion.
Two years later, I went into the army to do my national service. With what high hopes I went in! I was going to stand up for Jesus, come what may, and for a start I did just that. I joined up with an Army Scripture Reader and tried to get the boys to chapel. But soon, when the Scripture Reader came into the barrack room, I would slip out. Drinking, smoking and partying took over, and I led a double life. Home at weekends, I was the model Christian young man. I went to the meetings with the girl who was to be my future wife, and then went back to

my other life. Life went on like this until I was demobbed.

Life then changed and I turned over a new leaf. When I was 22, and my fiancée was 21, we married. Life was good. First we had a girl, then a boy and then another girl. We were happy. Then life started to go wrong. My wife, Vera, started to get pins and needles in her legs. Things got worse; there were many hospital visits. And it was at one such visit to Southend General that we met a physio who was the head of the department and did home visits. He gave us much advice and one piece of advice was that Vera should get drunk as this would relax the spasms in her legs. As she couldn't drink by herself, I of course drank with her. The next 2 or 3 years were a round of clubbing, drinking, dinner dances etc. Then a major operation, and, 10 years after the start of things going wrong, Vera was in a wheelchair for the last 30 years of her life. But God had His hand on us and He led us to people who believed that God was as real today as He was in Bible days.

To backtrack for a moment, after Vera's major operation, we both gave our lives back to God, but it was harder the second time than the first. Life went on and we travelled the country. Then, after 51 years of married life, God took Vera to be with Himself; and even in that God's hand was in it. But I praise God He has brought me through a dark valley, and now, after two years He has brought me to the mountain top, where the sun is shining, and you know if you face the sun, the shadows are all behind you. God has been so good to me; I can't begin to tell the half. Praise God from Whom all blessings flow. I am blessed.

John Maycock

Thank You Lord For What You Have Done For me

People have often said "If only I could live my life over again!" My only regret is that I never knew the Lord earlier in my life.

Of course I always believed in God. When I was in my early 50s I suffered with nerves and very deep depression. I was under the doctor and taking tranquilizers, which were not doing much for me. Sometimes I felt worse. I had all I wanted, a good husband, a nice home and no money problems. I should have been happy but I wasn't. Nothing satisfied me.

I have never been out to work, so I had lots of time on my hands to do what I wanted. I kept myself busy at home doing all my own decorating and gardening, always busy with different hobbies. But I always felt lonely and empty and felt something was missing in my life. I felt so depressed, my only thought was to end it all.

One night before going to bed I snapped and took an overdose of sleeping tablets. My husband found me the next morning and couldn't wake me. I don't remember what happened in hospital. I only know that when I came home I felt very guilty and ashamed to think how selfish I was to do this to my family.

My family were grown up. My four children were married and settled down. My youngest son Jeffrey, decided to work abroad, and after some time went to Israel to work on a Kibbutz. After a while he came home, and said he had met a nice girl (Maria). She was a born-again Christian and spent a lot of time having Bible Studies. Then he gave his life to the Lord. I never understood really what he meant by that; I only know there was a great change in him. Then Maria came home to England and they were going to get married. She wanted to find a church. So I started to come to church with them.

I found it good. I felt uplifted with everything that was said. Then I suddenly knew what it was to have the Lord in my life. Things had some meaning in my life. We always sat at the back of the Church, and many times we were asked if we wanted to come forward to the front. I felt hesitant about this, (although I wanted to) but I felt embarrassed, because I was feeling old among the congregation. Most of them were very young, so I never went forward.

One Evening Jeff asked me to go with him to some special meetings at the church in Laindon. He said there was going to be an evangelist there. I didn't want to go. I was in a lot of pain with my knee. I suffered with Arthritis and could hardly walk at times, so I said, "No!" but after some persuasion, I went. Someone picked us up in the car, so that was fine. The speaker was very good but all of the time I felt he was getting at ME, and I felt sick and uncomfortable.

At the end of his talk he asked if anyone wanted to come forward for healing. Several people went forward, so up I went too. My knee was really throbbing with pain but something inside me said, 'You won't have this pain tomorrow'.

I felt very shakey and nervous, not knowing what was going to happen to me, but at last I was up the front. As I stood before the speaker, he asked me why I had come forward. He then said "Just pray, a personal prayer between you and the Lord." He then put his hands on my shoulders, two people behind also laid their hands on me. I felt a strange feeling, as if his strength was in me. After the praying finished he walked to one side, and beckoned me to walk forward. I cannot explain the

85

feeling. I felt I was walking on air! No pain! I felt numb. It was wonderful!

As I walked back to my seat, the speaker asked those who wanted to come to the Lord, to raise their hand. While praying I suddenly felt my hand being pushed up. Since then I have never regretted it. I know I have the Lord in my life with his great love for me there is fullness of joy. Praise His Wonderful Name! What a friend we have in Jesus! He is changing my life, as I put my faith and trust in Him. I know my days of misery and emptiness have gone. The Lord has filled my life with peace and contentment.
Thank you Lord for what you have done for me.

Rose Ouwehand

An Encounter in Greece

In the June of 2001 I was made redundant after 24 years in the same job, and I thought "My God help me." By the end of June I had a new Job and I thought, "That was a bit of luck." Luck?

I had always believed in God, but never made the absolute commitment. I was a Catholic, but I found that was not enough, so I drifted away from God. But I always believed He was there.

My husband and I went on holiday in the September of that year. The holiday went fine. We went to a beautiful Greek Island called Paros. We had been to many Islands and were always looking for somewhere to settle down when we retire.

It was two days before we were due to come home, and I felt awful. I really didn't want to come home. We were on the beach and it was 4 o'clock in the afternoon. The beach was empty and a couple came down, with their dog, and sat right beside us (as people do when there's an empty beach) I felt really fed up. "Oh", I thought "I can't make conversation."

Well, the next day (our last day) I was really in the dumps and the same couple came down, with their dog, and sat right beside us again. But they started to talk to another couple that were near by us, whom we also knew. The other couple had asked the people with the dog "Are you English?" and "How did you come to live here in Greece?" (they obviously lived there because they had the dog) and the minute she started to speak, she began to say how Jesus had changed her life - that she had found Jesus - and the whole story of her life.

At the beginning of her life she had been a manager, doing very well – nice house, car - and how she had found Jesus, and didn't need all that. I was absolutely transfixed. Her name was Barbara, and she said she had written a book, about her life. And I said, "Where can I buy the book?" Barbara replied "Well, I've got them with me." So I bought a book and the other couple bought a book.

And I read that book - I just could not put it down. It was fantastic. But by the end of the book I was in floods of tears. I was so ashamed - I couldn't even remember the Lord's Prayer and I felt so ashamed. I kept crying and crying.

Before we left Paros, Barbara came back to our apartment, looking for us and she said, "I need your address because I need to send you a receipt for the book. But while I'm here I'll write down my e-mail address in case you need me." So she wrote her e-mail address inside my book.

And did I ever need her? Because after that, I had these feelings, these different feelings and I was 'on top of the world', and I thought "What's happening here?"

When we arrived home in England, I e-mailed her and explained everything to her and said "Help, I don't understand what's happening!" And she explained that she thought I had truly found Jesus, and the tears were tears of me repenting, and the joy of starting a new life!

So, we were e-mailing backwards and forwards to each other and she was telling me what to read in the Bible: Matthew, Mark...I couldn't get enough. I was reading everything and I thought, "this is fantastic!"

Then Barbara e-mailed me and said "It's about time you got out and found yourself a church".

I wondered – "where would I find the right church?" So, back to the internet - and thank goodness for technology (for once). I looked on the Internet and there was a local church website, and I thought, "This looks good."

So I e-mailed Barbara and said "Have a look at this website, and see what you think." And she e-mailed back and said "Yes, get along there, they sound great, just what you need."

And that's how I came to be at Gun Hill, and the Fellowship has welcomed me so much.

I am at a point now that I not only believe - I know! I know Jesus walked this earth. I know that He died for me and that He rose again - and He is here with me constantly.

Jan Morley

A Wounded Soldier Remembers

I am now a 98 year old bedridden man, confined to one room in a BUPA nursing home but until 94 years of age, I was looking after myself and my late wife, Violet, in our 3 bedroomed house in Leigh on Sea. We had a gardener and a cleaner in for an hour a week.

I lost my wife two years ago when Dementia took her from me after 70 years of marriage. We were married on 10th April, 1940 at Christchurch, Pall Mall, Leigh on Sea shortly before I was called up for World War II and had just set up our first home.

In June, 1940 I enlisted at Warley Barracks and went away for training for approximately two years which I mainly spent in Dorset. Eventually I was posted to the 16th/5th Lancers (the Scarlet and Green) at Catterick Barracks and embarked with them at Clydeside, Scotland bound for Algiers in November, 1942. Following 10 days at sea, we landed and spent all week unloading tanks and vehicles, finally settling in a field with a camel. That night the heavens opened, the field became a quagmire and we were moved to a stadium in Algiers before spending months in heavy fighting in the Tunisian Campaign. I served as a tank driver.

In January, 1944 we were redirected to the Italian campaign. We landed at Naples on 14th January in torrential rain which turned the vineyards into gluepots of mud. Tanks got bogged in ruts and furrows but it was our task to protect our Infantry from the enemy tanks in the advance to Casino. In February, I was with B Squadron resting but we were under fire from German and Italian guns firing from the hills. One of the shells fell among the tanks and exploded, killing and maiming many of our soldiers and ending the war for me.

I awoke to find myself in a hospital tent having received several pints of blood and morphine for my pain. I had suffered shrapnel wounds to my chest and leg but it was not until a comrade gave me back my wedding ring in Naples Palace, which was temporarily in use as a military hospital, that I discovered I no longer had my left forearm. A doctor explained that they had patched up my left leg as well as possible and told me it might last me five years. God must have stepped in because I still have it.

Whilst in hospital, I was aware of a brilliant red glow and loads of smoke and sparks. The staff and those who could stand were able to watch and tell me about the Eruption of Vesuvius on 15th March, 1944.

I received a visit from the Hospital Chaplain who read Psalm 118 to me and I desperately claimed the words in it for my situation, "I shall not die but live and declare the works of the Lord". That was the turning point in my illness. Three weeks later, I was well enough to be shipped home to Roehampton Hospital to be fitted with an artificial arm and hand.

Back in England, my wife received telegrams from the War Office, firstly saying I was missing in action, then that I was gravely wounded and lastly that I had lost limbs and was being sent back to England. Eventually I returned home to meet my first son, Trevor, then aged two.   More children followed; a daughter named

Rosemary, after my wife's twin sister and our youngest son, Peter.

I was allowed to return to work on the railways as a signalman and eventually completed 42 years with them. I led an active life, cycling to the station each morning, painting and decorating my own house and even re-laying my garden when I retired. . My brother-in-law and I also worked allotments to produce vegetables for our families. .

When I was almost 70, I found out that I could have a car specially adapted so that I could drive again. I made enquiries and was soon in possession of a three wheeler, which gave us back our independence. For several years I used it to go shopping, visit relatives and take us to the Leigh Elim church which we attended most of our married life. I was also able to help as a sides man there but I no longer played the piano for them although I did manage to attach a cork to my false arm so I could play one note with my left hand.

Life was good and we had 11 grandchildren, mostly living nearby, who visited regularly I currently have 13 great-grandchildren and see them all from time to time, when they are brought in to see me, some from as far away as Australia and New Zealand.

Three years ago, I broke my hip when I was unable to save myself from falling due to my missing arm and I am now only pain free in my bed. The staff are kind and I am regularly visited by family. I also receive visits from a lovely Christian man who reads the Bible to me, prays and talks with me and gives me great encouragement.

I look forward to the day when I am reunited with my dear wife and loved ones. Jesus spoke to me shortly after my wife died and He told me He has got her safe and I know I shall be with her in heaven one day.

Raymond Alexander Creasy,
Thundersley, Essex

The Car That Fell on Me

After working a year or two mixing shrimping with other jobs (as I had a family to support), shrimping alone could not support a growing family, I took on the job of unloading timber barges when they arrived at Theobald's Wharf in Old Leigh. This work on its own could not support my family, but it helped.

There was no "hand-outs" in those days, you either worked or you didn't eat. I was also asked to sort scrap metal for a chap I knew quite well at Basildon. I accepted this job on one condition which was simply this. My time belonged to the Lord and I would only work the hours that He permitted me to work, although while at work I would put 100% effort into everything I did. I was brought up that way and applied it to my life at work or at home. If a job was worth doing, do it with all your might. As a workman I gave good value, more so as a Christian. I was given a large warehouse with a yard to work in. That was my area.

One particular day I found three cars stacked one on top of another just outside my compound, and as usual, all the wheels had been taken off. I went outside to see who had done this, as there was no need for these cars to be stacked so close to where I was working, as the yard was very large with plenty of room. As I stood alongside the stack of cars, I heard the noise of a crane working on the other side. As the jib of the crane was turned, it knocked the top car off of the pile As I stood around the base of the stack, I looked up to see the dislodged car heading directly overhead. I had no way of escape, and the heavy car came down on me, landing on my shoulder, just missing my head. I lay under the car with just my head and shoulders showing. It caused great panic amongst the workers, the owner's son was shouting, "get the crane and lift the car from his body", and someone else shouted "get an ambulance".

My father, working near and doing the same sort of work that I was employed to do, rushed out hearing all the commotion, and saw me lying underneath the car. He grabbed hold of the car bumper, and shouted "in the name of Jesus", and with the help of my Guardian Angel, he lifted up the car while the others looked on, and shouted "drag him out", at which the confused workers did just that. With the call "get him to hospital", I said "just get me home".

I was taken home, about 10 or so miles away, and I was just put into a chair in my kitchen. It was now late Friday afternoon, and the weekend lay ahead of me. As soon as the pastor of the church heard the bad news, he came straight down to pray for me. I felt like I'd been put through a crusher, my ribs were hurting and my whole body ached. I just sat still in the chair. Saturday, I just sat still in the chair. Sunday, I just sat still in the chair. Monday morning came, I still sat in the chair, until about 7'o'clock. I then stirred, got back into my work-clothes and shouted to Grace "I'm off to work".

We all rejoiced at what had taken place, and praised the Good Lord for his healing power. Great surprise was on the faces of my fellow workers, as I got out of my car and strolled around the compound which I had left so tragically three days before. Not an ache in my body, not a pain in my side. My God had just worked wonders. I believe the Angel Of The Lord lifted up that car while the men dragged me clear. The sceptic would say, " could not God have prevented this happening at all" . Of course He could have, but I would not have been left with a living testimony, of the love and the power of a wonderful saviour. He is the same yesterday, today and forever.

"The Angel of The Lord encampeth round about them that fear Him and delivereth them."

Graham Turnidge

Six Years

Being asked to provide an occasion when God answered prayer has led me to think about specific times when God directly answered prayer for me in a significant and positive way. My story about answered prayer does involve specific answers to prayer but it is more about God answering prayer over a period of time. The answer to prayer I wish to convey covers a time period of six years.

It's a time which began when I left the relative security of being employed by an independent evangelical church. Having worked for this church for nine years it was not altogether obvious what God wanted me to do next. I knew two things I was not to do. I was not to be a Pastor and I was not to work for another church. I had a desire to do further study and I had a sense that my future lay in the area of Christian Education for Churches – but that was it and neither of these hunches would readily put food on the table for us.

However, it was time to live by faith in a way I never done before. We all live by faith; that is what we do when we trust in Jesus, but this was different. Now I had to trust that God would lead me and provide for me and my family at the same time. I began this venture in 2008. We are now in 2013. I am now a Director of a small Christian Educational Charity. We still, by and large, live by faith.

So the question is how have we survived these last six years? I actually struggle to give a comprehensive answer to this. Some people and some churches have been very generous to us and been the channel through which God has provided. The State Benefit System has kept us out of poverty. Income from preaching engagements and short courses which the charity now delivers has helped supplement our income. But when all this is added up there is still a shortfall which God has somehow filled. It hasn't quite been by raven as when Elijah's brook dried up, but it has been quite miraculous nonetheless. From cash gifts to the provision of a lawnmower, fridge-freezer and food items, to payment of my study fees, God has given us what we need when we needed it. The big answer to prayer of God providing for us is therefore made up lots of little answers to prayer. My story of answered prayer is summed up by the words of a hymn, *'All I have needed thy hand has provided, great is thy faithfulness, Lord unto me.'*

Andrew Burress

I Cried Out to God For Help

When I came out of the Royal Air Force in 1961, we spent a few months in Lincoln waiting to find a flat in London. We were successful in getting a one bedroom flat with shared bathroom in a place called South Lee in London south of the River. We moved down and took possession but we had a problem I did not have a job to go to.

The first port of call was the old firm I worked for before going into the Forces. They offered me a job immediately. However, I wanted a change of occupation, I wanted to change course. I explained this to my old manager and said that although I wanted a job it would only be for a short time while I looked for something else. Obviously he could not offer me a job under those conditions.

After that came the hunt for work. I found a job but could not start for a while which left me in a severe situation. I had to pay rent, and I needed food for myself my wife and two small children. This deeply concerned me and one morning I got up and was so desperate that I knelt down in the kitchen and wept, crying out to God for help. I was still on my knees when the doorbell rang. My wife went to the door and standing there was my former manager. He needed someone to fill in for a couple weeks. Would I like the job? Would I! Alleluia, Praise the Lord.

Fred Maynard

"If Anyone Lacks Wisdom, Let Him Ask God, Who Gives Generously To All, Without Finding Fault!"
James 1 : 5

Wisdom is one of the most valuable things we can acquire in life – it keeps us out of unnecessary trouble, helps our relationships, broadens our mind, and gives us something to contemplate when a power cut darkens our homes and TV screens. It is unfortunate that the normal method of acquiring it is by trial and error. It seems that we only become receptive to wisdom after we have caused sufficient pain, expense or embarrassment to ourselves or others. It's as if wisdom is always there waiting for us, but we have to be ready for it.

The biggest step towards wisdom I took came at the end of a long and frustrating period when everything seemed to be turning to dust in my hands. My marriage was in trouble, my career had taken a nose-dive, my normally buoyant self-esteem had taken a battering. I felt as if I was walking along a narrow cliff path in a small pool of light in the midst of darkness, with every step becoming more difficult as the path got steadily narrower. On one side was an unscaleable cliff face and on the other a dark abyss. It could only be a matter of time before I had to stop altogether, and then what? It was then that a good friend suggested to me that I trust my life to Jesus. "What have you got to lose?" they asked.

I had known of Jesus since Sunday School, and had been attracted to him many times, though never to the point of commitment. I had learnt that many thoughtful people had come to put their trust in Him, often after a personal crisis of some sort – people whose intelligence and integrity I respected. Partly because of their example but mostly, I must admit, out of desperation, I decide to trust – and stepped off the cliff.

Nothing dramatic happened, there was no crash onto the rocks below, but I knew from that moment my life was different. HE was there, in a way He had not been before. I was no longer on my own, no longer the lonely captain of my own ship. Indeed there was now a new captain on board, and I soon learned that He was far better at navigation than I was. What a relief I found it to be the first mate instead of the man in charge! No more lonely responsibility. No more grim struggles in the dark! I began to learn that being second-in-command was a much easier and more rewarding path to be on.

I also discovered that wisdom comes to those who ask. There were many things I wanted to know and get sorted out in my mind. The biblical world-view is very different from the typical modern western understanding of life, based on human effort and self-salvation. Previously it had all seemed too difficult, but now it was as if a light had been turned on. I started to find the answers that had been there all the time – for those willing to ask.

Peter Donoghue

The Power of Prayer

I've been a Christian for many years and believe in the power of prayer.

However, a couple of years ago my husband and I were due to go on holiday abroad and we had to cancel it because I was overcome with a terrible fear about flying. My fear was so intense I thought I would never be able to fly again.

One particular Sunday at church, the sermon was about "Trusting God in all circumstances". The message touched me and I could not stop thinking about it! All I could do was PRAY and I remember experiencing great joy and excitement afterwards.

I had to put God's plan into action and trust Him.
Once again we booked a holiday abroad and in the weeks and days leading up to it I regularly prayed. I had to let go and allow God ......

The peace I experienced before and during the flight was amazing. Yes God does answer prayer!
I was taught a lesson, I realized it was ok for me to pray within my comfort zone but I had to learn to pass on all my insecurities to Him through prayer.

> "What a friend we have in Jesus,
> All our sins and griefs to bear,
> What a privilege to carry *everything* to
> God in prayer."

Elsbeth

Old Joe – Part One

I was living in the old town of Leigh on Sea with my wife Grace and four children. The cottage was very small but it was cosy, and the rent was only 8 shillings a week. We both had come to know the Lord Jesus and our main objective in life was to be a witness of his love and goodness to us. The good days of earning money and making a good living on the water were past, and we were struggling to make enough to pay the rent and feed a family of six. The Lord was showing me, that after 300 years of family fishing, I was to be the last in the line. Engine repairs on my boat were getting regular, and larger bills were coming my way. There were times we would spend all night on the river Thames, and catch very little. Even with cockling, shrimping and picking up scrap iron, a living had to be earned.

I got into conversation with an old mariner, who I'd often seen around Leigh, and he lived not far away from us. While talking to him one day, the Lord came into the conversation. Eventually he asked me if I could paint up his boat, and get it sea-worthy for a long trip. I agreed and I went down to the boat at the first opportunity that

I had. Grace would come with me, and we soon found that they were Christian people, just as we were. They were born-again but did not go to a church. They had been having fellowship with a chap calling himself an evangelist, and he took advantage of Joe, moving into his cottage, with his three wives and children. Joe was nearing 90 years old, and befriended a younger, very frail lady who kept his cottage tidy for him. This preacher had convinced Joe and his friend Muriel, who he later married, that the Lord Jesus was soon to return to this earth and would stand on the mount Olivet, and the boat had to be ready for the journey to the Middle East.

That is where I came in and that is why the boat had to be shipshape and sea-worthy. The scriptures were as he said, that Jesus would come and stand on the mount Olivet, but it does not say that we all have to race out there to meet him. For the faithful church will be taken to meet the Lord in the air, before he returns with ten thousand of his saints, and sets his feet on Mount Olivet. This preacher not only got his scriptures confused, but did not live the life of a born-again believer, having multiple wives and children. Just after we came on the scene, the evangelist left, taking his wives and children with him.

Joe and Muriel, and Grace and I, became real friends, a friendship that would last until the day the Good Lord took them home to Glory. They still did not go to church, but I felt that my ministry was for those believers that were on the outside of the established churches, and although I put 100% into my local church, I always felt an outsider, mainly because the dear people who attended regularly were set in their ways. I was a young convert and was determined that my life was to be a life serving my saviour, and not for just filling a seat in a church once a week.

You might say I was a rebel at heart and would not conform to the ways of church-going people, sincere as they might have been. I felt with Jesus in my heart and in my life, I had so much to offer in this world of darkness without the Lord. Although I was on the boat to work, we spent much of the time talking about the Lord Jesus. We would sing hymns and praise the Lord. Joe wrote out one of his favourite hymns and Grace loved it, and we had not heard of it before that day, and we sang it with all our hearts. The words were

"Hallelujah, yes 'tis heaven, 'tis heaven to know my sins forgiven. On land or sea what matters where. Where Jesus is 'tis heaven there." And the verses that went with this inspired hymn were a blessing to us both. All this was happening in a boat, not a church.

Our friendship grew but Joe had to move his boat from the foreshore, just past the cockle sheds, as the local council were beginning to move all houseboats and such like from the sea wall and surrounding areas, in a clear-up operation. Joe decided to sell his little cottage in Billet Lane, and he bought a cottage in Woodham Ferrers, close to the river Crouch. It was a cottage set on its own, surrounded by trees, with a pathway leading down to the river, where he also had a summer-house and a mooring for his boat. The cottage was completely on its own with no neighbours, a wonderful place in the summer, but as we were to find out, it was a desolate place and very lonely in the winter.

I still had my boat, and Joe asked me if I would tow his boat around to his moorings in the Crouch. It was to be the last trip at sea that I would have with my boat,

"HEATHER PAM" named after my two elder sisters. The door had closed for me as a fisherman, but other doors were opening where I could be a better witness for the Lord. I was mainly at sea on my own, and it was hard work and dangerous at times being on one's own, with no communication with the shore. The Lord was even in this event. He was guiding my life and all I had to do was to be obedient and follow. My father had retired from fishing, and spent most of his time carrying a banner with "JESUS SAVES" on it, around the towns of Leigh and Southend. It's what he wanted to do, and felt it was a ministry for him.

When I told him that I was going to tow Joe's boat around to the Crouch, he volunteered to come with me, and I'm sure pleased he did, as I was not familiar with that part of the river. It was in this last journey in my boat, that I saw the greatness of our God. We set off on the flood tide as we knew it would be a very long journey. We were heading for the Southend Pier, when it shut in thick fog. This was our worst enemy. Dad asked me to get out the compass which I kept in the cabin. I went to get the compass, and then realised that I had taken it ashore to clean it. This meant being at sea in thick fog with no compass could be disastrous .We passed the Southend Pier and headed east down the river Thames, Dad said to me in a confident voice "We will just have to trust the Lord He is the Great Shepherd" .We kept motoring down the river and I laid on the bow of the boat, looking ahead, just in case anything loomed up ahead of us that I could recognise.

There were river Buoys, and beacons and the Boom Defence at Shoeburyness , plus the high sands , plus a wreck or two we knew could be in our path. I saw nothing as I kept staring into the thick fog. It seemed like hours lying on that deck. All of a sudden Dad said

"Look out for the West Buxsey buoy" which I knew to be a red and white chequered buoy. Within minutes of Dad telling me to watch for the buoy, it suddenly loomed up ahead of us. We were bang on course, I was simply amazed. It was the first object I had seen since passing the Southend Pier, except for the occasional sea gull sitting on the water, which loomed up like a small boat. From the buoy it was much easier, as the land soon came in sight. The banks of the River Crouch standing out clearly through the mist. My father was one of the best fishermen ever to work on the River Thames, but this journey without a compass was beyond the capability of any man. God was in this journey right from the beginning to the end. He had been our shepherd that day for certain.

We left the boat on the moorings Joe had prepared, and headed back to Leigh. The fog had now lifted for our journey home. That day we witnessed the power of God's love to them that trust in Him. On leaving, Joe asked me if I could take his old mooring chains over to him, at which I agreed. The following Saturday morning, I went down to where the boat had been moored just past the cockle sheds at Leigh. Other boats had been moved also and there were plenty of mooring chains lying in the soft mud, but which belonged to Joe I had no way of knowing. The following Saturday I tried again but I gave the job up as I could not cut up a chain belonging to someone else.

I thought then that Joe and Muriel had moved away out of my life, but I was so wrong, as I was to find out later. The Good Lord had plans I knew not of at the time, and Joe would stay involved in my life until the Good Lord took him home at the age of 100 years. I felt very concerned that I could not deliver the mooring chains to Joe. I was not a person to let people down, even before my conversion, and more so now that the Lord had come into my life. It started to worry me a little, and as much as I tried to put it out of my mind, the more I began to feel guilty. I felt that I had failed Joe, and although he had moved to Woodham Ferrers, 15 miles away, I took no consolation in that.

A few weeks passed, then one night I had a dream. It was so real to me, I saw a bus coming down Belton Way towards Leigh Station, and sitting on the bus was Joe and Muriel, and they were waving their hands at me. The next morning, I felt that the Lord had prompted me, I sat down and wrote a letter to Joe apologising for not doing what I had told them I would do. I explained the reason for this, and posted the letter at the first opportunity.

Within the week a large parcel arrived at my home. It was a large box of apples from Joe and Muriel. The misunderstanding had been dealt with and we were still friends. God has many ways of showing us his will for our lives, all we have to do is be obedient. It is then that we see the blessing of the Lord. We do not always see the result at the time, that will come as we trust him. It is a life of faith in the Lord Jesus. We took the journey out to see them and the cottage was lovely and peaceful, but it was summer and the weather was hot and we knew not what the winters would have been like. There was no main road to the place. We just followed a pathway at the edge of a field until the cottage came into view. It was just a track, but in our car we would finally get to Joe's cottage.

We kept in touch by phone and occasional visits. After the hot summer we had a very cold winter, and the year was 1963. One of the coldest winters on record, even the creek at Leigh froze in that cold spell. The journey to

Joe's cottage in thick fog, could be illustrated in this fashion. The driver of a car living in the Southend area being asked to drive to Clacton, 30 miles away, blindfolded. Needless to say, if you were the best driver of a car in the whole world, it would be an impossible task, far beyond the skill of any man alive. Like so on the river Thames, with hundreds of river Buoys and obstacles scattered on the river, it would be impossible for any fisherman, however skilled he might be, to make that journey to the river Crouch in thick fog. With strong tidal currents and no compass, and also towing a boat larger than the one we were in, it was a miracle of God, and Jesus the Good Shepherd took over the rudder.

It is things like this that we see how awesome God is, and our faith is strengthened by such events in our lives. *The Lord is my Shepherd I Shall Not Want*

Old Joe – Part Two

It was the middle of winter 1963, and Joe and Muriel still had an important part to play in my life, and the wonders of God were about to be revealed in the lives of many. But to see these wonderful things we must be obedient to the voice of God who speaks to our hearts. It was on a Saturday evening and Grace and I had just retired for the night after a busy weeks work. We were now living in a council house in North Leigh, which we had exchanged for our little rented cottage in the Old Town of Leigh.

The Good Lord had moved us out of the place we loved, and out of the job that I loved, but it was important to us, that we keep in the way the Good Lord would lead us. He is the shepherd of his sheep and he knows the way we should walk. The house we moved to had the luxury of a telephone, (at least it was a luxury to us).

On this Saturday evening the phone rang, and on the line was a frail voice which was full of concern. It was Muriel, and she cried "Graham, can you help me, I think Joe is dying". I jumped out of bed and said " I'll be there as quick as I can". I got dressed and Grace said "where are you going", to which I replied "I am needed at Joe's place". Having dressed I looked at the clock, it was 11'o'clock in the evening. I looked out of the window, and while we slept there had been a heavy fall of snow. The road and my car was covered and it looked very bleak. I started my old standard vanguard and set off for Woodham Ferrers, about 12 miles away. Conditions were terrible but I was on a mission for the Lord, and felt honoured that I was felt wanted in a time of need. I was on a service for my saviour.

The roads were covered with a fresh fall of snow and I reached the Rettendon Turnpike about midnight, where I branched off on the old road to Woodham. Very few cars adventured out in those conditions. I found the turn-off for Joe's property, and set off across the edge of a field. How different was the journey to Joe's cottage. In the summer it had been so easy to find, but this was winter, after midnight, with a covering of snow on the roads and all the pathways. I edged my way around the field with just my headlights guiding me, and into an open space. I was lost and had no idea where I was, and it was now 2'o'clock on Sunday morning. Suddenly my steering spun out of my hands, I was sliding down the bank of the river Crouch. My car came to a halt and I stopped the engine and cried "Oh Lord, where am I", and I asked the Lord to help me. I got out of the car and looked, only to find my offside wheels very close to the river. I looked and saw the cold water running past only yards from my car. I prayed again and took the car into reverse and it pulled back, away from the river bank.

With praise in my heart I then had to find Joe's cottage, and as the snow stopped falling, I could see a light in the distance. It just had to be Joe's place so I headed towards it, and to my great delight I had finally reached my destination. The time now was past 2'o'clock in the morning and Muriel was waiting for me. I went in and Joe was in a coma, I could not wake him and he had been like that for hours. I felt his brow and I feared the worst. Joe was 92 years old, and a miracle was needed here. I prayed for him and sat talking to Muriel for a while, then decided to leave for home.

I followed my tracks back, making sure that I avoided the river. Reaching home in the early hours of Sunday morning, I was pleased to get back into my bed, but found it difficult to sleep. Sunday morning I rang my best friend Fred, and told him of the situation. We decided to meet at Rettendon Turnpike and he would follow me down to Joe's place. This was a day that we missed church, Grace and I, and the children set off for Woodham Ferrers meeting up with brother Fred and finally arriving at Joe's cottage by the river Crouch. We went in where Muriel was still sitting beside Joe, but he still had not moved or opened his eyes. We gathered around his bed and we all prayed, and the Good Lord heard our cries for help. Then Joe suddenly sat bolt upright in his bed, and started talking to the window in front of him. He then turned to us and said "I've been talking to Jesus, and he told me my time is not yet", and then he laid down. While with Joe, we all rejoiced as God had answered our prayer, and everything that had happened the night before was all worthwhile. It was as though it had never happened. But it was so real. Fred and I, with Muriel, had to make a big decision.

We had to get Joe out of this cold damp cottage. Fred decided with his wife Gladys that Joe should stay at his house in Corringham until the cold winter was over. We put Joe in a chair, and carried him out to my car, covered in warm blankets. He sat in the passenger seat, and Grace sat behind him with her arms around him to steady him. Fred took the rest of us in his Bedford Dormabile and we were ready for our journey to Fred's house. The ground was covered in snow and ice, and my wheels began to spin, and my car could not get a grip to pull away up the steep incline. Then all of a sudden a chap appeared in a tractor from out of nowhere, he threw us a rope and he pulled us clear. What was that tractor doing out early on Sunday morning with not another house in sight. It must be the work of the Lord, or one of his angels.

God is so good and his plans are perfect. We got Joe safely to Fred's house, and he stayed there for the winter. We all had a part to play in this miracle of God's power, and there was much blessing in all our lives for the small part we played. God is so good. Joe got well, according to his vision, and he was soon out preaching with us at the open air meetings and at the gypsy camp which we visited often. The Good Lord used Joe and his wife Muriel.

At the first opportunity Joe sold his place in Woodham, and his boat, and moved to a detached bungalow in Rochford, where he lived until the Lord took him home to Glory, at the age of 100 years. For his centenary birthday, we had a small party in his house, where he was proud to show the letter of congratulations that he had received from The Queen.

The next phone call I had from Muriel was on a much sadder note. She had asked Joe to move a big upright piano, but the strain was too much for him. I picked up my friend George and we went over to see Joe at

Rochford, but when we arrived the doctor was just leaving and had pronounced Joe dead. We stayed a while with Muriel to give her some comfort. George, had had experience as a young man with the flu epidemic of 1918, and together we prepared his body for burial. It was a sad day for me to lose such a friend, but I was privileged to play just a small part in this wonderful testimony of the Grace Of God in the lives of those who had committed their lives to JESUS, THE KING.

Graham Turnidge

I Call Her My Little Miracle

It was a Black Day when my little nine year old grand daughter was diagnosed with cancer. It was cancer of the liver and, according to the scan, the cancer had grown quite big and was the size of a bag of sugar! My poor little grand-daughter couldn't stand up straight, as due to the cancer it pulled her down in stature so much that she walked in a stooped fashion.

As you can imagine we were all appalled by the news. Our nearest hospital referred her to a specialist in London who also examined her and he recommended three sessions of chemo before the operation and six sessions of chemo afterwards.

Many churches were praying for her complete recovery. Thankfully Jesus heard and answered our prayers.

The operation was carried out by a children's hospital in the Midlands, which specialised in these in operations on the liver. The first thing the surgeons did was to take a specimen of the good part of the liver and send it to the laboratory for examination to ensure that it was unaffected by the cancer. Thank God it was all clear and they were able to carry on with the operation and they managed to get rid of all the cancer.

She had come through the operation with flying colours. Of course she still had the six sessions of chemo to get through, but the main thing was that she was alive! Since then, the after care has been fantastic, she goes to the hospital every 3 months for a check up and is still clear.

She has recently passed her driving test, she is studying hard for her "A" levels and after that university. She leads a normal life and I call her my little miracle!

A very grateful Grandma

I Didn't Want to be Around Anymore

From a young age I was brought up in the church and moved around a lot with my parents. As a youngster I was always quiet and took interest at church, enjoying the stories I was told. My parents would also encourage this in our home life, reading the Bible, singing songs and through discussion.

As I approached my teens, my older siblings had all left home and I had few friends from school, which left me feeling quite lonely. I was slowly filling my life with pointless interests, as teenagers do, spending less time thinking about church and God, although He was always at the back of my mind. I had made a commitment to God back in 1992 at a Christian camp and I took it seriously but I was still young, still having a lot of growing up to do and things to understand about God and His ways.

From the age of 16 to around 25 I still attended church occasionally with my parents, but kept it separate from the other social part of my life. I had no young church friends to spend free time with, but dated throughout.

Half way through my third long-term relationship and after a lot of tough times mentally, I chose to start attending church regularly with my parents as I felt so lonely and unfulfilled in life and in my relationship. Things got so bad that I didn't want to be around anymore, I just wanted out. One day at my lowest, after an argument, I spent time alone crying out to God about my life not knowing where to turn, I'd lost myself and felt a real failure. My parents had always been there for me and offered good advice, but I had to make my own mistakes, which I did.

After that point things got a little better but my boyfriend at the time began to start blaming my church life for some of our problems and tried to encourage me to stay at home more. Over time it occurred to me that the situation was wrong. That wasn't where I wanted to be. Due to many issues we ended up separating......

I decided to attend more church courses and join a House Group to learn more, and re-confirmed my commitment that I made in 1992. I was eager to increase my knowledge and grow closer to God. At the age of 26 I finally decided to take the step of getting baptised, as I had been considering it for many years.

From that point on I feel I have grown as a Christian, having a deeper understanding and an inner peace that I had never experienced before that helps me through life. Yes, I do struggle sometimes with my emotions, but I know God is always there to help me through.

Anon

From Obligatory Prayers to Freedom!
My Christian Journey

My earliest memory of prayer was with my mother, just as I was getting into bed at night. This was the Prayer: *God Bless Mummy and Daddy, God Bless Granny and Grand-dad*, then follows a list of asking *God to Bless all the relations and friends usually by their individual names* – this can go on for quite a time! Finally finishing with the words *"And please Baby Jesus make me a good boy, Amen."*

For the first 45 years of my life I was a Roman Catholic, which meant that my life was to be lived according to the Laws and Rules of the Roman Catholic Church, which stated that I *had* to go to Mass every Sunday, it was a sin not to go! So for the first 7 years of my life I went to Mass every Sunday with my parents. In those days the Mass and all other Services were in Latin, so we had prayer books, or missals, which had the Latin with an English translation beside it.

Soon after I was 7 years old, I was sent to St. Martin's Prep School, Nawton, North Yorkshire. One of the lessons was "Catechism", which was learning about my catholic faith. I was taught about Confession and Holy Communion, this teaching ended with making my first Confession to a priest, and followed a day or so later by taking my first Communion, I suppose I was about 8 years old by then.

I was also taught how to be an Altar Boy, which meant saying the responses to the priest at a Latin Mass, (all services were in Latin until the mid 1960's), lighting candles, serving the priest with water and wine, ringing the bell at the Consecration (which is the time when the Communion wafer and wine are turned into the Body and Blood of Jesus Christ), more responses and finally blowing out the candles after the Mass had ended. On some special days the Mass was sung, which meant that the priest sang all the words, this was a longer service!

On February 2nd we had our throats blessed, as it was the Feast Day of St. Blaise. On Ash Wednesday we were anointed on the forehead with an "ash" cross. The ash was made by burning the old palms left over from the previous year's Palm Sunday.

On Sunday evenings we had Benediction, again in Latin, which was a Service of Adoration of the Eucharist (the Communion wafer of the Body of Jesus Christ). At other times we were taught how to pray The Rosary which was a "necklace type item" which held different coloured beads, for example:
1 Red bead = The Lord's Prayer
10 blue beads = 10 Hail Mary prayers
1 green bead = 1 Glory be to the Father prayer.
To pray the whole Rosary was to pray all the above bead prayers 5 times, while contemplating on a specified aspect of Jesus' life.

All of this is very hard when you are a young child, but I *had* to do it! In Catholic Boarding schools in those days it was a "punishable crime" to try and deliberately miss any of the church services without a valid reason – I was beaten with a cane!

After 2 years at St. Martins, I had to leave as my parents were moving to Steeple Bumpstead. I then attended Dame Bradbury's School in Saffron Walden. So for the next 2 years my church going was restricted to only once a week on Sundays for Mass and going to confession occasionally.

In 1953, I started a new school – St. Hugh's, which was the Preparatory School to St. Edmund's College in Hertfordshire. It was at St Hugh's where my class and I were prepared for Confirmation. This is about being strengthened by God's Holy Spirit. We were told that Bishop of Westminster would be the one to confirm us. In The Confirmation Service the Bishop, we were told, would tap each one of us on the cheek and say *"Pax Tecum"* (Peace be with you). Of course it didn't take too long before some "wag" in the class said "we should tap him back and say *"Tecum Pax"* – oh, how we did laugh!!

After two years at St. Hugh's, I progressed to St. Edmunds College. Here I was introduced another Prayer Service – "The Angellus" which was a short time of prayers to Jesus' Mother, Mary, these prayers could be said wherever you were and not necessarily in church when you heard the Angellus bell at 12 noon and 6.00pm.

It was while I was at St. Edmunds College that I was introduced to another type of the Mass – Sung High Mass which was celebrated by more than one priest at the same time. There was also incense being burnt and, at times, the smoke was so thick you couldn't see across the church! After one year here, I moved school again, this time to:

Blackfriars School, Laxton, Northamptonshire, where I stayed until I was 18, except for school holidays, of course! Another school meant another new Service which I was introduced to: Compline. This was a Service with Psalms and Prayers all sung in Latin of course and all out of a book. I remember asking at the time "Why can't we pray in our *own* words, rather than out of a book?" But none of the teachers had a satisfactory answer for me!

Finally, after seemingly a lifetime, I left school at the age of 18. My life in the outside world began and I was still a Catholic, so my week contained a Sunday morning Mass and also Mass on Holy Days of Obligation. It was still a sin if you missed Mass on any of those days! My Religious life continued in this way until I was 45 years old.

One day I was invited to attend an Open Air Songs of Praise here in Steeple Bumpstead, which I enjoyed, as I love singing. This event was followed by another invitation, this time to a Christian Singing Group which met in the Lecture Hall on Thursday Evening at 8.00pm. We were learning new Worship Songs, which I later found out were being sung at the Congregational Church on the following Sunday morning! So, here I was a practicing Roman Catholic going to a Congregational Singing Group on Thursdays and then still going to Mass on Sunday mornings!

After about 6 weeks, I decided to try just one Service at the Congregational Church. I crept in at the back of the church and kept a low profile, which is hard for me at 6ft 6". It wasn't many minutes before I was invited to join my friends from the Singing Group and sit with them! When the Service started I realised that I was finally *FREE*. My prayers had been answered, I was free from set prayers in a book, I could pray my own prayers of what I was feeling at the time. It took me 45 years to realise what Religious Freedom meant to me and I still like it!!!

I realised that prayer is talking to God, just like you talk to your best friend. You talk to them and you listen to their reply. We can't just tell God everything we want, like a shopping list, without waiting for His reply!

Bill Hybells, the American author of *"Too Busy Not to Pray"* wrote that there are four types of prayer, which are best remembered by A.C.T.S. which stand for:
A – Adoration, **C** – Confession, **T** – Thanksgiving, **S** – Supplication.

We should start our prayers by:
- Saying how much we **A**dore, Love, Worship God our Father, Jesus and the Holy Spirit.
- **C**onfessing our sins to Him.
- **T**hanking Him for His divine goodness in forgiving our sins.
- **S**upplication, this means asking God for our needs, what we need for ourselves and for other people.

When I was meditating about this, I had the following discussion with The Holy Spirit:

Holy Spirit: Who are you?
Me: I am a child of God.
Holy Spirit: Who is your father?
Me: God is my Father.
Holy Spirit: Out of all your children and grand-children, which one asks on behalf of all the others?
Me: They all ask individually for what they want.

So, I believe, it is with God and us, all humans are all equal, no one person is better than anyone else.

If we can think, we can pray silently in our hearts.

If we can talk, we can pray aloud, as well. After all prayer is talking to God.

We can also pray with other people in Group Prayer, but we must always remember that "Prayer is the soul dealing with God, and when one prays in order to attract the attention of men (or women) it is blasphemy." *(An Exposition of the Whole Bible by G. Morgan Campbell).*

In "His Sermon on the Mount" Jesus said: *"And when you come before God, don't turn that into a theatrical production either. All these people making a regular show out of their prayers, hoping for stardom! Do you think God sits in a box seat?*

"Here's what I want you to do: Find a quiet, secluded place so you won't be tempted to role-play before God. Just be there as simply and honestly as you can manage. The focus will shift from you to God, and you will begin to sense His grace.

"The world is full of so-called prayer warriors who are prayer-ignorant. They're full of formulas and programmes and advice, peddling techniques for getting what you want from God. Don't fall for that nonsense. This is your Father you are dealing with, and he knows better than you what you need. With a God like this loving you, you can pray very simply." (The Message Bible – Mathew 6:5 – 8).
You don't have to be in church to talk to God, you can be anywhere, anywhere at all.
Talk to God in the mornings when you wake up.
Talk to God all the time, as He is always with you.

Talk to God before you go to sleep, and if you go to sleep while you are praying, then you are sleeping in your Father's arms, what better place?

Some years later, another challenge came my way. Our Pastor, Derrick Potts, was talking of leaving. Shock, horror – oh please don't go Derrick, we implored! "I will stay another year if you guys: Ron Bentley, Adrian Burr, Kim Cresswell and Chris Stirling will each take a Sunday Service occasionally," he said. This was a real shock to me!! How do I do it?

The answer: is to Pray to Jesus, and pray to the Holy Spirit for inspiration. Then, sitting at my computer, when I have received an idea for the theme of the Service, then I need to look at the Bible for the suitable Readings, then the Hymn Book for the Worship Songs to link the Readings with The Message and finally the prayers, which of course none come from a book! After a many hours, with lots of Divine Inspiration, my Service is ready for when it is required. It is the Holy Spirit who gives me the confidence now to stand up, lead the Service and preach, I can't do it on my own!

I am working for Jesus,
may I go on for as long as He wants me!!

What a wonderful God we have.
All Praise and Glory goes to Him!

Christopher Stirling

God Knows my Size

I was brought up in a Christian home, the youngest of four children of a long-distance lorry driver. My mother was very special; although we never had much in the way of worldly possessions, we had just so much love. Mum became a second mum to almost everyone she met. She used to say, "If you can't bring your friends home, then maybe you shouldn't be going out with them".

We lived in a four roomed house and the only room in the house which wasn't a bedroom served as living room, bathroom, etc. We didn't have a bathroom or drains so mum would draw water from the well, fill up the big boiler in the yard and light a fire under it so there was plenty of water for baths and hair-washes. Then she would drag the big galvanized bath into the 'lounge', bath my sister and I first, then add water for the boys and finally drag the bath into the bedroom, adding more water for herself and dad. The water had to be lifted out in buckets and emptied onto the garden, since we had no drains.

We didn't have a TV, in fact, like many country families, we didn't have electricity. Our evenings were spent singing around the piano by an old Tilley lamp or candlelight if we had run out of paraffin. Sometimes we listened to Biggles or Larry the Lamb on a very crackly radio, when we had enough money to have the accumulator charged. During the long, hot summer days we spent most of our time on the common near our home with a bag of jam sandwiches packed for us by mum. We had a wonderful childhood and often saw the hand of the Lord supplying our needs in miraculous ways. Mum would say, "Lord, you own the cattle on a thousand hills, please sell another cow".

We attended church three times on Sundays, alternating in the evening between the Pentecostal church and the Methodist church which my Gran attended. I loved church and dreamed of being a missionary. On one occasion mum urgently needed new shoes and she prayed about this. That same afternoon as she passed her sister's house, she called out that she had received a parcel with two pairs of shoes in it and they didn't fit.

She replied, "They will fit me. God knows my size". Guess who had two pairs of shoes that were a perfect fit?

I asked about going to Bible School but was told I could never afford it so I started work in a children's home. I had always wanted to visit Switzerland so when I saw an advert for a youth holiday, I began saving. Then a pastor visited and invited us to give up some of our summer holidays to help take the gospel to Belgium. Would I have to cancel my trip to Switzerland? I was called to the homes' Southampton office, expecting to be sacked. To my surprise the boss greeted me with a smile and informed me I was on lower pay than I should be. I left that office praising God for his wonderful provision, with enough money for the trip to Belgium, a camera and spending money.

I was the only one of the family who wasn't married, so I asked God for a partner. On the Belgian holiday, I saw a picture of myself in a wedding dress with a husband by my side. I said, "Lord, that's no good, let us turn round so I can see who he is. We turned round and I recognized the church pastor from Oostende, to whom I was married for over thirty happy years.

I was happy to marry in a suit but remembered that in the picture I had been wearing a wedding dress. Where to get one my size was a problem I turned over to God. I looked in the Southampton Echo and there, sure enough, there was one in my size, but no price. I worked out my finances, £12 in total! I thought to myself, "Don't be stupid, who is going to sell a wedding dress my size for £!2?

My brother drove me to Southampton and a lady showed us a heavy white brocade dress with a long train. There was a beautiful coronet with it. "Try it on", she said. "But I doubt if I can afford it", I said. It fitted like a glove and she said, "I paid a lot for the material and had it made. You will have the coronet and veil as well won't you? You can have it all for ....£12. "Thank you, Lord!"

I had everything except shoes and needed a size 9; rare for a woman. One rude assistant suggested I needed canoes!. Eventually I went to Chance's shoe shop in Totton where the assistant offered a pair of white satin shoes in size 8. To my amazement, they fitted and I bought a pair of navy ones, also size 8 for my honeymoon. They were really comfortable. Afterwards, Mum suggested dyeing the satin shoes and wearing them for occasions and I went to try them on but they were far too small. God had allowed my feet to shrink so I would have shoes for my wedding!

Jennifer Desmet,
Southampton

Footnote:

Jenny has worked in children's homes, as a personal secretary and as driving instructor. She and her husband, a pastor who was formerly a monk, worked in Belgium, Portsmouth, Havant, Holywood, Dublin, Tramore, Waterford, Sunderland, Totton and Cyprus. She has also written a book entitled, 'Lord Sell A Cow' in which she shares more of her life story. One of our church members was with her when, aged 21, she met and prayed for a stranger, a lady with a withered arm, on Southsea seafront. The arm was instantly restored.

It was impossible that I should be born

In August 1940 my mother and her friend Lena Smallbone wanted to go into St Michael's Church in

Basingstoke, but they felt they ought not to as they were not wearing hats. During the time they would have been inside, German bombs fell and damaged the church. Their lack of headgear quite possibly saved their lives.

But my mother had an infantile womb and was unable to bear children. However, she persisted in prayer, and in trailing from doctor to doctor, till she found one who was willing and able to help. And so on the evening of Wednesday, Christmas Day 1946, at my home at 295 Worting Road, Basingstoke, I came into the world, attended by two doctors in dinner dress to a background of the Salvation Army outside in the road playing *Silent Night* - the only child of Dinsdale Thomas Young and Isobel Kate Young.

One deep impression that abides from my childhood is that I was loved. No one reading these pages will form the impression that my parents were perfect, but that they loved me is beyond question.

My conversion took place when I was alone at home. When I was 11 or 12, I still had a vague belief that God existed, but He played no part in my life or thought. I "prayed" nightly, because this had been ingrained in me from earliest childhood, but my prayers were no more than empty repetition of the same formulas, and I got through them as quickly as I could.

At the age of 13 or 14 I began to think more seriously. Soon, I became convinced that there is no God, and that those who believed in Him were quite below my own level of insight!

In time, my father gave me a book about life after death, acquired at the preparations for a jumble sale, and I bought another book about spiritism at the same sale. Through them I became convinced that there is indeed an afterlife; with this persuasion came also a head belief in the existence of God. It went no further than the idea that He existed - He still played no part in my life.

As I had had piano lessons, I was able to play several of the easier tunes from "The Methodist Hymnbook". One day I was playing hymn 452, and at the same time reading these words of Charles Wesley:

> *I long to know and to make known*
> *The heights and depths of love divine,*
> *The kindness Thou to me hast shown,*
> *Whose every sin was counted Thine.*
> *My God for me resigned His breath:*
> *He died to save my soul from death.*

It was as I was reading line four - "Whose every sin was counted Thine" - that I saw that they are true words. It was for me a sinner, that Jesus had died on the Cross. God had shown me, opening my heart to believe. And so I became a Christian - humanly, perhaps Charles Wesley's last convert.

I do not remember when I went to Cambridge for my interview. I was interviewed by Dr Robson, who later became my tutor. We spoke of politics and of religion, and I came away somewhat downcast, for he tied me up in knots, certainly on politics (he was a historian), perhaps also on religion. I did not feel I had done well. When I was working at Basingstoke sorting office, my father came one day to tell me that we had received a telegram from Trinity, saying I had gained an exhibition. I was also awarded the closed Philpott Exhibition.

My mother was so proud! Everyone had to know that "David is going to Cambridge." I recall her horror when a local paper mistakenly reported that I was going up to Cambridge to read Theology. She urged me to consider what my father's clients might think if they heard he had a son who was going into the ministry: it might adversely affect his business as an insurance agent. Perhaps my father's undated note to her, found after his death, stems from this period, in which he writes, "May all your worries about David be gone!" Paradoxically, there came a time when my father said to me quietly, out of my mother's hearing, that I should continue to preach, and had his approval in it.

David Young, MA,

Scripture and Other Books Comforted my Heart

I have often been asked how I came to be involved with Albania, a closed Communist country. At the age of 18, when I was in Backnang, Germany, I saw, in a vision, a 'man of Macedonia' calling me to "Come over and help us". I started breaking down and teaching myself the Albanian language, not knowing what God had in store for me.

I was looking for full-time secular employment, with a view to serving God in connection with the Albanian calling, including travelling again to the Albanian people. Meanwhile I was not idle in attempting to earn extra money for the family's needs, and gave private German tuition in the first three months of 1977.

I applied for thirty-three posts and had interviews at Shillingstone (where the headmaster seemed tipsy), Cottenham, Gravesend, Hurstpierpoint, Melksham, Bedford, Eastleigh and Ruabon,.at Lindisfarne College.

On 30th April 1981 I went into Hunter Ward at the Wrexham Maelor Hospital to have two fairly simple operations done at the same time. But when Mr Crumplin the surgeon opened me up he found cancer. Wisely, he removed it there and then, but woke me up later from my drugged sleep following the anæsthetic to secure my retrospective consent.

I shed tears at the thought of death, of Margaret being left a widow, of my fatherless children.

Passages of scripture and of other books comforted my heart with the hope of a cure. Mr Crumplin said twice that the way the cancer was discovered looked like the working of Fate, and the doctors told me there was a 96% chance of full recovery.

On 15th May, in accordance with the word in James 5, Mr Harding and Frank Collins, came and anointed me with oil and prayed for me with the laying-on of hands, asking God that in one way or another I should be fully healed. We felt a sense of the presence of God.

A visit to Christie Hospital, the specialist cancer hospital where the actor John Wayne went for treatment, followed. I came out on 4th June, and returned to work at Lindisfarne.

On 21st October I learnt that the cancer had spread to one of my lungs, where it was euphemistically called "a secondary deposit". Three years previously it had always been incurable; now it would be incurable if it returned after the treatment I was to receive. So I now faced the prospect of four months of feeling ill, of losing all my hair, of unpleasant chemotherapy at Christie Hospital. Isaiah 14:3 refers to a time of "pain and turmoil" followed by God-given rest. This was what I expected.

On 8th November I went back into Christie and my treatment started the next day. It consisted of a régime of four cycles of one week in hospital and two or three at home.

As the chemotherapy broke down my immune system, I began to suffer from whatever was close by. I began to be delirious; I thought I had a pile of noses on my face. My mouth got thrush, and I had a horrible taste in it at all times. It was very hard indeed to feel warm, though I achieved it by lying on the settee beside the fire, with the central heating on and a quilt over me.

It became hard to find a vein into which to insert a needle for the chemotherapy drip. Needles were sometimes inserted into my foot instead of my arm. One doctor, on failing to find even that way in, put his head in his hands and said, "Oh God! What am I going to do?"

I was allergic to one of the anti-sickness drugs used during chemotherapy, Maxolon: it made me feel very ill. Maybe the hospital staff thought this was my imagination, but they discontinued it for me; then one evening a nurse gave it to me, and though I did not know she had, the same feelings of illness and queasiness immediately followed.

My arm swelled up so badly in reaction to Bleomycin that they discontinued it. Indeed, my reaction to the treatment was so severe that it was mooted that it might be stopped, in which case I would have died.

When it was all over, I had to increase the amount of fluids I drank in order to flush out my kidneys: beer, I was informed, was one of the best drinks to achieve this. But I was told to tear up my donor card, for no hospital would now wish to use my kidneys.

My second spell in hospital was from 30th November till 4th December. On Sunday 13th much of Britain "was turned into a giant disaster area", according to *The Times*, as a wave of blizzards swept in from the West. North Wales suffered the worst conditions for eighteen years; many roads in both North and South Wales were blocked.

The whole period was exhausting for Margaret, who had me ill, the children aged 7 and 4. As I often slept a good deal of the day, I sometimes woke up in the night and wanted to talk, or to satisfy my craving for blackberries and ice-cream, which she duly got from the freezer for me. She made herculean efforts to make Christmas as jolly and joyful as was possible.

Two days after Christmas, on Sunday 27th, I returned to hospital in Manchester for a further week of treatment. Margaret cried as she saw the New Year in alone - the children in bed and an unknown future.

It was not possible for me to come home from Manchester at the end of my third week of treatment because of the snow. I pleaded to be taken to Wrexham with Dr Read when he went for his Wednesday clinic for outpatients, but I was refused on insurance grounds. In the end, Margaret phoned one of the teachers at Lindisfarne, a devout Catholic, who put a spade and walking boots into his car, set off for Manchester and brought me home. This is the kind of friend I would like to be to people: "Go thou and do likewise."

Other friends visited during my illness. One almost carried me to the doctor's surgery in Wrexham as I was too weak to walk. Others came from Kent, Sussex and Yorkshire - friends from Cambridge days. I appreciated - and still appreciate - all these tokens of genuine friendship.

By Sunday 10th January Wales was almost isolated by snow and ice after thirty-seven hours of continuous snowfall. The Prince of Wales interrupted his holiday to visit Wales and see for himself the havoc wrought by the worst blizzards in living memory.

127

I feel like a plant going into winter: the upper, visible part dying off for a while, but the roots remaining and in some way being deepened or strengthened.

After that winter ended, a new chapter of my life began, leading to a pastorate and then to full-time work for Albania, but the next four years brought more fragmentation to our lives before the pattern finally became clearer to our minds: and to that story we now turn.

In February 1983 I began to have what I called "intrusions". I was not unconscious. If I was speaking, I continued to speak, though I was unable to recall afterwards what I had said. If I was driving, I continued along the road, rather as one might when a normal memory pops into one's mind. Strangely, it seemed to happen a number of times as I drove to the junction of Ffordd Môn and the main road to Llay, and in time I began to be anxious about that junction, in case an intrusion occurred.

What more might I say to describe the intrusions? I leant on the wall or work surface in the kitchen one day and told Margaret I could see creatures crawling all over the kitchen. Then the intrusion passed, and I couldn't remember anything about it. That is what it was like. It was very alarming.

Dr Read told me that I was probably suffering from temporal lobe epilepsy, which is often caused by a brain tumour. I was to have tests for these, and meanwhile I was forbidden to drive. Often, when I was on house duty, my father, already aged about 80, would turn out at 11 pm to drive me home.

House duty was from 9 till 11 pm, and four times this was also done for me by other staff. By half term, at the end of May, I felt once again in full health, and not tired.

I began to believe that the intrusions I had had in February and March were brought on by the devastating effect of House and school duties in the early part of the year, and by deep tiredness. Mark Diavastes wrote to me saying, "The work you do would make any person very tired."

In April 1983 I could finally look back over the first two terms of the school year. I felt as if I had passed along a dark tunnel, a time of strain and pressure. School duties had continued, the classroom behaviour of pupils had degenerated, cancer treatment had battered me the previous winter, and now the doctors believed I had succumbed to epilepsy.

Thus by the first half of 1983, I had finished my cancer treatment

By May 1984 I was able to write to my parents:

> *They told me that if I survived two years I would probably be all right, and it is now nearly 2½ years since I came out of hospital; so probably I am as safe from cancer as anyone else...*

> *Although I was never diagnosed as epileptic, I have had no more of the "turns" since March, last year, except for a few days back in November, during a month when I was on duty late at school one day in three and became very tired indeed. However, the possibility of being diagnosed as epileptic plays on my mind much more than the possibility of the return of the cancer. It would be difficult to get another job with a background of both cancer and epilepsy, and being my age.*

On 6th April 1987, in the school holiday, the new headmaster spoke with me and said that he wished to replace me with a full-time teacher of French. He said

129

that if I agreed to leave, he would arrange generous compensation; if I refused, he would compile a dossier of complaints and dismiss me. Not long after he was sacked himself.

By the end of 1988 - an outward pattern was at last almost completely in place that would continue well into the next century:

- My health seemed fairly secure, as nearly seven years had passed since my cancer treatment had finished.

- School teaching had finished: I had escaped.

- Our marriage had undergone a period of creeping separateness which we would not have suspected when we married fifteen years earlier.

- Margaret had arranged to start work at the estate agency Thomas C. Adams, thus greatly helping our financial situation.

- My rôle as a pastor had been exercised for a second time in my life, and ended.

The call to Albanian work had come to dominate my working life, and to set its pattern for a period of time which, as I write, has still not reached its end. Folly, weakness and the character of a failed earthen vessel have been often in evidence in my life, and surely, in the words of Charles Wesley, I have "grieved him with a thousand falls." But in his infinite mercy God granted me a part to play in "shaming the strong" in the matter of Albania and its release from Satan's seemingly unbreakable grip.

God's call to eastern Europe and then to the Albanian people was in fact quietly working itself out, unrecognised but always persisting. I have every reason to sing the hymn, "All the way my Saviour leads me... Jesus led me all the way" He does it: we do not always see and know what he is planning and creating. We need to learn to trust him.

Finally, I end with the expression of my gratitude to my wife Margaret for her continuing sacrificial involvement in the work, and to God for all his mercies to me, an unworthy servant.

David Martin Young, MA

Wrexham, North Wales.

Footnote:
David Young preaches in many countries in languages including Albanian and Welsh.

During the years 2000-2010 alone, David made 22 trips to Albanians in Italy and Sicily and drove over 66,000 miles within Britain as Director of Albania Evangelical Trust. As a result there are full time Christian workers and churches in Albania today. The full story can be found in David's book, "Turned East-half a life for Albania".

God is Constantly Helping His People

But the trouble is that human nature being what it is, the acts of God are often explained away by some plausible answer, or by some "scientific" reason....I must confess, that I have in the past, been guilty of this failing.

I can well remember an incident that happened to me some time ago. I had entered our garden by the back door of our house and made my way down the path, to our portacabin which I use as an office. Some time later I needed to get back into the house, but arriving at the door and turning the handle, found it well and truly locked!

Fortunately I had access to some basic tools in our garage, and came back with them. Using a screwdriver I removed the door handle and tried turning the key on the inside, from the outside with a thin screwdriver. But all this was of no avail. Had Linda been in the house, she could have opened the back door by turning the key but she wasn't at home that day and would not be back until after 10pm.

I continued with my endeavour to get the door open, becoming more and more agitated at not being able to do so, and praying all the time "Lord help me, help me". After three quarters of an hour of hectic manoeuvring with the tools I had, it became obvious that the door was not going to be opened by my efforts. I lost heart of trying any more and became resigned to the fact that I would have to wait until Linda got back with her bunch of keys.

But then, I casually turned the door handle, for what reason I cannot tell, and although I had turned the handle many times previously, THIS TIME IT RESPONDED. The door opened and I stepped into the house!

In all that I had been trying up till now there was no mistaking that the door had been well and truly locked. I had not IMAGINED it to be so. And there was no

"SCIENTIFIC" reason for the door being open now. No, NOTHING that would provide an answer....Apart from the fact that it was opened by a MIRACLE...! I CAN QUITE BELIEVE THAT THE Archangel Gabriel who stands in heaven's throne room would have smiled knowingly and said on my behalf, to Jesus, "Master, this time you have convinced him!"

You might be wondering to yourself "Will God help ME?" The answer is of course He will, all the time, every time, a thousand times over until you are convinced that miracles are a reality today.

David Clapp
Pickering, North Yorkshire

Footnote:
David Clapp was born and educated in India and came to England to fulfill his ambition of becoming pilot. He missed this job after telling the interviewer that he would re-apply next year if unselected. Later, he left the RAF to become a full-time Christian evangelist and printer and has trusted God for support for his family. He says he has never taken one penny from the UK government. He is a skilled carpenter and builder and does all his own work on the house he and his wife own in Pickering.

I Saw The Ambulance As We Turned into Our Road

With my heart feeling as though it was coming out of my chest I accelerated hard and pulled up at our house. Jumping out, I raced up the path, but a man in uniform wouldn't let me. I looked at the man's ashen face and his next words caused me to collapse into his arms.

He said, "I'm afraid I have some sad news, Madam. Your husband has passed away. It was 1982 and I was almost fifty.

The days passed slowly and painfully, stretching into long weeks of emptiness. I sat around the house a lot. Family and friends offered comfort, but my heart ached and I began to cry out to God. "Give me something to do," I prayed. "Please!" He must have heard, for the very next day, a friend called round with a book called 'Appointment in Jerusalem' by Derek Prince. In it he told the story of his first wife's call to live there and rescue Jewish and Arab children. I was captivated by this Danish woman who gave up a comfortable life to be the adoptive mother to several children of both nationalities. A strange feeling began to stir in my heart and I said to my youngest daughter, "I believe the Lord may be calling me to Israel". "Don't be silly, Mum," was her response. "It's just your imagination. Put that book away." Over the next days and weeks I mused on this unexpected desire to go to Jerusalem. "It seems a strange place to send me, but I'm glad it's not the Soviet Union". Labour camps and torture were not things I wanted to face.

I took a holiday in Israel with a friend and one night I woke up. I was wide awake and suddenly, from all around the ceiling came voices, "Who is this man Jesus?" The voices repeated the question over and over again. Then I felt I heard the Lord say, "My own people-they don't know me". I began to cry. I could have stayed, but I wisely returned home, until a short time later I received a letter from the International Christian embassy. It said, "Come out for an extended time and see if God opens a door for you". I was so happy and arranged to go out for six weeks.

I was given a list of organizations in need of volunteers and visited each one in turn, asking God to get me invited if one of these was for me. The last was a home for children with severe mental and physical disabilities. I started there in October, 1984.

I became involved with the Jewish people and with groups seeking to enable Jews to return to their homeland, if they wished to do so. I visited several countries, at one time being followed by and managing to evade the KGB by following God's instructions. We never know what amazing adventures God has in store for us. Flying in old Russian helicopters and planes in a war zone, sleeping under kitchen tables and delivering vitally needed food and clothing were all part of my life.

Then came the Gulf War and I became used to the sirens and the bother of carrying gas masks everywhere. The War ended at the Feast of Purim and tales of miraculous escapes began to emerge. A baby was found unharmed and asleep having been protected by falling masonry. Another family could not enter their shelter as they had lost the key. They stayed indoors and a scud missile took the roof off the shelter where they would have been hiding. Thirty nine of these missiles had been fired and there was only one reported fatality. It was a joyous Purim that year!

Esther Lever
Monks Risborough

Footnote: At the age of 80, Esther is a Regional Representative for Ebenezer Operation Exodus which seeks to help Jewish people wishing to return to Israel in fulfillment of Biblical prophecy. She also visits churches, speaking about Israel. She has written several books and we have included quotes from "The Ingathering of Israel" with this story

He Hears and Answers....

There are so many instances of where God has answered prayer that it is embarrassing to say that I don't remember them all. Of course I am extremely grateful, because in writing this I realise afresh that who and what I am - at least the good bits, are answers to prayer.

I'll recount two specific answers at either end of my adult life (to date!); New Year's Eve 1975 found myself and girlfriend Cheryl Self gathered with other Christians in a farm house just outside Braintree to pray and celebrate in the New Year in worship. The leader, Dave MacAdam, now pastor of a very large church in the USA, spoke to us about God granting the desires of our hearts because if we were truly following Him, our desires would be His desires. He then encouraged us to bring to God the desires of our hearts. I did, and so did Cheryl. The answer for both of us came in August the following year when Cheryl Self became Cheryl Mizen! There has followed (so far) almost 37 years of answered prayer in ways beyond our "imaginings".

The other is very recent (March 2013), having had an unplanned change of circumstance during 2012 I/we have found a new way in which God answers prayer, He does so by answering before we ask! Through a very difficult time, God has gone before and prepared paths which have at times astounded us not only in their outcome, but also in the healing these paths have brought.

At the beginning of 2013, we both felt that we needed to settle into a "home church". Having finally found the church we believed to be called to, we felt we needed to join a cell group, the only problem being that the groups were all at the beginning of the week which is when we are away from home. We eventually decided that perhaps if we got away from work on time, then we could make the Wednesday group just a little late so "pushed on that door" of joining. Just a week after taking the step to join, we were asked to change our shift pattern and start an hour earlier in the morning because of changing needs of our work. Of course that means we can now leave work an hour earlier ....

More and more I/we find that walking with God, listening and being obedient, means that the emergency praying for ourselves reduces. When we listen as we walk, and walk as we hear, then God has what He asks, faithfulness and obedience......I wish I could say we were that all the time!!

IM/CM

I left him and ran to my Mum

I spent my childhood in a happy Christian household, going to church every Sunday and Youth Group most Thursdays. I read my bible every day and had never known any other way of life.

This all changed drastically when my father left my mother in favour of my 17 year old 'best friend'. Up until that moment I had adored and greatly respected my father. I felt my little world shatter and I turned my back on God.

I moved to Zimbabwe where I met and married an agnostic bigot. He kept me far from my family, from the church, and I lived a godless life and marriage for 15 years. We had three beautiful children who were never christened as we couldn't falsely commit to bringing them up in the church.

Not surprisingly, my marriage eventually failed. I left him and ran to my Mum, who was taken from me a few months later by cancer. I had no money, no support and no faith.

Almost two years ago, in complete and utter despair, I got down on my knees and prayed to a God I hadn't believed in for over twenty years. The very next day God sent what I then believed to be an angel to my door. He showed me the first act of selfless kindness I had received since my Mum died and handed me a wad of cash. No strings, no questions. God had told him to come to me, urgently, and he had obeyed.

Turns out he wasn't an angel but a humble, God-fearing, deeply committed Christian and, with his help, my life has been turned around. My son believes, my eldest daughter asked to be baptised last year and my youngest loves Jesus with all her heart. Our God is indeed a Mighty God, Praise His Name, Amen.

Rebecca Pretorius
Zimbabwe

Footnote:

'Reb'Pretorius originates from Essex and graduated from Colchester Institute. She went to Zimbabwe initially to teach French and music and has played in their National Orchestra. On her ill-fated wedding day, a squall blew up as she and her husband sailed off for their honeymoon and she was swept overboard from her husband's yacht in her wedding dress. She and her husband ran a Safari Park near Bulawayo but this was seized by Mugabe's government, together with other land in their valley. She and her husband spent four years at sea on a small yacht with their two young children, visiting many countries but finally returned to Zimbabwe.

Jesus Speaks to Me

Whilst I was never baptised as a Jehovah's Witness (and I never intended to) it is true to say that in the time that I studied with them I became indoctrinated, very quickly (which was the aim).

I remember suffering with toothache during my year of book study, even though I asked Jehovah to take the pain away, nothing happened. I saw the dentist eventually and was operated on.

Eventually, I reached a point in my life where I cried out to God Jesus to forgive me for my sin, I need You in my life, come into my life and make me a new creation in You. And He did. He started a thirst that was for me to read the bible and it's a discipline that's still with me today. He came to live on the inside of me and I read from John 5:24 where Jesus said "he who believes in me has passed over the judgement from death to life," I knew from that sudden moment that when I died I was going to go to heaven.

The toothache used to reappear now and again. one night in 1990 I laid in bed with toothache and a voice in my head said "say 'I am cleansed by the blood of Jesus' 3 times, then something like 'Holy Spirit come and heal me'. So I did what the voice said and on the third time, the pain just fizzled out.
I learnt quite quickly about the power of Jesus name and pleading the blood of Christ. One night as I was reading a Christian book, I felt a terrible presence in the room, full of fear. I called on the Name of the Lord Jesus and it left immediately. The Lord was teaching me about Himself in a very practical sense.

Just last summertime the Lord was showing me about

the relationships I have with those who live in the same house. I run errands and amongst others I collect bottled water for one of my parents. At times my father has rubbed me up the wrong way so often that I thought to myself "I can't collect the water anymore". I distinctly heard the Lord Jesus in my spirit speaking, "I know you can't do it for him, and I don't expect you to. I want you to do it for Me". My reaction was "I can do that for You Lord". I get the water for Jesus now, and I experience a release in my spirit from that.

My unbelieving, ex-Jehovah's Witness sister has said to me about my relationship with our earthly dad (in between criticism) "I think you're very gracious to him Jane", out of her eyeshot, punching the air with my fist "Thank *You* Lord " I whisper (italics mine).

It's not always easy...but keep your focus on Jesus, trust and obey and never let go of His Hand. He's worth it!

Jane Searle

In 1993 We Found Out My Dad Had Cancer

He had treatment (chemo) but it didn't work. Then they tried radio therapy, this shrunk the tumor so dad was able to breath.
Dad told the Doctors that every time I was there with him he felt well. I told Dad that it wasn't anything to do with me and that it was Jesus' healing powers working.

I became a Christian in January 1991. I prayed so much for my family and my mum and sister to be able to get through this and for dad to be healed. I clung to God in those months from when Dad was diagnosed and I was going through different emotions of sadness and special moments shared with my wonderful Dad. Taking him to the Sea side and out to lots of different places before he became too weak to go out.

I asked people to come and pray for Dad from my church. In the last few months of his life When Dad went into the Hospice in Bury St Edmunds to give mum a rest. We would go over and be with him every day and when I came home I'd leave the Bible open on 1 John on his bed. Mum told me that she told Dad I think Karen wants you to read this. :)

Dad told the Doctors that every time I was there with him he felt well. I told Dad it's nothing that I do to make you feel well it's Jesus that makes you feel well when I'm around, not me. But Jesus living in me.

When Dad came home again, he would sit in his car just listening to a cassette tape that I had given to him that I got from a Christian event called 'Easter People'. It was recorded during one of the worship celebrations with lots of Christians singing. My family and I were present during the recording. He used to turn up the volume and just sit listening :) .

One day when I went to visit Mum and Dad I told Dad that I wanted to speak with him so we went into the sitting room and I told Dad that he needed to ask Jesus into his life. He agreed that it was the right time and the right thing to do. I went through the steps of salvation with him. Dad asked God to forgive him for anything he had ever done wrong in his life and he asked Jesus to come into his life and to be with him and live in him through God's Holy Spirit. I laid my hands on Dad's head and asked The Holy Spirit to come and fill Dad from the top of his head to the tip of his toes. I told Dad that when he died he would go to Heaven and be with Jesus. (John 3 verse 16) and that on the day when Jesus comes back he will be raised from death to life and have eternal life.

In November when Dad was very near the end of his life I kissed him on his forehead and I said these words ... Now I lay me down to sleep, I pray the Lord my soul to keep. If I should die before I wake I pray the Lord my soul to take. (I have no idea apart from God prompting me, why I said that prayer. I had heard it before years ago but it just came to my heart to say it). I hugged my Dad before leaving to go home to sleep. Before I went to sleep I tried to picture Dad's face but I just couldn't see him. Around 5 am on the 14th November 1993 Remembrance Sunday, I woke up opened my eyes and my Dad's face was right up close to me, the room was dark, but I could see him so clear. I woke my husband up and told him that Dad's face was right in front of me a few minutes later the phone rang, it was my sister telling me that Dad had died a few minuets before ... But I already knew and through the sadness and tears I had a joy in my heart because I knew with out a doubt that my Dad was at peace and not in pain and that he was with Jesus sleeping in Heaven till one day we will meet again. I felt as though Dad was saying to me " it's ok Karen I know what you wanted for me was right and true and that he was with God.

I have no idea why God chooses to heal some and not others physically ..... But I believe that when we are in Heaven we will have new bodies and on the day that Jesus comes. There will be no more pain or crying or sickness we will all have new bodies. We will be healed.

Karen Tann
Formerly of Haverhill, Suffolk

No Matter What Situation You are in

The earliest memories I have are of South London immediately after the war, where we children played on bomb sites and tram lines and lived in a sparsely furnished flat in which I and my brothers shared a double bed. Our annual 'holiday' was in Kent, hop picking with other families from our street. We would collect a few pots and pans, blankets and clothes and head off for the fields where our hotels were sheds with piles of straw for bedding and we cooked on open fires in the field. I can remember this as a happy time when I never felt out of place as there were lots of other children in the same circumstances.

My world came to a standstill at the age of four when my mother died of cancer and we were taken in by a half-sister aged about 20. My father had previously died-on my first birthday. She found that she was unable to cope with three boisterous lads amongst the dangers of Central London. Thankfully we were kept together but we were taken into care and placed in an orphanage in the country near Tiverton, Devon. I longed to return to my 'roots' in London but this was not to be, for when I was seven, we were transferred to another orphanage, this time in Lancashire. It was grim up north and the harsh climate was reflected by the harsh conditions in the home.

At age 12, I brought back my school report, which read '3', a surprise to everybody and not least to me. The Vicar was so impressed that he gave me a two-shilling piece (10p) for my improvement in reading and I thoroughly enjoyed the sweets I was able to purchase with it, but two months later he found out that I had been placed in a group of three for special coaching due to my inability to read!

One of the high points of my youth was joining Sea Scouts and forming bonds with the scouting 'family'. Two lovely people, Mr & Mrs Brown, took my brother and I into their home and my brother obtained a job as a mechanic for a while, before moving on to the Merchant Navy. I missed him and though I took a job in a nursery and had friends, I could not settle and moved back to London. When I was three and a half I had watched a homeless couple climb into a bomb ruin on a snowy night and cuddle together with two potato sacks for bedding. I'll always be thankful to God that I had shelter as a child and for every night I am blessed with it now.

Shortly afterwards, I also joined the Navy and became a fairly typical seaman, travelling the world and spending a short while with my half-sister while on leave. I switched to cruise liners-then to tankers, learning a lot about life as I travelled the world and playing a lot of practical jokes on my fellow seamen.

My elder brother was now married and on a visit, I was introduced to the love of my life. I couldn't get her out of my thoughts but I couldn't write to convey my feelings. She was so kind to me and often showed up at unexpected times. I couldn't bear to leave her and return to sea. When I did so, I asked for a discharge on medical grounds and the sympathetic officer, sensing that I was in love, agreed. Not only that, he paid me for the remaining term of service on the ship and covered my NI contributions.

We married and settled in London but we realised that we would never afford our own home, so we looked elsewhere, finding an opportunity in Suffolk. I found a job as a butcher....then as a milkman, but the milk kept disappearing and I could not make a proper wage, so I had to quit and moved from job to job.

About this time, my wife was on the verge of needing a blood transfusion to save her life and this did not suit the Jehovah's Witnesses we had joined on account of their friendliness to us. I consented and faced the consequences, leaving the JW's as a result. Life went from bad to worse and work in a factory finally sent me into a breakdown. From then on my life revolved around tablets... I became lost in a world of psychotic medication, for which I blamed myself. There were brief periods when I could work and we attended a local church where the people were very supportive. My wife thought she had said goodbye to the man she had known and loved.

In 2003, I made a decision and announced to my wife over breakfast, "I cannot live my life without Jesus in it!" I said goodbye to her, went into the bedroom and cried out to God in distress. I told Him I was sorry I hadn't let Him in all my life and I needed Him now more than ever before. A great calming effect came over me and I 'felt' His presence inside of me and sensed all would be alright.

My wife had contacted my doctor and I received a call to attend the surgery. To my surprise, the doctor told me that he had never known me so calm and I didn't need to attend hospital. I took no more medication and my weight dropped from 18 to 10 stones in six weeks or so. I was tested for diabetes but I knew that my appetite for food had been replaced with one for prayer. My total dependency was now firmly in Christ. I began to read. The Bible became exciting and I longed to know more of what was happening to me. The physical strength I have now and the skills I have gained have blessed me and others. I have recently completed a Foundation for Christian Service course, which I found had already been paid for when I attempted to pay!

One issue I had to face was that of debt. My illness had caused a great deal of strain on my family, both emotionally and financially. Whilst I was ill, I had made bad decisions in how I handled money. We approached a company called Christians Against Poverty and started our journey to financial freedom. Another was the stigma of mental illness but I am proving myself to those who have doubts about my sanity. I also help with various Christian charities in town.

Because I know I am released from my sins, I am able to write this story. No matter what situation you are in or what background you have, I encourage you to call on Jesus Christ for your salvation and for any healing you need. By taking this step of faith and receiving Christ's love and forgiveness, your life will become purposeful and fulfilled.

Gordon Savory,
Haverhill.

Footnote:
Since his healing, Gordon has, with help, been able to write and publish an account of his life, a book he has called, 'Tell It As It Is'.

My Saviour had surprised me and God has heard our Prayers

Call to Me, and I will answer you, and show you great and mighty things, which you do not know.'
Jeremiah 33:3

Greetings to you in the name of Jesus Christ

1. Two young women and a young man were baptized through our prayers in the year 2013. These students belong to our Sunday school since their childhood. Praise the Lord since all the three of them came from Dalit (Hindu-untouchables) background.

2. Sister. Aruna (age 40 yrs): She was possessed by evil spirit. She was so sick that her family members spent a lot of time and money on her by visiting several hospitals as well as to witch doctors. One day in our prayer meeting, I delivered the word and the evil spirit came out through name of Jesus. She is perfectly cured now. God has answered through this miracle.

3. Grace Orphan Home: We have been praying since 5 years for the construction of the building and the office. Here, 16 Orphan children are currently sheltered through BGM. We prayed and the Lord answered our prayers and helped us complete ~ 80% of the new building in the year 2013.

4. There were many incidents of healings in cases such as evil possessions, cancer, and sickness. Broken hearts and many helpless souls received miracles through Jesus Christ name and they were blessed.

What Are The Benefits of Prayer?

Prayer is powerful (Luke 18:1; Exodus 32:7-14)

a. Much Prayer – Much Power!
b. Little Prayer – Little Power!
c. No Prayer – No Power!

I thank all those who have supported, prayed, and participated in Bethesda Gospel Ministries as well as Congregational Church Members and friends. I am also grateful to every one who has sent their donations to ensure the success of our ministries in India.

I am sure that the book will share the message of our helping God in times of troubles. I congratulate the committee for their efforts and wish them all a grand success.

May the Blessing of our Lord and Saviour Jesus Christ and Almighty God lead us to build a stronger Bethesda Gospel Ministries team through our prayers.

Your friends in Jesus,
Rev. John Prasad Vallori, President & Founder - BGM
Rev. K. Dinakar, General Secretary (BGM) INDIA.

God's Heart of Love for Each One of Us

The Father's heart of LOVE towards each one of us, individually, is more powerful and much deeper than we could ever imagine

I was in the middle of a very busy day. Washing machine busy - ironing board out - potatoes for tea bubbling on the stove. as I stopped for a breather, I heard the gentle voice of the Holy Spirit speaking to me. "Go and see P........ " (my friend in the next village) No Lord - that is impossible - look at all the things going on and what I have left to do. But the gentle voice would not give up. SO I turned everything off, changed, washed and combed my hair and went. When I got to my friend's house she was about to call the doctor. Her leg was encased in plaster after an ankle operation and she had severe pain in her calf muscle. "A blood clot....." "thank you Lord" We prayed together and the pain went and she felt better. We both knew the Lord had healed her, and removed the clot.

His love for her involved my obedience of course - but He would have used someone else if I hadn't obeyed and I would have missed a blessing. For seeing the outworking of His love strengthened my faith. and encouraged me greatly.

On another occasion I was visiting a friend who was looking after a neighbour's little girl for a few hours. We were discussing something when we heard a crash and a scream. It was difficult to know who was the most terrified - the baby or her baby-sitter. With an instinctive motherly compassion I reached out to stroke the back of the child's head - when suddenly my whole body was encased in an exquisite envelope of love that was almost unbearable. The child turned to me and held out her arms and I held her close - both of us wrapped together for a few seconds in the very heart of God. THEN JUST AS SUDDENLY IT EVAPORATED - and I was left with just me. My companion frowned, wriggled, pushed herself down on to the carpet and went off to play. I had experienced the healing power of Jesus. In fact I believe that it was HIS presence. I couldn't tell anyone for ages what had happened - because not only did I want to keep the experience glowing in me - but I thought no-one would believe me.

But I KNOW the reality of that love.

It is up to us to keep ourselves within that love by prayer; reading and absorbing His Word; by obedience and by listening to the Holy Spirit.

GIVING   is part of our natural Christian life. Our fellowship with each other - our mutual sharing and caring - is evidence of this. But there are special circumstances in our lives in which God asks us to give more than we think we have. Does that sound nonsense to you? Well think about this: The most precious gift that God's Holy Spirit can give us is the expression of the love of Jesus in this sad world. By pouring out this love into the lives of the people we meet we can show them a little of the heart of our God.

Oh Lord - you are my love - the precious hope that lingers   in   my   heart   from   day   to   day. But more than that - much more than that - as each day quickly goes.

I SEE - YOUR COMING ISN'T VERY FAR AWAY

DWT

How Did I Get Involved in the Religious Field?

Well that's a question but it could be addressed to a number of scientists, not just me. The great scientists of history, not entirely, but to a large extent, have been Christians; not just in name but in their experience and life. I could quote people like Galileo, whose private papers I've had access to, he clearly had a dynamic relationship with Jesus Christ. Or people like Kepler, who as an astronomer discovered a thing called Keplerian ellipses, which indicates how planets go around the sun and things like that. All these people were Christians. Michael Faraday, the man who sort of laid down the principles by which we now have electric

150

light, and his successor, James Clark Maxwell, were both vibrant Christians.

I began my questioning from the point of view of design, what we observe in life. How was it I could look down a microscope and see a pattern, and I could look up into the sky, the two extremes in terms of spatial size, and I could still see patterns and organisation. That was the first question I asked myself. So there's lots of illustrative evidence there. But the ultimate evidence is in one's own heart. That's where it counts; and that's where it happened with me. It was the establishing of a heart centred relationship with a God - who previously I didn't even believe existed. But suddenly I knew was there.

I think the starting point was for me to say this. I was brought up to go to church. My parents had decided we needed some religion in the family so I was sent to church. That was the essence of it. But as time went on I began to discover that my church going, I was living an illusory sort of life. Nothing I did in my church or religious life seemed to have any bearing whatsoever on what I did in the rest of my life. And I drifted away from any religious concept, if I could use the word religious in that context. And then when I went up to do research at Cambridge I found myself sat at the knees of great men and I discovered that none of them seemed to have any interest whatsoever, or ever made any reference to anything that was religious, to God, Jesus Christ, the Bible or anything of that sort. And they were very focused people. I decided, well if this is how they achieved greatness, if I was ever going to achieve greatness, which incidentally I didn't; if ever I was going to achieve greatness then I would follow the same path. I would dispense with any concept of God - so really I became an atheist to the point that I was prepared to go out, which I did, onto street corners, where I would find people on soapboxes preaching and I'd challenge them publicly; and I used to do quite well at it actually. So I was very hardened in my atheistic ideas, and it was at that point, I was just finishing my research at Cambridge at the time living in a village just outside. A mission came to the village, of which I had no interest whatsoever; and it was during the course of that week that my eyes began to be opened to the fact that there were people around me, in particular the speaker who I personally disliked; the missioner certainly had something in his life, which I'd never seen before. And then to my horror I realised that what he had I wanted. And that led me down a fairly short path, an agonising one in a sense, where I tried to disprove the existence of God, from a scientific perspective. I mean I'd spend most of the week doing that and finally, late one night about two o'clock in the morning actually, I was in bed and was unable to sleep, and I had what can only be called a revelation. I saw a vision to be quite frank, and I heard the voice of God speaking to me. Now for somebody who didn't even believe the existence of God, to hear a voice, and not so many people do hear voices, you know, my first thought was, gosh am I drunk or did I have too many pickled onions for supper. But I knew this was real, and within eighteen hours I had made a commitment of my life, not knowing where it was going to take me, to the God whom I didn't even know, but in the moment of commitment, I realised that not only was he real, but he showered me with the most amazing sense of peace and fulfilment. He gave to me a joy inexpressible if I can put it that way. And a sense of destiny, although I didn't know what that meant. But I knew my life had been changed fundamentally and it stayed that way ever since.

Professor Roy Peacock
United States of America

Footnote:
Professor Roy Peacock was Nav Air Research Professor inAeronautics at the U.S.Naval Postgraduate School and, Aerospace Sciences Chair, at the University of Pisa. His 'home patch' is in the field of thermodynamics. "I'm mainly interested in Gastro Irons. And have been involved in researching them and designing them over most of my life". He has been an advisor to the UK, United States, Indian and one or two other governments. We would like to thank Sarah J and Cross-Rhythms Broadcasting for providing this material for our use.

Healed by Prayer

We were at a small prayer meeting, one week before Christmas, a few years ago.

Dennis joined us. He was in so much pain having had a stack of hardboard sheets fall on him, five days previously. He had been taken to hospital and stayed overnight for assessment. He had chest bruising and two broken/cracked ribs. At the end of the meeting he asked for prayer for healing – and my heart sank as I had struggled in the meeting, being a working mum and all the busyness of Christmas filling my mind.

Dennis' faith was strong and expectant – mine was very weak. However we prayed, asking Jesus to heal Dennis through His blood shed on the cross. We ended and Dennis rose from his chair, moved his arms up gradually and then pumped the air with his arms and danced and praised God for his healing.

I was overwhelmed by God's love and power – Dennis' faith had been sure and God's love and healing was awesome.

Anon,
Haverhill

My Proof God Exists

It is so easy to blame God for all disasters and say he doesn't exist, but many times God has proved himself to be so real to me. I would like to outline one of these events.

Back in the early 1990's when I had just passed my car driving test, I was very keen to meet my father to show him I could now drive. We lived only 40 miles apart, me in Haverhill Suffolk, and my father on a farm off the A14 near Swavesey, (Friesland Farm). We arranged to meet half way, at the Cambridge machinery Sale in Cambridge. I drove very carefully there and felt so proud of my new freedom. On meeting my father I got out and closed the car door (Renault 21), then realised I had self-locked the driving keys in the car. I was completely stuck.

My father also felt so helpless at that time and no mobile phones were available for public use to call for help. My father had driven in with his tractor, and only had tractor keys with him. However, he felt he should pray over his keys, which he did, then went to the car, tried the tractor key in the car door, and it instantly opened the door.

We were both completely amazed, and on comparing the two keys, the keys were both totally incompatible. The tractor key neither worked again in the car; it was only at that point of need. I just know God was there.

and....

Events I cannot Explain, But God Exists

I remember getting a very bad neck ache in my early twenties. This ache was so bad I found it difficult to move, or even lift my head to get myself out of bed. It was at a time when I was staying with my brother, who wanted to take me to his church that morning. (Cross Roads in St. Ives). I did not know anyone in his church, I was purely a visitor. Having struggled to get there we walked in late, and instantly a young girl spoke up on the front row. "There is someone here who has a neck ache that is radiating down to the shoulder, God wants heal them". I had never met this person, she neither saw me, how did she know I had an ache? I couldn't believe what I was hearing, and neither my brother. God had sent a message to this person. I was then prayed over. The ache did not disappear immediately, but without the prayer it may have continued. What meant more to me was knowing that God had given this message. His is so real.

Lynn Bond

For many years I suffered from stomach pain...

For many years I suffered from stomach pain – acid indigestion. I took advice from doctors and followed it by taking medication. I am an electrician which entails a lot of bending. I would feel burning pain every time I bent down. I could not eat certain fruit like raw apples because of the acid. If I drank a cold drink, or a hot drink, I would have pain. If I would lie in bed facing the wrong way, I would have pain.

I have been a Christian from the age of 12 and I believe God heals. I had prayed for healing many times. People prayed over me. I attended a Meeting where Evangelist Oral Roberts prayed for me, all with no effect.

Eventually I gave up praying and settled for taking indigestion tablets whenever I had the pain. I told the Lord I had prayed long enough. After a few more years, I began to realize that I was not getting the pain anymore. I did not need the tablets!

I no longer suffer from any stomach pain. God has healed me. Praise His wonderful name!

I can eat *anything* now with no ill effect. I have now been free of that for around 15 years. I really do believe that, sometimes there comes a point when we have to stop praying and simply trust with patience.

God always hears the prayers of His children but often makes us wait, why? Only He knows and, sometimes, shows us why in His time.

John Staff
Lindfield, Sussex

Footnote:
In addition to his electrical work, John Staff formerly pastored a church in Canewdon, near Southend. He has been involved in radio work for many years. He has a particular interest in hospital radio, formerly in Essex, and later in Sussex where he now has his own radio station.

From Being a Fraud to an Honest Christian

I was born within sound of Bow bells and therefore I am a Cockney, as anyone who has heard me speak will discern. Later, my family were able to move to Greenford, a much better district. We endured the trauma of war with all the other London families and my parents eventually separated.

At the age of 17, I became curious in spiritual phenomena in crossing the divide between the living and the dead. My interest was aroused by a News of the World article about Harry Edwards, the spiritualist faith healer. I bought Spiritualist magazines and sought enlightenment the Spiritualist church, experimenting with faith healing, spirit writing and emptying my mind to be aware of spiritual vibrations. One night, after playing cards and watching the Coronation on TV, my friend decided to hold a séance as his parents were mediums. A spirit guide, manifesting as a Chinese Mandarin, appeared, who smiled and told me that the material trappings of life, particularly money and success, would be my primary interests until the age of 50. But then my life would take a change of direction. I was told that my spirit guide was an American Indian names Silver Birch and if I stared into a mirror, I would see his image instead of my own. I was wary of this but occasionally attended the weekly séances at their home.
I also became interested in ballroom dancing and met and married my first wife before entering the RAF and travelling the world. Later, on leaving the RAF, I settled into a very successful career in sales which had a drastic effect on my home life.

I awoke one morning during Lent, 1983 and again contemplated a problem that had been troubling my conscience for some while. My tax affairs were under investigation and although I knew I could lie and cover up my evasion, my better nature was telling me to confess and make a clean breast of my embezzlement despite the risk of imprisonment. Today was different – I just didn't want to tell another lie. I hated the deceitful creature I had become. My accountant would always explain the previous year's results by turning to the profit and loss page of the annual accounts. I mused that any supernatural being I might have to account to would not judge the commendable bottom line figures presented, but rather the methods used to achieve the results; before passing a final judgment of worth. My wife and I owned two sports shops and a health club in Cambridge as well as being wholesalers. We installed gaming machines to an extremely diverse market and I was currently negotiating with the council to open an amusement arcade in the city. Six years into my second marriage we were settled into an imposing house furnished with expensive luxuries. We indulged in regular holidays because I had not declared my true taxable income. I was well on my way to being a self-made millionaire by 50 years of age. I could clearly see I was materialistic and self indulgent. As an employee I had deceived my family and cheated my employer and now as an employer I was cheating both customers and the tax authorities. I was physically fit having three times won the local Squash Championship and having played for Cambridgeshire and England, also coaching in UK and overseas. We also ran about 50 miles per week and entered many half marathons. Superficially, I appeared to have everything going for me, an attractive younger wife and plenty of money but inside, I was a mess. I married at 21, divorced at 43 and left my wife to raise three teenage children. Perhaps all the years of heavy drinking in the RAF, combined with 23 years in the Round Table and in Freemasonry had dulled my sense of decency. All that I held as desirable and respectable had turned to ashes. I realised that I was morally bankrupt.

Suddenly an authoritative voice impressed itself upon my ears:-

'Alf Droy, I know every thought you have ever had and I am aware of all your deeds. You believe that with your quick wits and your silver tongue you can persuade your way into eternal life by charm. You have never acknowledged Me as Lord of your life. I am the Lord Jesus Christ. You are responsible to me only, for your life's work. If you surrender your life over to me and repent of your sinfulness and accept My forgiveness offered by grace and not performance; if you will declare your dishonesty publicly and make restitution, I will grant you a place in heaven beside Me.'

I realised that my life was an open book to a Holy God and that He knew the reason for every action I had, or had not taken. There is a redeemer and He wanted to save me! I am nobody's fool and I can recognise a good deal when I am offered one. Walking away from a failed marriage had not solved any of my problems, I had only washed my hands of the responsibility for failure. I could not turn over a new leaf and avoid punishment without repentance for my past sins. I was morally and spiritually responsible for my own behaviour to an omniscient God. I leaped from my bed determined to be obedient to Jesus' possible final offer. My wife was taken aback at my revelation although she calmly accepted my decision to confess all to the tax authorities. Later that day, whilst wondering over the consequences, she felt compelled to read 1 Timothy, Chapter 1, verse 19: *'And keep your faith in a clear conscience. Some men have not listened to their conscience and have made a ruin of their faith'.*

Spiritually this day was the most significant in my life, the day the Lord revealed Himself to me. He released me from a bondage to sin of which I had previously been unaware. I knew what it was to suffer the pangs of a guilty conscience and to find relief through appeasement, but this release was totally different. Accepting Jesus Christ as a living Messiah meant the restoration of all broken relationships. The instant I had genuinely repented of my sins, I experienced a peace in my heart beyond human understanding.

I visited the office of the Inland Revenue without making an appointment and asked to see Mr Heap the chief tax inspector, who was investigating my tax returns for the year ending April, 1982. I had obtained a large mortgage on our house having increased its value by building an extension and paying for the cost out of undisclosed profits that I had embezzled from my various companies. Mr Heap was dumb-struck when I place before him bank statements for a secret bank account in which I hid the money I had secreted away. I asked of him, 'What happens now?' I had fully expected him to call for a policeman, who would hand-cuff me and lead me to a prison cell. Mr Heap said the fraud was too big for his jurisdiction and that the Fraud Squad would have to be informed.

Later that day, I wrote a letter to the Worshipful Master of the Masonic Lodge of which I was a member, informing him that I had become a 'born again' believer and no longer wanted to be associated with freemasonry. At that time I was unaware that if I progressed through the 33rd degree as a Freemason, I would have been calling on the name of Satan (Lucifer) for my guidance!

Some weeks after my conversion, I found that my conscience was still troubling me. I had been invalided from the RAF owing to a lower back problem. It was the continuous receipt of my pension that was troubling my conscience. I had lost 30 pound in weight since taking up squash and was no longer troubled with back problems. I wrote to the War Pensions Office and told them that I was now perfectly healthy and no longer qualified to receive this pension. My action placed a great strain on my ability to meet all our bills. .I came into a period of revelations from God and as I saw myself in a huge congregation worshipping God, I understood my own body as being a temple belonging to the Lord.

I met with a Mr Warner for investigative interviews and told him that I no longer wanted to hide any of my previous cunning and devious nature because the Lord had told me to reveal all. He was sceptical and I produced a dummy invoice book and told him about the duplicate Passport I had requested to hide my numerous visits abroad. My accountant was advised that I should contact the VAT office at Harlow and I did so, resulting in a further bill of £6,500. The Inland Revenue finally settled on a penalty of £100,000. We agreed with the directive to sell our house and move into rented accommodation to pay the bulk of my fine. Eventually the house sold and we moved into a small flat. We dealt with all our debts during a trying seven year period, experiencing many divine interventions and finally we were free from the control of the banks.

I have hesitated in writing this, not because I thought the message contained in it was irrelevant, but because, in my opinion there was too much of me and too little of Jesus. The Lord has given me a greater liberty than I have ever known, to testify to His goodness towards me and to show His outstretched welcoming arms to all others who would receive Him.

Alf Droy
Cambridge

Footnote:
Alf and his second wife, Pauline, live in Cambridge, where they have run a successful B & B for a number of years. He is active in Christian work and evangelism and is often used supernaturally in ministry. He has also written several books.

This story is taken from:
'The Lord is my Shepherd' by Alf Droy,

With God, Nothing is Impossible

The voice of the doctor rang in my ears, 'You may as well give in, take my advice and have a hysterectomy now. You will never carry another child' I was about 35.

I had produced my first two healthy children at home without too many problems (except the doctor and my normal midwife being on holiday and the relief midwives arriving with empty gas and air cylinders) However, my daughter and son had arrived within 18 months and my new doctors were determined that there would be a longer gap before we had any more. They wore us down until we agreed to take preventative measures. I was never happy about this and eventually had to have minor surgery at Rochford Hospital as complications arose.
The short gap we had envisaged became a long gap as I had four miscarriages in a row after that, one on the only occasion we went ski-ing in Switzerland with our friends. . When we moved to Pickering in North

Yorkshire, I was sent for tests and informed that at some time my womb had been repaired. The only time this could have happened was by unauthorised surgery at Rochford.

Our doctor was a very arrogant character who regularly worked at a local hospital in obstetrics and gynaecology and he was very firm in his judgement. He must have been rather shocked as I replied that I definitely would have another child and that I would bring it in and show it to him when it arrived. 'Absolutely no chance. With a condition like yours there will be no more' I quietly replied that when I married, God had given me three names for my children, not just two, and I knew the name of the third-Lydia! I forget what he promised to do if that ever happened but I didn't hold him to it.

A year or so later, I arrived at the same surgery and was told I was again pregnant. Still he was adamant, 'You have wasted your time. You will not carry that for more than three months at most' This time I told him I was not prepared to allow any internal examinations as my first gynaecologist had disapproved of these after the first few weeks. He hissed and fumed and finally agreed. Seven months and two weeks later, Lydia arrived, confounding the opinion of his partner who had told me he had never been more certain of a baby's sex and to go and buy the trousers now. He came to our house twice to reassure himself that I had produced a girl. She was a remarkable child and is on record at Pickering clinic as saying 'Ello' at six weeks old and 'Goo' girl' at 8 weeks. The staff were called in to 'Hear this tiny baby, talking to its mummy'.

A short while later another girl was on the way but for no known reason I lost her at 24 weeks and was told on my birthday that the baby I was carrying was dead.

Doctors feared septicaemia and I had to carry the baby and then have a drug-induced birth-an experience I am glad I shall never have to repeat!

Then came the bonus. I had been brought up as an only child and didn't want my children to experience this, so I prayed for another child to grow up with Lydia. Bethany, another miracle child I could never carry, came into the world in 1983.

The doctor's comment was priceless. 'Well, you always have been determined to re-write the medical books, haven't you?' And indeed I have done, on many occasions, as God has intervened in my life and the impossible has become possible. With God, nothing is impossible.

Yvonne Creasy

The Reality is Jesus Christ

We were a large family comprising two sets of boy and girl twins and three other girls and we were brought up in Thornton Heath. My two older sisters were both 'on stage' in the West End of London and I started work at the Faraday Building in Victoria Street, the main London Telephone Exchange, on the French Section. Occasionally, I recognized the voices of Government Leaders as I connected calls, particularly the distinctive voice of one Winston Spencer Churchill. I would dearly have loved to thank him for all he did for us in WWII but as a timid young operator, I thought he would probably shout at me and tell me to get on with my job.

I remember passing a signboard on the way to work, bearing the scripture text "Seek ye the Lord while he may be found" and thinking to myself, "That's ridiculous, nobody can find God" The little I knew of God was from casual visits to the little mission down the road. Sometimes I had a feeling of being 'watched' as I passed St Paul's Cathedral and I felt very uncomfortable as I saw people genuflecting as they passed the cross opposite Blackfriars. I thought, "My sins put Him there." Later, I started to be quite bothered about my sin and crept into St Dunstan's Chapel in St Paul's Cathedral for the 7.30am communion. There were two of us there and afterwards the Dean asked what was the matter with me. When I replied that I was burdened with my sin, he told me that I was a good living young woman and that I must not take religion so seriously. I had a good friend named Helen and I suppose you would have classed us as 'teddy girls' but we were not into anything really bad.

The spiritual one was my father, Hal. He used to receive 'visits' from 'emissaries' who named themselves as 'Moses, Elijah and Aaron and bowed down to him and told him they were his 'spirit guides'. He was a spiritist healer, as well as having many visions. He predicted the terrible flooding in France which he and his brother in law both foresaw in a vision. After I had appendicitis I went to live with my Uncle Nick, and he started to get me interested. He and Dad used to listen to Harry Edwards and pray with him at 12 o clock, 3pm and 6pm and one day as I listened I felt "utter sin" all around me. Uncle Nick had led the family into spiritism after a spider landed on a rock near him in the desert during WWII, causing him to race away from the area. A few minutes later a shell exploded on the rock and Nick vowed he would join the first church he found on his return to England-a Spiritist church. Towards the end of Nick's life, my brother Andy visited him at his home in Kent to try to persuade him to renounce Spiritism and accept Jesus Christ. Andy could get nowhere and left saying to him, 'If God himself showed you, would you believe then?'. Nick replied that he would and a month

165

or so later when the family assembled for his funeral, his wife, Con, gave Andy a book of hand written poems entitled, 'Jesus Christ my Guide' and told him that Nick wanted him to know that he had died believing in Jesus as his saviour.

I missed speaking French and met up with a young French girl. Yvette ridiculed those simple enough to believe God could hear prayer. I learned afterwards that her father was a high ranking government official and a communist. It made sense, "How could God hear prayer?" and with this new thought, I joined the Communist Party and got on with my nursing. Two weeks later, I woke up in the night and felt a Presence in my room-God! This happened a couple of times and I took codeine to get sleep. One morning I awoke to find the sister tutor standing over me, demanding to know why I was not on duty. She put me straight in the sick bay and ordered psychiatric tests which proved there was nothing wrong. I persuaded a visitor to bring me a small red Bible from home Somewhere around then, I completely stopped eating and sent all meals back with a polite, "No, thank you."

A Christian girl named Betty Holder was also put on the ward, suffering from a slipped disc. She spoke of her friend, "Jesus" and I assumed him to be a foreign friend with that name. One day, when I sent my meal back, Betty spoke up, "Leave it." I was shocked but her next words shocked me more, "Bow your head". She prayed and I ate the meal. It was a Thursday in November, 1960. We prayed and read a part of St John's Gospel. At 2am I awoke to a Presence. This time I prayed, "Don't let me die until I'm forgiven". Then saw Him-on a cross and heard Him say, "I took your place". I prayed. All my burden and torture went! Oddly, when I told Betty in the morning, she already knew! In a couple of days I was out of the sick bay and back to work. I became secretary of the Nurses Christian Union and one night I was half asleep when I heard footsteps I assumed to be an early morning window cleaner-until I realised he had come through a locked door. The 'person' stood by my bed and I feigned sleep until I heard him say, 'What's that rubbish by the bed. Burn that Bible'. I was paralysed; it often happens when spirits are present and then I heard awful laughter and felt a hand around my throat pressing me into the pillows. I couldn't speak but over and over in my mind, I spoke the name of Jesus, eventually managing to vocalise His Name. Next, I was surrounded by angelic beings and light filled the room. The spirits disappeared as quickly as they had materialised. After this I regularly spoke to young people around Soho when I saw them playing with Ouija boards and warned them off these activities.

I was invited to a conference at High Leigh, led by Dick Carter and George Breckon. Someone spoke out a 'word from God' which said "Someone here comes from a home in spiritism; God will save all your family". I claimed that promise. A few days later I had what I suppose was a vision-"Today your sisters will come in". Babs lived nearby and she accepted the Lord. Pam was living at Worthing, with her young baby and never visited or contacted us. I opened the post and there was a carton of Milo drink with a note-from Pam. She described how a strong wind swept through her room and she committed herself to God.

I invited my mother to church but she was content to go at Christmas and Easter and thought that was enough. Instead she joined dad in his spiritism and the house went very strange. Doors opened and shut for no reason and there was often an evil presence in the room. Then mother became very ill. Dad summoned up a couple of spirits to come and pray for her, two Chinese men who laid their hands on her for healing and for a short while she seemed to improve. Then she took a rapid downturn. Her legs were badly ulcerated and bandaged from top to bottom and now a heart condition appeared. We were all really worried but she insisted on returning to work at the hospital where I found her one day leaning against the wall, blue all over. She had suffered a heart attack but would not let me alert anybody. In despair, I went back to my room in the nurses' quarters and cried.

Christian friends of mine came to Drury Lane to hold an evangelistic and healing meeting and by this time mum was in such a state that she was prepared to try anything. Colin, the speaker, said, 'Does anyone here have a great need? Does anyone need God's help? Mum responded and he prayed for mum's legs and heart. She cried and cried and found her way to God. When she sat down all she could say was, 'Thank you Jesus. By His stripes I am healed' At home that night we heard mum praising God out loud in her room. She described how a voice said to her, 'Ellen Strevens, praise my name'. Next day, she got up, removed all her bandages and found her legs were totally healed. Her heart had also regulated itself and she went off to help Pam and her baby down on the South Coast. What a transformation she had. For years she had been in pain and was always shouting at us. Now she was totally full of peace and joy, praising God. My sisters Jan and Tessa, who was a doctor, avoided us like the plague and Tessa often dived through hospital doors to avoid speaking to us. One day, in a dream, I stood by an old kitchen cabinet cutting bread and Jan came into the room. One look told me she was different and I said, 'You've accepted Christ, haven't you?' To which she replied, 'How did you know?' A couple of days later, that is exactly what happened and Jan who was about 15 described how she had been woken up by a grey lady walking into her locked room. She was so scared that she fell out of bed and pleaded with Jesus to come into her life. Tessa was impossible to talk to, so we sent her a Christian tract with a birthday card and she also found Christ.

This left Dad with a family of mad women; all five daughters and his wife had become Christians and were full of it. He had a three day Spiritist conference coming up and was really looking forward to it, so he paid no heed when we tried to dissuade him from going and replied, 'I've got more reality than all of you put together and I am not going to miss this'. We replied, 'But we have peace in our hearts'. On Friday evening dad put on his coat and headed for the bus stop and I whispered to Jan, 'Stop him'. We huddled behind a door and began to repeat the name of Jesus, over and over again. When we slipped into the living room we found dad in his armchair...asleep. He was angry when he awoke! Next day, he again got ready and went to the front door. We hid again and repeated the name of Jesus as before and to our surprise we again found dad asleep in his chair. David was in and he couldn't believe what he saw, although, as usual, he was cynical and sceptical. This time Dad was really furious. He shouted and swore; he just couldn't believe he had missed the second meeting. Sunday came and he was really determined not to miss the last meeting. He went out and stood at the gate. We hid and prayed again and could hardly believe it when he came in, sat down and fell asleep. He went ballistic when he woke up; he had missed the whole conference!

Dad became very depressed and eventually mum suggested he asked his spirit guides who denied there was a devil, what they thought about Jesus. Did he really come in flesh? He said no more but obviously did and got the reply, 'We've been here thousands of years before him'. One spat at him as he said these words. Dad was in turmoil. As he stood on Streatham station an audible voice spoke to him, 'I am the Lord your God and you shall worship no other god' Next Sunday he came to our meeting and although I didn't witness this, I was told they cast ten devils out of him. His spirits came back in force and put their hands around his neck, trying to strangle him in the night. He called desperately on the name of Jesus for protection and they went. Next day he started a fast without food or water and really 'met God' He never returned to Spiritism.

My brothers were still at home and shared a bedroom. Andrew worked for Matsui bank and had no time for God but woke a few nights later to find a real presence in his room. The bed shook and he shook until he fell out of bed and asked Jesus into his life. Later that night David came in, fag in hand, sat down and leaned back on his elbow. The same presence filled the room, so he quickly stubbed out his cigarette as the room shook around him. Andy was asleep, so David ran for mum and asked her to pray with him. The change in our family was obvious and after avoiding us for a few months, our neighbour, a local bank manager, and his wife knocked at the door and asked if they could join us, saying, 'If you cannot beat them, join them' They were the first of many.

I have been asked what would I say to others in my situation. It is this, 'Don't do it! We have been there and it is not worth it. There is a counterfeit and there is reality-the reality is Jesus Christ.

Linda Strevens
North Yorkshire

Not Just For Sundays

As our Father, God only wants the best for us; if we allow God to be involved in our everyday lives, He will be with us all week, not just on Sundays.

He will be there for us, even in the everyday things, if we want Him to be; not to command our every move but to gently guide and steer us, as we listen to Him.

As parents, we invest so much into our children and though we don't need to know every situation, decision or aspect of their lives it is nice to be involved, especially when there is a big decision to be made or event happening; it's also good to know about the little things. Yes, God sees and knows all, even before we do, but if we feel left out of the loop when our children don't confide in us, doesn't God have the right to feel just as hurt when we don't show Him the same courtesy?

Or do we think that He's too big for that?

Speaking from experience, it is so easy to take Him for granted and just as easy to be 'too busy' and, before you know it, the day and even week has gone by and we haven't even given Him the time of day. I spent the New Year in Germany with my two Grandchildren. When it was time to leave, I realised I had taken the time I had spent with them for granted and I was heart-broken.

So many times we take God for granted in our actions or acts of omission; when we go through the same it is then that we can relate to how God, our Father, must feel when we hurt Him.

If only we would talk to God about our situations and decisions, involve our Father in our lives and spend intimate time with Him. If only we would ask Him what He thinks about the decisions we need to make. After all, what concerns us concerns our Father; that doesn't mean we have to want Him to make decisions for us.

God has given us free will and wants us to be strong and bold to do that for ourselves, but He wants to be confided in and 'included'.

God has a purpose for our lives; if we don't talk to Him about things how will we be sure we are following His path? Our plans change but God's plans for us never change. (Jer 29:11- 14) and (Prov 19:21)

Father, thank you for Your unconditional and perfect love. Thank You that You're always waiting for me to talk to You about everything. Thank You for Your peace when I confide and include You in my everyday life and decisions, help me not to leave You out of anything.

I will trust You for all and in all things, by the power of Your name Jesus. Amen.

Tricia

My Early Life Was Spiced with Dreams

The Bible teacher painted vivid pictures with his words. Sitting in that class, I could hear Peter say "look here. " My mind's eye pictured the expectant initial look on the man's face. He hoped to receive money. Disappointment changed to wonder when Peter, staring at him declared his inability to help financially. My childish credulity "saw" the halo of anointing on Peter as he ordered him to "walk in the name of Jesus. " There was suspense as, a few seconds later, Peter helped him to his feet. The excitement in the man as he discovered he could walk, rippled through the crowd. It even came into our Sunday school classroom. I decided to do the same experiment the next day, on my way to school. To my horror, it did not work. As a result, I made two decisions. One was to give my allowance for school to beggars thereafter. The second was that, no matter what it took, I would become a doctor. I was committed to striving towards that goal. However, the loss of my father when I was sixteen seemed an insuperable setback. After the sharp edge of sorrow had worn off and the dust had settled, I decided to acquire metaphysical power. Unfortunately I did not realise that being a regenerated man was inconsistent with occultism. My objectives were simple. I was the oldest boy of the family and I needed power to defend my mother, younger brother and two older sisters from devilish attacks. I had. two contemporaries at school who had knowledge in this area. I consulted them and they gave me various magazines to read. Through these journals, I made contact with an Indian guru who sold me books on Yoga and occultism. As soon as I left school in 1951, I embarked on intensive studies of these books. Apart from a six hour interlude at a civil service job, I spent most days in acquiring this esoteric brand of knowledge. I learnt control over various parts of my body's metabolism. I also learnt thought transference and telepathy, clairvoyance and clairaudience, healing and transcendental meditation.

My style of life was highly ascetic, being an absolute vegetarian and indulging in protracted fasts. Mahatma Ghandi's life-style, for instance, was very attractive to me. About eighteen months after embarking on these studies, however, I became disillusioned. My mother had burnt my books, because they had become passionate obsessions for me. In addition, an aura of sterile holiness had surrounded me and somehow prevented my erstwhile friends from coming close. I missed their company so much that I started to compromise with regard to my asceticism. In fact, by June 1954, I started indulging in occasional alcoholic escapades and there were a few cases of sexual debauchery.

For many years there ensued a swing between these extremes.. This pattern continued unabated for twenty-one years. There was a curious marriage in either of these states with the external observances of the Christian faith. I sang in the choir and took part in other church activities. I became a regular member of "sound" Christian societies at the University without relinquishing my interest in the occult and/or licentiousness. I envied many of my friends who knew Christ securely and had a consistent stable relationship with Him. Many of them did not twig my double-mindedness, as my other activities were often clandestine.

I had hoped to earn a grant to pay for my training by dint of hard work. The loan from mortgaging my mother's house was finished. I was at a loss to see how I would continue. A Mr. Barker, employed as Education Attaché at the Nigeria Office in London visited his son at Baliol College. He called on him early in the morning while his son was on the river rowing. He decided to fill the time with some useful activity. He had read flattering accounts of me in my tutor's recommendations for a grant. He wondered how an "undistinguished" black got into Magdalen. (My father was not one of the Nigerian "big names. ") As he knocked on my door, I was "whooping" over the Broadbent prize letter. "They must have made a mistake" I said, aloud. "How can you give a "wog" like me a college prize. " Quietly, he said "I am Barker from the Nigerian Office in London. Can I have a look?" I gave the letter to him still mumbling to myself. "Your getting into Magdalen was like a camel getting through a needle's eye. And this is something else. Can I borrow this letter?" He did, and that was how, eight months and several letter battles later, the Nigerian Government gave me, first a loan scholarship and in 1961 a full scholarship. That solved my financial problems. Before the money arrived, I was literally starving, since I could not do factory work with my backlog of academic requirements.

At the end of January 1965, the hospital authorities felt it would enrich my experience as a Senior House Officer to change places with a colleague in the Department of Medicine. So it was that professor G. L. Monekosso became my head of Department. I was working in the Outpatients Department one afternoon when I heard him. "Hello, Isaacs. I would like you to consider a proposition. " "What is it, sir?" I queried. "We know you have a good degree in Animal Physiology from Oxford. We would like you to start work next week on the 1st April as Junior Research Fellow in Physiology. We will regularize your appointment later by interview. " This was how I made the crossing from service posts to academics in medicine.

That's how I went to Cambridge in October 1965. To medical scientists, sitting under the lectures of Krebs, Le Gros Clark, Florey and Liddell at Oxford should be enough good fortune for one man. Dr. Lehmann's laboratory rapidly opened more avenues for good intellectual contacts. If genius could be transmitted through skin contact, I should have acquired some. Fred Sanger and Max Perutz and a host of other brilliant and Nobel-rewarded men provided formal and informal training through lectures and discussions. Indeed, I gained invaluable insights due to the innate humility of most of the great men I met at Cambridge. This privilege showed me the world from which C. S. Lewis had recently departed. We had to work extremely hard as Postgraduate students. When in my second year, I decided to combine abnormal haemoglobin work (for which Professor Lehmann was famous) with tissue culture work, I had to labour for a little under twenty four hours a day. This was true for most days of most weeks in my second year. The methods for defining the structure of proteins which had been invented by Sanger were still new then. The newly found haemoglobins (sent from all over the world to Professor Lehmann) which we struggled to characterize, resulted in "discoveries" for us when the work was complete. I was involved in defining human types, as well as horse, donkey and mule haemoglobins. A contemporary of mine in that laboratory broke entirely new ground when his work explained for the first time a whole group of diseases. He has been rewarded now with an appointment as Professor of Haematology in the University of Cambridge. His predecessor in that post, Professor F. G. J. Hayhoe gave me my opportunity for a breakthrough.

Professor Lehmann had asked him "Could you train Isaacs in routine haematology for his second year?" A Christian gentleman, he had agreed. In sophisticated Cambridge, I was given a whole room to myself as well as a laboratory assistant. I decided to make the best of it. The laboratory of Professor Hayhoe was famous for many things - leukaemias, cytogenetics and cytochemistry among others. I decided to investigate a pet idea of mine - to breed blood cells in the bottle with the idea of changing their genetic make-up. In particular, I was anxious to see whether sickle cells could be induced to change into normal cells. It was not as easy to get off the ground as I had thought. To start with, cells from blood forming tissues always reverted to a more primitive type in the bottle, by the techniques available then. After extensive consultation as well as trial and error, I was beginning to get somewhere. I desired to clinch this development by repeating the experiment in a more measurable way. That time, however, I could not obtain any samples of bone marrow from the accident department. I decided (for the fifth

176

time) to have my marrow removed by a colleague as material for my experiment. I set up the experiments.

The design was simple. Two bottles, each containing my bone marrow in a suitable fluid which would supply nutrients lay side by side in an incubator. The only difference between both bottles is that whereas one had a minute amount of the male sex hormone in it, the other only had the oil in which the hormone was dissolved. I had to take samples for study every three hours, because radioactive matter was tagged on to the haemoglobin-making cells. Lo and behold, the first sample after three hours sprang a surprise. The innocent bottle (devoid of hormone) contained cells which were shaped like blades of grass (with sharp edges). I knew I was a carrier of sickle cell haemoglobin but my cells were usually the normal doughnut shape. The requirement of the system for oxygen was so heavy that the atmosphere was robbed of its supply of oxygen. Carriers of haemoglobin S would produce blade-shaped cells under these conditions. The only surprise was that it was so early. When however, I had examined the contents of the other bottle repeatedly for about an hour, I began to sing the "Magnificat and Nunc Dimitis" alternately at the top of my voice. As I cycled home, it was a wonder that I was not arrested for disturbing the peace of the sleeping population of Cambridge. It was 1:30 a.m. and I continued praising God uncontrollably at the top of my voice.. " Why was I so happy? Many great men of Science had worked on sickle cell disease. And now, almost casually, the solution to the terrors of this disease seemed unveiled.

The long hand of providence gave me a hard push. Not only did that goal materialise, but I soon became a specialist. It did not end there, but one breakthrough after another led to some modest measure of prominence. I had become a workaholic, interested only in the exciting fruits of academic research. Quite unexpectedly, on a certain afternoon, the name of Jesus brought healing to a polio cripple in my laboratory. Rediscovery of the old-time religion therefore turned my gaze to a different type of research. Was this healing authentic? Is it repeatable? How did it operate? What are the ingredients which stimulate the genesis of faith for healing? Would everyone get healed? What are the limits, beyond which a would-be adventurer may not explore? These and many other questions raced through my mind. They prompted a new line of research which almost entirely displaced scientific medicine. The question, "what makes Jesus tick" became an overwhelming curiosity. This research project continues. Indeed, it must continue till we arrive at the other side of the vale. The interim findings may interest you. One conclusion stands out. The same hand of providence which brought realisation of my initial dream, seems interested in wholesomeness or making people whole. The realm of the miraculous remains a mystery.

I was a Buswell Foundation Fellow from April to July 1972 under Professor Robin Bannerman of Medical Genetics who was formerly my tutor at the Radcliffe Infirmary, Oxford, England. I was also offered a job under Professor Titus Huisman and Augusta, Georgia as Assistant Professor of Medicine and Director of Sickle Cell Anaemia Clinic. I was anxious to return home to Nigeria and I turned it down. What is important, however, is that providence had pushed that hope-starved man in rural Nigeria (1955) to this position in 1972 - seven University degrees and diplomas and an international reputation. I recognized vaguely the hand of God upon my life. My academic career was interrupted in September 1979. The stoppage is for an undefined period of time. I had worked too much and my health broke down. I was forced to make a choice.

For to God, nothing shall be impossible. Luke 1:37

I did not plan to be a minister. Indeed, I never thought I was worthy enough to be called of God. My long history of backsliding had put such wild thoughts out of my mind. And yet did God not say "my thoughts are not your thoughts, neither are your ways my ways"? (Isaiah 55:8.)

After I returned to the Lord Jesus fully, I began to see the words of scripture with new eyes.. There was created in me a tremendous and new zest for living. I was not immediately made pure in thought, word and deed. Indeed, I continued to be a slave to many passions for quite a few weeks. I still masturbated often. In fact, I failed badly in that there was a sexual debauch with an American visitor soon after my decision. I was simply too weak to resist temptation. I indulged in tobacco and alcohol almost continuously. And yet, as the word seeped into my spirit, a supernatural strength was born in me to shake off all these enslaving instincts. Suddenly, (and it seemed dramatic), I was free.

Five months after my re-conversion, on December 12th, 1973, I had a strange encounter with the Holy Spirit. On getting home, I knelt by the bed. The house was quiet, for it was about midnight. I rushed through my prayers. I could not sleep. Indeed, somebody (an inaudible voice) started after an interval, an interrogation within me. "Please get up and show me from the Bible where I gave instructions as to the class and magnitude of problems which would qualify to be brought to me. " I was patient at first. Later, I started to squirm inside and this turned to cold fury. After some time the question echoed again in my head. "OK. " I said, a little frustrated "there is no such passage. " "Thank you", the voice seemed to say. "Now show me where I indicated that I would need a recovery period after any exercise of my supernaturalness. " Again, I was stumped. My irritation knew no bounds. However, I decided to have my revenge on the voice. "Look here," I said inside, "I suffer from hypertension, duodenal ulcer, asthmatic bronchitis, chronic sinusitis and enhanced susceptibility to malaria. I have drugs for all of these, I will no longer take these drugs. If a man cannot reasonably hope to be logical about simple things, you God will have to heal me or I'll not believe that it makes sense." There was no a priori reason why God should have taken any notice of me. The incredible thing was that He did. That was the last of those pestilence's.

The new year saw a total change in my life style. I became much more involved in fellowship meetings. The curious aspect of it was that I was usually the only one from my age bracket at those meetings. My big need came from my depression at the end of every day's working session. There I was, returning home daily to my miracle-working God. But I usually left at the hospital some patients with cancer of the blood-forming system and similar ghastly problems. What was the use of my getting all that help if I could not pass any of it on to those helpless patients? Could there be a way of becoming so full that the power of God would literally ooze out of me? I had read some books. In fact, I had made up my mind that all I wanted from God was the gift to heal. I certainly wanted nothing to do with "tongues". Loonies in the psychiatric ward sometimes had "tongues" and I did not wish to be confused with them. I did not know enough about the other gifts to hanker after them.

Late that December, I had an encounter with the Lord Jesus. I was on my knees, with my arms spread on the bed praying. There was an appearance before me of brilliant light caused by a blazing human form. I was too terrified to pick the details. He motioned to me and I bent down, petrified. As He was bringing the shining sword in His right hand down on my left shoulder, I remember protesting that I was very unworthy. "Arise, for you are now my knight." I could not even rise for so great was my prostration. The vision had faded, but it was all repeated about a month later. Such then was my "ordination" into the ministry of the Lord Jesus.

A little later, in October, I was involved with testing sickle cell disease children. An old illiterate woman came in with a little boy of four. "Thank you for curing this boy from painful spells" she said. I explained that it was only a control and that it was the product of scientific research. However, she stood her ground "If you can remove the pain, you can also make the boy walk." The boy's right thigh and leg were wasted and he could not walk. In vain, I tried to convince her that I was no magician. "We do not have money, or I would have offered you" she said. It was this insinuation that I needed financial encouragement to do my trick which galvanized me into action. "Please come away from the corridor", I said, as I shut the door to stop the embarrassment. "The truth is that I can do nothing for your grandson's polio. However, I have seen my friend Jesus deal with such problems when other people have prayed. You hold on to the right thigh of the boy and I will put my hand on his head. Tell Jesus to repair the leg and I will pray along with you." I gave the instructions hurriedly because I wanted to get rid of her. When we had prayed, both of us supported the boy, as he staggered a little. "Take him home and as you exercise him, he will improve." To my mind what I was talking was rubbish, but they believed me and left.

Two weeks later, there was a greeting from the open door to my room. "Yes, good afternoon." I replied, burying my head in my work. The greeting was repeated. I was irritated because I was busy. "Can I help you?" I asked, rather unfriendly. "Don't you recognize us?" she asked, pushing a little boy towards me - the boy ran towards me. "No, I don't. I am sorry; I see a lot of people all the time. Madam, I already explained that I am busy." "Don't you remember praying for a crippled little boy two weeks ago? This is the boy. " I started to cry. It was too wonderful for words. That was the first spectacular physical miracle I had seen at close range. I almost could not believe it. When did Jesus comet in? My laboratory is an untidy place, not suitable for such things. How did He do it, in spite of my unbelief.

That was the beginning. Two months later, in the December, the grandmother of a sicker patient of mine was brought in. I had referred the old lady (almost 60 years old) to a Consultant Ophthalmologist. Now, they were reporting back that the problem was brought too late. She was already blind. She was in despair, as she only lived to look after her grandson. Because of the healed cripple, I offered to pray. But she was a fanatic Muslim and she rejected the idea outright. However two weeks later, she was back in her desperation. After stalling for time to make sure she had faith, I called her in and prayed a simple prayer. There was a slight difference after the prayer. The old lady returned. There were altogether seven visitors in my room, excluding Christian brethren. I was so afraid to ask about her sight. Indeed, I complained to one of my student mentors. "Why does this woman not leave me alone. I have done all I can for her. "This was in the corridor, and on my way back into the room, the Holy Spirit charged me with cowardice. "What will you lose by inquiring after her health?" the inner voice said. "But there are so many people" I countered. In any case, the Spirit prevailed. In a very small voice, I asked "What about your sight?" "I can see now" she replied. And I burst into tears again. All the seven visitors present which included four Muslims, gave their lives to the Lord Jesus right there.

In my medical career spanning twenty-five years, I have seen a lot of illness and a lot of deaths. In just over fourteen years of ministry, I witnessed a lot of miracles of the Lord Jesus. Clearly, not every ill person has been healed. However, listening to the Holy Spirit better has made the percentage of failures very small. Indeed, I never usually have the opportunity or the boldness to minister to those God did not plan to heal. This is all a far cry from my beginnings in medicine at Magdalen College, Oxford. My vision was confined then to living in smart society and perhaps making a lot of money. I wanted to serve in 1948, when I first met Christ intimately (my first altar call). That is why I came through thick and thin, the hand of providence being upon me, to become a doctor. Backsliding distracted me for a while, but He had always foreknown me (Romans 8:29, 30). For fifteen and a half years, I have been back. My prayer is that I will apprehend fully that for which I was apprehended (Phil. 3:12b). And that I will always trust Him whatever He brings, for He has been a wonderful Father to me.

C. S. Lewis used the word "miracle" to mean an interference with Nature by supernatural power. I have been describing true stories of events in which I believe one Supernatural power, the living, glorified Jesus was involved. At the start of my ministry (1974-1975) Jesus appeared to me three times - first to ordain me, second, to heal me of giant cell arthritis (or a three week continuous migraine) and third, to show me the "rapture". Why have I been so blessed? I do not know why. But I can suggest why not. It is most certainly not because I was good. Indeed, I have committed more terrible sins more frequently than many other people. It is not because I have been more industrious, popular or more trusting than others. An unkind friend once asked me - "Why are your testimonies always larger than life?" I said I was sorry to have given offence, but that I was at a loss how to behave since I do love and serve a God who is "larger than life". It is also true to say that not all sick people I have prayed for got healed.

The miracles cited in this testimony are a small fraction of what He (Jesus) did in my life since He called me. Since August 1989 two more times the risen Christ has successfully "confronted" death with me as an observer. I believe in miracles of Jesus Christ today. I also believe that Mark 16:17 and 18 are true today.

Rev. Dr. W. (Bill) Isaacs
Sodeye, Wisbech, Cambs.

Footnote:
Rev. Dr.'Bill' Isaacs fled to England from Nigeria in 1993 as his life was in danger during an Islamist uprising. He settled near Cambridge and was immediately involved in ministry in Anglican and other churches in Cambridgeshire, Norfolk and beyond. Further details of his activities and ministry are available on his websites and in several books which he has written to tell people of the miracles God has performed.

The problem was too big for us

My partner and I found ourselves needing a larger vehicle fairly quickly due to the imminent arrival of our 4th child and an upcoming holiday to Devon, on which we were likely to be taking a school friend. After finding a 7 seater within our price range and being pressured into an agreement by sales staff, my partner and I arranged to collect the vehicle the following weekend after checks and repairs were done and MOT and Tax had been obtained. Although we had not paid in full, the sales staff require us to leave a £500 deposit to secure the vehicle as they had other interested buyers. They pushed my partner to cancel viewing another similar vehicle in the area and after three days we received a call saying the repairs and inspection were done and the vehicle was ready. I found this unbelievable as they were to have it checked by a Volvo main dealer to verify that repair work had been done properly.

We arrived as arranged and found the vehicle missing, although we were expected. They claimed it was being valeted and after an hour's wait it arrived back, looking as though the boss had just popped down the road in it, not as though it had been professionally valeted. As we waited to sign, the boss bowled in. asking the salesman if he had informed us some of the car's internal electrical features were not working. Shocked that these had only just been checked, I stopped my partner signing the paperwork as I was unconvinced that the company would keep their promise to fix these later and we left empty-handed.

After several weeks of unreturned 'phone calls we looked into the possibility of fixing the issues ourselves at the company's request, as they were unprepared to meet the cost of the repairs and kept dodging our 'phone calls. We even offered a slightly lower figure for the car and the option of us arranging the repairs ourselves but they declined saying they could not make enough profit. They were intending to do the repairs and sell it again for a higher figure, well above the recommended value of the vehicle. They offered a refund, pretty much stating they were pulling out on the agreement. Very disappointed, we had to agree, although not sure of the legality of them doing this as they had turned their backs on us and wouldn't answer our calls. At least with the money back we could put it towards another vehicle. A bank transfer taking 3-5 days was promised providing we e-mailed bank details. This we did immediately but a week later no money had been refunded. We made several calls after that, which were either dodged, or if we did speak to the salesman, he claimed he hadn't received the e-mail from us. One of the e-mail addresses given was a bogus one which bounced straight back, another, it was claimed, had gone off to a different sales department with my partner's bank details (despite the small family-run company having only 3 members of staff and one address).

We were forced to take our holiday in our existing car, which had been playing us up and we were unable to take my daughter's friend with us. Calls to the company were even made from holiday, chasing up our refund. If anyone answered, we were fobbed off with lies such as, 'The boss is busy, not in today, will call you back, or has sent the refund out today'. And it will reach you in a further 3-5 days'. It was like a black cloud hanging over our heads for months and I couldn't see an end to it. The last straw was my partner being angry upon being told a cheque was in the post, despite us remembering afterwards that they didn't have our address, so couldn't send one even if they tried. I could not believe a company would treat us so unprofessionally and be so badly run by men with their own families and supposedly caring, let alone stealing our money from us when I was obviously just about to have another child. After my partner left for work one morning, I realised that I was too worried to go back to sleep and that there was no alternative but to involve third-parties, which would take time and money. I did the only thing I knew to do when something was beyond my control and to hand the problem over to God.

I prayed quietly in my bed, just telling Him the problem was too big for us especially with all the concerns and day to day problems of everyday life, financial struggles and the impending new baby. I lay there thinking for no longer than 2 minutes after praying until I had the thought of e-mailing to boss myself, telling him he was committing theft and the whole transaction was fraudulent. I was considering hitting him from all sides, the bank's fraud dept, trading standards, car sales regulators and possibly *Watchdog* so people knew how his company were treating people. It seemed very clear that I had to tell the boss this directly and let him know we considered them very dubious and were not going to take this treatment lying down and just lose £500 deposit to them when they had let us down. Then I thought that I had just handed over the problem to the

Lord's hands and why was I trying to solve a problem I had handed over to Him. Now a further thought occurred, sometimes God directs you and gives you the tools to use. What if I sat back waiting for the money to come back, expecting God to do it all for me when He could be giving me my answer now and I was ignoring Him? I wrote an e-mail there and then, asking God to help me control my anger at them so it wasn't a personal attack by an irate woman and to give me the ability to word it professionally and use legal terms so it looked as though I had already sought legal advice. I was able to keep my temper and use several different angles of attack to show that it could threaten their business reputation and ability to trade in future.

I only told my partner that afternoon as I had an e-mail back from the boss which I was too nervous to read. I expected a backlash and abuse as I had reported the company and threatened their business. However insincere, the e-mail offered apologies and said a registered cheque had been put in the post that day and wished us good luck with the baby.

To our astonishment, the cheque arrived 2 days later and a week later, actually cleared. My partner fully expected it to bounce but I had felt sure for the first time in months, knowing there had been some kind of divine intervention. After months of lies and ignorance, I had a polite response directly from the boss the same day, the cheque arrived as stated and needed to be signed for. Even better, it didn't bounce as many people jokingly said it would!

I honestly do not believe we would have had the refund by now if I hadn't prayed and had my prayer answered. If anything it would have been a lengthy and costly process to try to retrieve the money from this company.

Anon
Haverhill, Suffolk

Born Again

I have now known the Lord as my personal Saviour for sixty three years and have found him to be real in many different experiences that I have been through.

I cannot remember just when my parents' marriage began to fall apart as I was very young, but I do remember lots of fighting and unhappiness. When I was six I was sent to live with my grandmother on my father's side, until they could save enough money to get a divorce. In this country divorce was hardly ever heard of and when they finally managed it, it took them three years, which was the time you had to wait back then. It brought such a disgrace and stigma they had to leave their hometown and go elsewhere to stay. They both married again and had family, so I was left with my grandparents, and there I stayed.

In my teens I met and married my husband Simon and neither of us "were born again" at this time. Soon Simon was called into the British army for national service and was posted to Trieste in Italy.

During that time, I went to a small Pentecostal meeting and heard what was to me the first time that I could be "born again".

I had always gone to church and as far as I knew I would get to heaven; that night I gave my heart to the Lord. When my husband heard that I had made that decision, the whole world changed and he 'wanted nothing to do with it' and tried to get me away as hard as he could, but I was changed. He was a different man now, used to drinking and living a worldly life; he had no intention of changing, so I had to rely on the Lord for my safety, when he had had too much to drink.

Through all of that I was conscious of the presence of God, and one day, while at his work God spoke to Simon and changed his life forever. We spent fifty five years together and most of them working and serving the

189

Lord, He has now gone on to his reward, and I am still here serving a great saviour.......

Wendy Cameron,
Peterhead, Scotland.

Footnote:
Simon Cameron owned a furniture factory, shops and vans. When he met Jesus, he sold many of his possessions and converted one of his vans into a mobile 'platform'. From which he and his family would tour North-East Scotland preaching and singing. They developed an international ministry and founded charity shops, a school, an old folk's home and a Christian 'drop-in' complex for the local community with the profits. They also upgraded orphanages in Romania and some of their family are now living there, rescuing unwilling victims from sex-trafficking. Wendy, his widow was always in the forefront of this work with him as well as caring for her family. She is known affectionately to hundreds as 'Mrs C'.

Wealth Did Not Stop me From Feeling Empty

"Surely God does not have any partiality in the way He treats us human beings. I would never have qualified to be one of His favourite ones, as I was brought up in a fairly rich and arrogant family. Rev 3:17 applied to us: You say, 'I am rich; I have acquired wealth and do not need a thing. ' But you do not realise that you are wretched, pitiful, poor, blind and naked. Wealth did not stop me from feeling empty deep within my heart. Nobody ever shared with me their own feeling of emptiness, because every person pretended they were doing fine and had a good life.

I was brought to the knowledge of the truth and I had to make the decision of a life-time. If God who made me says I am a sinner, I had no choice but to agree with Him and leave the lifestyle of pretence. Being religious did not hide the truth from me, as it could not fulfil the desire of my heart for something more satisfying than mere rituals. While I was struggling with this in my heart, I was invited to a meeting by fellow undergraduates. For the very first time in my life I was faced with the truth of how I was living, and also a knowledge of where I would end up if I did not repent and follow God's way of life.

All my Roman Catholic teaching about the ability of good works to give me a secure place in heaven failed to stand in the face of God's word. I knew deep in my heart, that God was giving me a chance to know what the scores were, and an idea of what His expectations are; as well as the way into His kingdom. I had always prayed that I may be allowed by God to live with Him in heaven when I died; the above scripture showed me clearly that I did not qualify! It was a big shock to me. The next question I had to answer was 'what would it cost me to live a life that would be pleasing to God?' The speaker that evening, made it clear that I would have to give up the ruler-ship of my life, and allow the creator of heaven and earth to be in total control of my life. That was not a bad cost for my life was totally meaningless. The life I had lived was one that manufactured lies as easily as one breathes. How can a seasoned liar live a holy life? Again God's word came to me from Romans 8:11 "But if the Spirit of Him that raised up Jesus from the dead dwells in you, He that raised up Christ from the dead shall also quicken your mortal bodies by His Spirit that dwells in you. " It could only have been God who put all of this together for me in one talk. After the talk I just knelt down quietly and asked God to forgive me all my sins, and take over ruler-ship of my life forever.

That was the third time I had asked Him into my life; the first was to get rid of a fervent Scripture Union school-girl, the second was to get prayer help for a boyfriend. Until I was prepared to follow my prayer with a commitment to obey God's word always, my life was unchanged. The word of God became my only manual for life in Jesus Christ. I have never regretted that decision, in fact I have discovered that my gains are more than my losses.

Mark 11:25-26 says "And whenever you stand praying, if you have anything against anyone, forgive him, that your Father in heaven may also forgive you your sins. But if you do not forgive, neither will your Father in heaven forgive your sins. "

He then instructed me to bless out loud to His hearing those from whom I received hurts. He then told me not to defend myself - in other words I should not bother to explain to people who had cut me off. He gave me the opportunity to give truthful answers to direct questions to those who cared enough to ask me for an explanation of my actions. God is not a liar He always keeps His word. God does not see the same way people see, people look at the outside of a person but the Lord looks at the heart!

Our God is a merciful God! He gives us more than a second chance, and He prefers mercy to judgement.

Bridget Isaacs.
Sodeye, Wisbech

Footnote:
Bridget is an Economics graduate and is ordained in the Pentecostal Church.

All Things are Possible!

On the 14 of January 2012 our lives as a family were turned up side down, we sat in a doctors waiting room, the oncologist said I'm sorry your cancer has returned; my wife having battled breast cancer in 2007 and now it was back!

She said "the news is not good, you have tumours in your liver, lungs and deposits in your brain, and the prognosis without treatment is 2-4 months." I remember feeling devastated, hopeless, sick and we were just numb.

The next few weeks..... We just prayed and worshipped. We listened to God's word on healing over and over and over. It was such a battle in the mind. Doubts and fears were so real, they spoke with a loud voice, but God's word also speaks and His truth changes our circumstances. It brings life and something was happening. We were beginning to become established in faith; faith was rising and fear was diminishing.

In every battle there comes a turning point and God brought it about in September something changed, a shift took place we were gaining ground! Then in February just over 1 year on, all the tumours had diminished and some had completely disappeared.

We are not there yet, but we know that God is faithful to His word and we continue to stand in faith for Jan's complete healing holding on to Him because all things are possible with him who believes !

Pastor Sandy Jamieson,
Castle Douglas, Scotland.

Footnote:
Sandy pastors The Lighthouse church in Dumfries, Scotland. He was formerly a hairdresser and he is one of a team of ministers available to conduct weddings at the many venues in and around Gretna Green. You are likely to have seen him in friends' wedding photos.

A Place of Miracles – Miracle Valley

I am a Yorkshire farmer, the son of a farmer and born and raised in Snape. As a child, I was a hopeless case and there are many in that village who would vouch for that. To be fair, I wasn't alone in the pranks I played. It took more than one to stuff a chicken down someone's smoking chimney, or to roll a five gallon drum of water to someone's door and prop it so it would cascade down the hallway when the door was opened. With that reputation It was understandable that a wave of relief swept the community along with the news that, at 14 years of age, I had been converted. Maybe it was the result of their prayers but I was the first out of my seat at a crusade led by Tom Butler. Unfortunately my 'conversion' was from the head not the heart and I had to be rather more discreet about my pranks in future. I kept up the pretence of being a Christian and was even invited to speak at the little Methodist missions, using a supply of sermons from a Christian periodical. The words were another man's, so was the conviction behind them.

On the way home from Ellingstring one night, we were laughing at the memory of our host's face after we devoured every scrap of food on the table. As we motored down the roads, we fell silent. Just as we rounded a bend a voice spoke to me, 'You've been preaching about me tonight, haven't you?' The other passengers were otherwise occupied and it dawned on me that God was speaking to me. That knowledge brought a leap to my heart and I thought I'd better answer the question.

'Mmm', I replied. Almost immediately, it came again, 'Do you really know me?' The six miles to Snape seemed more like 60. In a flash I realised I had been found out. God had known my heart all along.

It wasn't until a few months later I realised how much I had been blessed. I was 19 and visiting the opticians for a routine eye test. I had gone over the handlebars of my bike at the age of 6 and smashed my eyebrow bone, leaving me with faulty vision which necessitated wearing glasses. I also suffered severe migraines. This time something had changed. 'You've 20/20 vision, the surprised optician informed me. Your problem seems to have cleared up.

Eventually, I met and married my wife, Cynthia, who had been destined to go to the top in a singing career. She was so good that she had been offered free training but when she became a Christian, she turned down the opportunity, vowing to use her voice for God. We settled into the busy life of a small farm and God blessed us. But we had lessons to learn. 'I think we've got sick pigs on our hands'. Our pigs were bringing in more money than our crops and this was an enormous blow. A couple of days later as the Ministry men finished and left me bulldozing earth over a mass of lifeless pigs, I asked the question, 'Where did this terrible waste fit into God's plan for our lives?' Somehow, I thought God wanted us to give Him thanks, even in this situation.

Just then a doll's pram followed by our giggling two-year old daughter came hurtling through the door. The pram hit the table leg, spilling the milk and sending our Labrador scooting off. ' Be careful', I scolded. At which Cynthia said, 'Praise the Lord in all things, even when your two-year old is knocking the house down around you'

A friend, George arrived and informed me he had seen a vision of me looking out over vast acres of land. No chance. 'Sorry, George, but I think you have the wrong man. If God wants me to buy fields, He'll have to make two blades of grass grow for every one'. We were trying to get straight.

But at the end of the month, there was an auction and Hollybush Farm came up. As we sped past, I suddenly knew, 'I want that place for my glory'. I swallowed hard. O, Lord, where was I going to get that sort of money? As I drove Cynthia past the house, she saw an acre of phosphorescent light. 'Oh, Jim, the glory', was all she could say. With the help of friends and our bank manager, we became the owners of that 15 room farmhouse and land.

'This place shall be called a place of miracles-Miracle Valley-for here will I perform great and wondrous things, the likes of which you have never seen before. A place of miracles it shall be, for even as the sick and suffering come and step upon its holy ground they shall receive healing from the Lord'. Brian spoke this prophecy and what rejoicing that caused.

We held Friday meetings and at one, Mrs Hutchinson asked for prayer for her deaf ear.   Later, as she couldn't sleep for the ticking of the clock in her ear, she realised she was healed, go up put the clock on the landing and went to sleep.

There was a lady downstairs wanting prayer. As she stepped from the car, her foot touched the ground, 'In the name of Jesus'. She couldn't believe that she was already healed after all those years of arthritis. And so it continued, evil spirits left, migraines, kidney disorders, depression, varicose veins, breast cancer, paralysis. Truly it had become Miracle Valley. And it still is.

Jim Wilkinson
Newsham, Thirsk, Yorkshire

Footnote:
As the meetings grew Jim and Cynthia had to move the meetings from their house to the Granary, then to two converted cottages, a large barn and finally to a purpose built church in a barn style building. There is a large café on site, and also a caravan & campsite. Another barn houses a large charity shop with profits going to missionaries. In former years they erected a 1,500 seat tent each summer and people came from near and far.
Northallerton Hospital used to wait until after their annual camp before ordering medical supplies as so much came back from the camp.
www.hollybushchristianfellowship.co.uk

We are a Close Family, My Kids are my Life

I was born in Gloucester, in a family of six sisters and one brother. My parents split up when I was quite young. Mum sent us all to church on Sundays so she could get a break from us, so I knew about Jesus. Mum found it hard to cope with all of us, she had her hands full with all of us and so we got on with life and never showed one another much love and being in the middle of the bunch I never got much of a look in when it came to affection from mum. I looked elsewhere for affection and ended up pregnant at 15 years of age. Not good! My mum decided that the shame would be too much so she tried to get rid of my child but it never worked, instead she almost killed me. Anyway, the baby was born and looked OK, to mum's relief, but he had problems with his heart. They gave him six months to live but he survived until he was six years old, when we lost him.

As I was pregnant, mum then decided I had to get married and she arranged a marriage for me-to a Latin-American man. I have to say I did not like him, even though he was what most people would call good-looking. I thought, 'Give him a pair of horns and he would be satan'. Anyway, we went on to have five other children, three boys and two girls. I lost the first girl at eight weeks old.

All this time I still went to church when I could, always looking for something that was missing from my life. I was not a bad person. When I went to church, I got a good feeling, but it never lasted.

My husband did turn out to be satan. He would hit me when he had been out. He would come home and accuse me of all sorts of things but it was him who was doing it, not me. Anyway, I decided that I would leave him as soon as I could. I managed to get away from him and stayed with a friend. He knew where I was and kept causing rows at the house. I tried to get somewhere for the kids and me but the authorities said I had to go home as the house was for me and the kids and not my husband. So they talked to both of us and patched things up. One night I went out with my brother who had come down from Birmingham and he looked after the kids. My brother dropped me home and that is when my husband decided to put a hatchet in my head. I managed to crawl next door to get help. My neighbour was a nurse and I remember her putting a towel round my head and calling the ambulance. I was in hospital for a couple of weeks and my husband went to prison. They asked if I wanted to press charges against him but I said that all I wanted was a divorce. They said, 'You will get that, no problem'. So he got away with GBH instead of an attempted murder conviction. For years after this I suffered from severe pain in my head.

I looked for a council house exchange as far away as possible before he was released from prison and that is how I ended up in Suffolk, with four children, not knowing anyone. The children were aged 3, 4, 7 and 8 and I and I felt lost and drifted into another marriage. That didn't turn out much better. He had children from a previous relationship and I had my four. Anyway, he died of chest cancer, so it was me and the kids again. I was still looking for the missing piece in my life. My two oldest boys started getting into fights over their colour and their names and then they started smoking. Next they were into drugs, which caused untold trouble. I had to make my middle son leave home on account of this.

It was him who was out on the streets when someone said to him, 'Do you know Jesus and that He loves you?' The chap said, 'Do you want to come to a meeting with me?' He said, 'OK'. He went along and after a while, he got saved and then decided he had to save the rest of his family. When he visited from time to time he gave us what I would call 'a Bible-bashing'. Sometimes he made us cry, at others very angry. We thought we would go and see some people from his Ipswich group when they were in Bury. I have never been to anything like it; it was just a big hall with people in it singing songs I had never heard of and they were so loud and sang the same thing over and over again. I thought, 'I don't like this' but they sent someone to talk to us and got us to go again.

Then my young son went off with the older boy to an open-air meeting and he and his friend both got saved. It took me a while longer to get up the courage to take that step. It was hard to put my hand up to show I wanted to get saved and then walk down to the front to pray the prayer. I remember being at the stage, then one of the people bent down to say the prayer with me, then everything went black. I could hear everybody but not see anyone. We came home and didn't feel anything else – everything seemed normal. I felt lighter and a lot of problems in life had been lifted off my shoulders. I found the Lord talking to me and I would argue the point thinking it was in my head and not God talking to me, but when it still came back in the same way, then I knew it was not me but the Lord. Eventually I realised...from the time I had given myself to Jesus and 'blacked out', I had no further pain in my head! Praise God!

Everything was OK for a while, then, 'Bang!' My youngest son who had been saved before me, had never seen a doctor in his life and had never been a sick child, died in his sleep. I remember running outside and knocking on all the neighbours' doors to get help while waiting for an ambulance but it was around 2am and there was no answer. When someone did get there, he was pronounced dead. I was in limbo again. As I walked his dogs, I would imagine him waiting for us to come off the field with his arm across his chest, saying 'Come on'.

By this time, we had joined a church in Kedington, Suffolk and the people there helped me so much at this point meeting and talking with me and so I cried my way through it. I find I lock things away in my mind and forget about them but there are things that bring back the memories even when you don't want them to. You just have to give it to the Lord and He will get you through ANYTHING, but it takes time. I love being part of a Christian family who are always there for you no matter what happens, where ordinary family cannot help as much as they love you. When I saw my Christian family greeting one another with a hug and all the love, it took me a long time to take that on board but I grew to appreciate it.

When I found the Lord I found it very hard to accept that His Son would die for me and that God loved me more than anything, as I hadn't known a father's love. I struggle with God the Father and with people loving me as I hadn't been shown much of this in my life. I still get choked up when we sing songs with 'the father' in them. I don't know why!

Being a born-again Christian gave me my life back. I am a strong person but without the Lord, I could never have coped. Kids and life can throw so much at you that without the Lord you cannot cope. I have never been lost because the Lord was there with me, even before I knew Him.

Joyce,
Barnardiston, Suffolk

From my Darkest Hours to Joy in The Lord

As a child, my devoutly Christian Nana had a huge influence on me, she taught me to pray and bought me my first illustrated bible. Encouraged by her, my mother enrolled my brothers and I in a nearby Wesleyan Evangelical Sunday School, the Church of the Nazarene, where I went on Bible Camps two years running and can truly say I first came to know the Lord, indeed to the point of feeling called to the ministry.

Later, my brothers and I were moved to an Anglican Priory where we acted as Servers, Crucifers and Choristers, but the revelation by the man I called "Dad" that he was not my real father, when I was aged eleven, and his subsequent death by decapitation on a railway line impacted greatly on me, fostering doubt, suspicion, introversion and pent-up anger. I found my real "birth" father when I was sixteen by scouring the Liverpool telephone directories, only to be rejected by the alcoholic I encountered.

To escape an abusive and dysfunctional home life and violent third stepfather, I left home aged sixteen, naïve, unworldly, and whilst still at school.

Despite joining a Christian fellowship aged nineteen and becoming born-again, I must admit to falling away and I spent years lost in the wilderness. Drowning in personal problems, I suffered extreme difficulties with my nerves and had ongoing severe mental health issues, making several attempts on my own life, having become involved with drugs and dependant on alcohol, I found myself hospitalised on many occasions and even sectioned to psychiatric unit..

Low self-esteem, lack of confidence and a series of unhealthy relationships that involved suicides, a death from AIDS and a termination of pregnancy led me to my lowest ebb. I was a complete mess, I felt unable to carry on and that life was not worth living.

However, the Lord has and had always been there for me, especially amongst my darkest hours, even though I may have forgotten Him at times.

I turned to the Lord Jesus, repenting and confessing all my sins and He answered me, turning my life around and showering me with blessings, working miracles in my life mere words aren't sufficient to describe, although here I will attempt to do so. Throughout it all, the Lord has sustained and kept me safe; without Him and His abundant Love I would not be here today. He continues to keep me, today and every day and is my rock and my salvation. Without Him I am nothing.

Having truly invited the Lord into my life I can't describe the joy and confidence I feel I have been granted, peace and strength which seems to grow and flourish daily. I've found myself able to forgive and let go of past hurts, have risen from the quagmire of depression and feel physically and spiritually renewed. My faith has given me purpose, direction and real meaning to my life. I no longer wish to self-harm and although in truth I may still experience difficulties, I know I am never alone and that through Grace I have God beside me always. I can only thank Father God for this dramatic change in my life and wish to thank Him, Praise His Name and continue to worship Him in Spirit and in Truth. I've been given a new beginning and opportunity to start again, truly a second birth, so praise the Lord who died for me, taking my sins upon Himself, and bless the Holy Name of Jesus.

I'm just now so glad and rejoice in the Lord to be part of a family, community and truly loving church at Steeple Bumpstead, where I've made so many friends, feel so loved, accepted and not judged. I'm so proud be an active part of a spiritually dynamic and living church, which feeds bread and not stones, and enacts the Gospel.

The Lord has blessed me and worked wondrous miracles in my life. After a period of estrangement, I have a renewed and loving relationship with my Mum, and in answer to prayer, believe there has been forgiveness on both sides. I have been reconciled with my youngest brother, whom I haven't spoken to in over 3 years, until recently. I pray we can build on this foundation the Lord has laid before me, and know it is through His doing.

The power of prayer is real and tangible as I know, as I know Christ is my Saviour and Redeemer and in Him I am a New Creation. I was encountering difficulties with a fellow tenant at my address, and through prayer much sought-after new accommodation was provided. The hurdles of references, credit checks and initial finance to get started were overcome. When the removal dates clashed with the start of Spring Harvest, once again my prayers were heeded and the landlords agreed to give me the keys to the property earlier, so I could begin moving in and still be able to attend this Easter Event. People and friends came forward with offers of help, again an answer to prayer. Even today, I discovered a request I'd put in to the police for traffic cones outside the property in order to off-load and move in on a usually parked up main road had been granted. Since my baptism, things have moved on a pace and I indeed feel truly blessed and that the hand of God is at work in my life. He is showering me with blessings and prayers have been answered, as I and my friends can attest to. A close friend and mentor has called all of these events evidence of the Lord at work in my life, and I must humbly agree.

I just want to thank God for all He has done and continues to do for me. All Honour, Praise and Glory is due to Him. So thank You Jesus for your power at work in me, and changing me.

I'm so thankful to have this deep and personal relationship with the Father of the fatherless, and hereby testify to His Power and all-enveloping Love.

Praise the Lord!

Howard J. Downes
Haverhill, Suffolk

I Discovered The Bible Foretold History

I did not come from a Christian home or have contact, as far as I know, with people who were Christians. From an early age I grew up in a Public House as my parents were publicans. One of Tottenham Hotspur's directors regularly used our pub and in return, I was allowed to sit in the Directors Box whenever I visited. However, Bobby Moore's mum lived just across the road from my cousin and I mainly supported Man U.. I used to take Bob's mum to watch football at West Ham. and I had some prestigious autographs and photos in my collection.

Among the subjects I found interesting in at school was ancient history. I found it interesting to look at various sources on this subject one of which was the Bible. I found that there was a lot of history the Bible recorded which was at the time it was written was prophetic. I wondered if I could prove if the prophecy was correct and could I prove it from secular history?

I soon found that so much of what was written in the Bible was proved in secular history that there had to be a God. One of many such accounts was the fall of the Ancient City of Babylon. God named the person who would capture the city 200years before he was born and how it would be taken 70 years before it was built. Having researched it out using secular history as my source I found that the city of Babylon was taken by the person God named and it was captured just as the Bible prophesied, so for me there had to be a God and the God of Israel was Him. This was just one example. .

That led me to have a look at the Book of Revelation in the Bible to see what if anything was said about how things would develop in the world. I found that it had a lot to say on the final outcome of mankind. I also noticed that what the Bible called unbelievers would end up it what the Bible called the Lake of Fire or the Second Death. I had no idea of what or who were believers, so I just left the matter there.

Just a few years after leaving school I went along to a youth meeting at a local church, one of my friends invited me. The speaker for the evening spoke on a passage from the Book of Revelation and made the point if people, and by people I took it to mean me, were to die that night did they know where they would end up? I knew the answer to that question, It would be the Lake of Fire and eternal punishment, whatever that meant! He then made the point about the Lake of Fire would be the place for all unbelievers, however the good news was that by asking Jesus into your life you would spend forever with God and not in the Lake of Fire. All I had to do was to believe what God said about who Jesus was and accept HIm as my Saviour. The great thing for me was that God was the same God that I knew existed, the God of Israel.

It took me a while to make that decision that night but make it I did and this year, 2013, is my 50th year of being a believer.

I continued to study the Bible and the more I found out about it the more it became clear that it was a Jewish or Near Eastern book and there is a difference between that style of writing and the way we write in the West. This led me to find and research Jewish books that would give me a greater insight in to the Bible, after all it was the Jewish peoples' book.

The resources available are tremendous and made understanding the Bible much clearer because it explained what was meant with the sayings of Jesus, how He taught the Scriptures and as a result what was required of me to live as a follower of Jesus. It is not enough to have salvation and a head knowledge of God's Word, for me the real issue is not what I know about God, but how I live my life as a member of God's family, because it matters to God how I live.

Of course it does not mean I am perfect, do things right all the time or say all the right things. I would like to be able to say to anyone who reads this, Become a believer in Jesus and all of life just works out great', but that would not be true. However, through all of life's trials and tests God has promised He would always be there with me. I have found that to be true even though things have not always gone as I would like them to have gone, God has brought me through.

David W J Hilsley,
Frinton, Essex.

Footnote:
David and his wife, Carol, formerly lived south of the Thames and he is Treasurer and an Elder at his local church. He is in great demand as an itinerant Bible teacher and his scholarly but very amusing talks and his publications have been invaluable to the ministers and laymen and women in the UK.

I Was Searching For Answers to Life...

... and began to get involved with the music business, because I thought that was the route to happiness. I had a lot of questions and one day I had an invitation to go to hear an evangelist. I put it off for o a long while. It was the first time I remember hearing the gospel and I got saved that night.

Just over a year later, I was so excited at having met with the Lord, that I wanted to tell the world, but they didn't seem very interested. The more I read the bible, the more I realised that the people I was reading about had something I had not got. I decided I would go forward at the next Christian meeting. The speaker asked, 'What have you come for?' I said, 'I don't know, but I want something'

He asked, 'Have you been baptized in the Holy Spirit?' I replied, 'I've never heard of it ' So he prayed for me and I received. It made an amazing difference.

Back in 1977, I was at a meeting in a barn, on a farm near St. Ives, in Cambridgeshire. Before the meeting began, a woman approached me and said questioningly, 'Peter? 'Do I know you?' 'No, but I was sitting at home when the Lord told me to come here and give you a message, that you will take His healing message and power to the world. I live seven miles away and I had to call a taxi to bring me here. It is waiting outside to take me home'. And then she left.

The meeting began and I was in the middle of 200-300 people. Suddenly, in the middle of a hymn, Edgar Webb the preacher, whom I had never heard of or seen before, said loudly, 'Stop!' Then pointing to me, he said' You boy, come here'   I was terrified. Friends said I went white as I walked to the front, wondering what God had told him!   I thought, 'Lord, have I done something wrong. Edgar began to prophesy how the power of God would come upon me and I would minister in the power of the Holy Spirit'.

At the close of the meeting, an extremely fat man came up to me and said, 'Pray for me'. As I touched him, he fell down under the power of the Holy Spirit and because he was so big, he knocked everyone about him flying. From that day, more and more invitations came in and soon I could not continue a full-time job.

The word of the Lord was 'to take Christ's healing message and power to the world' God cares. He wants to heal our hurting world, body, soul and spirit.

My first overseas mission was in Tanzania. God did some great things there and I was invited back for several crusades. My favourite memory is of a crusade in Zimbabwe where five deaf and dumb boys from a special school were brought to the meeting. They heard and spoke in Jesus Name. The next day a pastor came up to me and said they hadn't been healed. 'I keep asking them questions and they just look at me blankly', he said. I replied with a smile, 'You've got to teach them, like babies. So he took them and taught them to speak Matabili. As we left the city, they were speaking more English than they could the local dialect. They were waving and saying, 'Bye-bye, Peter' The next time I went back they had been trained for over a year. It was amazing.

I was sent out from the Baptist church in South-west London where I was minister to the 2.2 billion who have never heard the gospel. I knew that I had to go. We use TV, radio and city-wide crusades to reach people. We also started a training school to train and equip others to go out and reach the world.
The Book of Acts, in the Bible has never finished. It is full of miracles done by and for the Apostles. God wants your life to be like theirs.

'Grant to your servants that with all boldness they may speak Your word, by stretching out Your hand to heal, and that signs and wonders may be done through the name of Your holy Servant, Jesus. Acts 4:29,30.

Dr. Peter Gammons

Footnote:
Peter was originally from Ramsey, Hunts. For over 37 years, Peter has been preaching the good news of Jesus Christ. He travels worldwide, currently to about 70 countries and has recently preached to a massive crowd of over 4 million in the Philippines (made possible by the use of radios, which they shared in groups.). He has also written over 70 books to tell of the miracles God has been doing and to enable others to follow in his footsteps. www.petergammons.org. , www.pgmi.org.

My Life with Him is Amazing

I became a Christian at the age of eleven. I had always lived in a Christian home. I thought I would go to

Heaven anyway because my parents believed. And all of a sudden there was a man from a young peoples' crusade standing in front of me and saying that now, if we are old enough to realise that Christ gave His life for us, then we *must* make a decision for ourselves, you can't get to Heaven on the wings of someone else. I tried to put it off, but God had a different idea, He would not leave me alone. I went home but I couldn't sleep, eventually I went down to the bathroom and there I gave my life to Christ. It was the best thing I have ever done, but don't think it was easy. I had about three weeks of torture after I became a Christian, the devil haunted me, I feared. He tried to taunt me to say that things didn't make sense. It was a truly hard time, but by God's grace I came through and my Life with Him is amazing.

Being a Christian does not mean that everything is a bed of roses and everything is easy, I truly believe we have a path to walk and God holds the key to life and death. When hard times come, the difference from a Christian to a non-Christian is that a Christian has a friend who sticks closer than a brother, who walks through life with Him and this is my prayer that I will always walk with the Lord, now and forever, and one day I will spend eternity in His presence.

Janice Cresswell
Steeple Bumpstead

God said "Don't be afraid"

My life after my husband died was not easy, if I needed to go anywhere I had to ask one of my daughters to take me, as we lived in a village with hardly any bus services.

Eventually I decided that I would take driving lessons and, hopefully, when I passed my driving test I would be more mobile. I had the driving lessons and took the tests but always failed. It must have been my driving, because I was always able to answer the questions on the High Way Code but sometimes not in the official way of explaining the law!

On the morning of my 5th Driving Test, I felt God was telling me to open my Bible and look at Isaiah 54:4, you can imagine my surprise when I read:
""Fear not; you will no longer live in shame. Don't be afraid; there is no more disgrace for you. You will no longer remember the shame of your youth and the sorrows of widowhood." (New Living Translation).

I was a young Christian, but it was then I realized exactly what God was saying to me and this calmed my nerves on this important day.
I had a driving lesson before the test and everything was fine. At the Test Centre they explained that I had to have a different examiner, as the one who was booked to examine me was ill. So it was with some trepidation that I went out to the car to take my test. Everything seemed ok, I was nervous but not as nervous as I had been on my previous tests, the "actual test" seemed to go well and then the questions.............. which I answered seemingly satisfactorily! Then came the statement which I was so hesitant to hear.......... "You've passed!"
At first the words didn't sink in, "Excuse me," I asked "what did you just say?" "You've passed!"

To say I was pleased was an understatement!! I was pleased, the staff where I worked were pleased, my daughters were pleased, everyone seemingly was pleased for me. I can now drive by myself, I don't need to ask anyone to drive me anymore!

I truly believe it was God telling me not to be afraid and it was His words that gave me the confidence to pass. Thank you Lord for my independence, now I can help others!

Frankie Smith
Steeple Bumpstead

What God has Done for Me

At the age of 25 I was at the cross-roads.
More like Spaghetti Junction!
I called out to 'God' whoever he was, as I only had a conventional idea of him, rather than what I realise now is a person with whom I could have a relationship with.

Life had dealt me some blows and had got complicated to the point of crisis!

He answered my plea by giving me Christian courses and kind friends who I met through these courses. One early lesson in particular stands out: Immediately God threw me a life-line. I attended Dick and Eleanor Ashton's Church, St Dionis, Parsons Green. An elderly lady needed help getting set up for the day. They asked if, on my way to work, I could help her once a week. 'Getting out there' saved me. With Alice's wisdom and a sense of humour I was always sent on my way with a chuckle. She did far more for me than I could ever do for her. Also, that 'being a human being is as effective as being a human doing!' He was telling me to 'be still and know that I am God'

In 2002, whilst praying with a friend in her kitchen, when the fish man knocked on the door, I saw a vivid picture of a flotilla of Tall Ships sailing on a beautiful sparkly river in front of our parish church,

St Margaret's, Tilbury juxta Clare. Indeed, a tiny tributary flows in front of it!

Church leaders and friends helped to discern the meanings of this picture.

The Ships represent people. Individuals.

The Masts represent God's integrity, a warning, to keep the ships/individuals upright.

The Sails are fully open and un-reefed. We must un reef our hearts and minds to allow God's Holy Spirit whose warm fresh lively breeze fills the sails, be the power in our lives.

Jesus is on the Tiller. We must allow Jesus to guide us.

The hulls are our hearts and minds. Above the water-line is what is seen.

The hull below the water-line and the keel is the unseen stuff in our lives. Good and bad!

The Anchors tell us we must be anchored in Love. Love each other. Love ourselves too.

Not to beat ourselves up. Christ has come to set us free.

The River is a River of Life. We must become free-flowing, allowing God's love to flow through us to others. 'A new command I give you: Love one another. As I have loved you, so you must love one another. By this all men will know you are my disciples' John 13:34

The Wakes are what we leave behind us. Our funeral wakes! (Help!)

Or 'Awake o sleeper and arise from the dead, and Christ shall give you light'. Ephesians 5:4 This is not a direct quote from scripture but was probably taken from a hymn well known to the Ephesians. Paul was appealing to the Ephesians to wake up and realise the dangerous condition into which some of them had been slipping.

Isaiah 60:1 We long for fulfilment, but we must patiently wait for God's timing. He is in control and he weaves together all our lives into his plan.

The fact that they are 'Tall Ships' means that he wants us to be mature in the faith, 'to get onto solids' and be confident in Him.

That there is a flotilla means this is for many people.

As the fish man was present during this picture, knocking on the door of our hearts, like Peter, it is suggested we are we to be 'fishers of men.' 'Feed my lambs, Feed my sheep' John 21.

The tall ships are fellowships, relationships, hardships, Little Ships (Dunkirk), lightships,
worships, battleships etc. This illustrates our purposes for each other.

Since the river tributary in the picture flows directly into the river Colne, it is suggested that this must be for people in the Colne Valley. A River of Life river
Its as if the constant lapping of the waves on the shores are relentlessly reminding us to get on. Where the estuary meets the sea is a place called 'Point Clear' Is our geography speaking to us? Is the Point Clear?

To that end, I sensed strong promptings to share this. God literally introduced me to Nena Harding. She advised praying over the river to as far as Earls Colne. Adrian Burr introduced me to his church, Steeple Bumpstead Congregational Church led by Ian Mizen, and their monthly evening service, Steeple Praise where there is a longing for revival. The source of the Colne is in Steeple Bumpstead ! Then I was told that during the 1980s Hedingham Baptist Fellowship had had a 'season of praying and longing for revival in the Colne Valley.' Maurice Jones in Castle Hedingham had written a trilogy about revival. So we invited all churches from Steeple Bumpstead to as far as Earls Colne, to 'alive@5' and on 6th September 2006, 80+ people gathered together to worship in unity.

215

God had filled our little church, St Margaret's, and as a non-public-speaker he got me there, knees knocking, to explain why we were there. He wants his name to honoured in the Colne Valley. It had been a major challenge to me to 'come out' with an invitation in our Village Magazine, and as I write this, www.colnevalleyalive.co.uk is being launched and the whole length of the valley is invited to the 15th alive@5 at Halstead Baptist Church. Father-like he tends and spares us, well our feeble frame he knows.

Through the friends he has given me, and my long-suffering husband, God has unravelled my 'spaghetti junction' and shown me a bit of Who He Is! He wants me to actively receive, his Love, Joy, Peace, Patience, Kindness, Goodness, Faithfulness, Gentleness, and Self-control. I can Sail on with that!

I'm only a little tug
Looking at the plug.
The Admiral of The Ship
Keeps giving me some lip:
"Some people out there need a hug!"
I cannot sit there and shrug.

God has spoken to many more people in the valley with pictures and words.

"Praise is the devil's death knell. Resignation, acceptance of my will, obedience, to it, have not the power to vanquish evil that praise has. The joyful heart is my best weapon against evil. Oh! Pray and Praise! You are learning your lesson. You are being led out into a large place. Go with songs of rejoicing. Rejoice evermore. Happy indeed if each day has its thrill of Joy. Talk to me during the day. Look up into my face - a look of love, a feeling of security, a thrill of Joy at the sense of the nearness of My Presence - these are your best prayers. Fear is the grim figure that turns saide success so

let these smooth the day's work, then fear will vanish." God Calling by Two Listeners

<u>In 2 Chronicles Ch 20,</u> King Jehoshaphat is alarmed to hear of the approach of a vast army. He proclaimed a fast. He was told not to be afraid, for the Battle Is The Lord's. He is with them. After consulting the people, the King appointed a choir to sing in front of his army, singing, "Give thanks to the Lord for his love endures for ever." This results in the enemy army becoming confused and it self-destructs. The valley becomes a Valley of Blessings.
Our prayer is that the Colne Valley will become a Valley of Blessings through Jesus, Saviour of the World.

"Sing unto me from a glad heart. Sing and praise My Holy Name. Praise is man's joy-tribute to Me, and as you praise, thrills surge through your being, and you learn something of the joy of the heavenly Host."
　　　　　　　　　　　　　　From: God Calling by two Listeners.

　　　　　　　　　　　　　　　　　Rosemary Watkins
　　　　　　　　　　　　　Tilbury juxta Clare, Essex

We Must Live Like Jesus

Born in Peterhead, Scotland, I am the oldest daughter of four children. I was brought up in Church as a Pastor's daughter and both brothers in the Ministry. I travelled in USA (35 States) for many years as part of a 'ministry team' with my parents and family.

My first husband was a builder and became a Pastor in one of the churches my parents launched in Scotland. We had three daughters. We were married for 35 years.

217

In later years, he contracted Leukaemia which left him very weak and eventually eight years past September, he suffered a brain haemorrhage and passed away without regaining consciousness. The lives of my girls and myself were shattered and we felt as if our lives were finished..

I worked as a pioneer in the building and launching of New Hope Bible College in Scotland along with my family. My father was the founder along with my mother, and we built together a large facility which was well known all over the world. After my father died I took over the 'humanitarian aid' side and travelled a lot to Eastern Europe.

For thirty five years I worked there and for ten years I worked as the CEO of New Hope Trust, the biggest humanitarian aid organisation in the North East of Scotland at the time. I had 36 workers and we provided an incredible place of ministry through which many thousands have been blessed.

After a family breakdown, and much heartache, my time there was terminated. I lost many family relationships and only by the grace of God was able to find another life for myself with a complete new beginning. The experience that I went through helped me to reach out and help others and I see the hand of God in it all now although at the time I was devastated.

I remarried for the second time, a man who had attended Bible School in Scotland and who had also worked closely with my family there. He knew the work I did and was willing to stand by my side through all the devastation in my life and I appreciated it very much. After two years, we were married on the condition that if I married him I would be willing to move to his country of Romania as he felt that God had called him there for this time.

Presently, I am pasturing, with my husband Sava, Kairos Christian Centre in Timisoara. We are working with many young people and God has been very kind to us .We meet every Sunday morning for church and in the evening we meet with our leadership team. When we started our work here, there was only Sava and I, and over the past two and a half years we have worked hard and now our 'Leadership team' has five people and we also invite members of our congregation to join for a three month period so they will know how Kairos is conducted and to get rid of the 'myth' of how leaders are 'perfect'. In Kairos our motto is 'Fara Masca' which means without a mask and we try our best not to allow double standards to creep in we have been totally honest with our team and we expect that if we want to attract people to the gospel we must live like Jesus did. Our congregation has now grown and is around 35 to 40 people weekly and growing all the time, for which we thank God.

I personally launched a 'Breakfast with Wendy' work with women and my aim is to reach 100 girls/ladies this year. We normally run around 25 so far and I have recently been invited to start another 'Tea with Wendy' in a small city around 50 kilometres from Timisoara. I believe that God can use my experience and wisdom (through much pain) to help girls not to fall into the traps that I myself fell into as well as working with them when they do. I also give 'mentoring' to girls who have asked me to help them in their business or marriages or just in their lives. I feel God is using me greatly in this field and I am blessed to know I can be used for Him.

We do not know how long God will ask us to be here and the pain of being separated from my daughters and 8 grand children is sometimes unbearable. But God has given my husband and I favour here and we are very blessed to have a large circle of friends, as well as my husband's family, who dearly love me.

I feel that once again, my life has meaning, and that God will continue to use us all over Europe as we place our lives in His hands. My husband is well known in the city of Timisoara and recently was asked to translate for Michael W Smith who came to the city. He is very charismatic, optimistic and full of faith and I thank God that He has given me another opportunity to serve Him..

I realise the sky is the limit in God, and can't wait to see what the future holds for us as well as for Kairos.

Wendy Tomin
Romania

They Prayed for Jesus to Bless Sue

Sue was a young Chinese girl who lived in a town in Eastern China. She had always experienced poor health, and after leaving school found work in a local shop. One day she collapsed at work, and as she lay in a semi-conscious state she vomited blood. She was taken to a hospital in the city and given tests and a blood transfusion. When her parents managed to reach her they were told their daughter had advanced leukaemia and had only 6 months to live. Remember that, in China, parents are only allowed one child, so Sue was their only hope.

Sue's mother was a devout Buddhist. At her temple she sacrificed and prostrated herself hundreds of times before the idol. But her precious daughter only grew worse, and on each visit Sue seemed weaker and sicker.

In Sue's ward was another young woman who was also seriously ill. Her loving husband visited each day and always read to his wife and talked with her while holding her hands. Sue sensed something about this couple, and one day when the husband passed her bed asked him what it was he read every day. He told her it was the Bible, which they believed was God's special Word. Sue had heard of the Bible but had never seen one, so he showed her his copy.

When Sue asked him about holding his wife's hands and them talking together, he explained about prayer. He told Sue that Jesus lives today and loves for us to bring all our needs to Him. He told Sue of some of Jesus' miracles and how He still works wonders for those who trust and love Him. This young man offered to pray for Sue, and so, each day, with his wife joining them from her bed, they prayed for Jesus to bless Sue.

From that day Sue began to pick up. Her doctors were amazed and could find no medical explanation for her recovery. Instead of dying in 6 months, Sue left hospital stronger and fitter than she had ever been. And she had Jesus in her heart as her personal Saviour and Friend.

Naturally, she wanted to share what God had done for her. She arranged a meeting in a local hall and 1,000 people turned up to hear her wonderful story.

She became an evangelist and shared the love of Jesus far and wide. And, today there is a Christian church of more than 6,000 members in her town. They meet in a building that, before the communist revolution, belonged to a British Christian mission that was expelled by Chairman Mao.

That's God for you!!! – Do you know Him?

Ben White
Whitstable, Kent

Ask Him to do Some Thing for This Man

One day a man returned from working in the fields to find his young children playing with the deadliest snake in Vietnam. Because it was small, they thought it was harmless. He cried out and tried to grab the creature below its head. But, he missed, and the snake struck out and bit him deeply on the arm.

As the snake slithered away, the man fell down howling in pain and fear. The frightened children ran off calling for other villagers to help their stricken father. The people quickly gathered, but they already knew there was nothing anyone could do. No one had ever survived a bite by this type of snake. Even the village witch-doctor didn't want to get involved, so the people did what they could to comfort his family and watched, helpless, as the poor man writhed on the ground.

In that village there were just a few believers in Jesus – remember Vietnam is still a communist country. Because they had given up their traditional religious practices, the Christians were persecuted by their neighbours; and they were oppressed by the police because of their faith in Jesus. So life was very hard for these young Christians.

But, on that day, they stood around with the other villagers, watching the dying agonies of the poor man on the ground. Then, one of the village elders said to them, "You Christians claim that your Jesus can still perform miracles, don't you?" "Yes", the believers replied, naturally fearful of where this may be going.

"Then ask Him to do something for this man," they were challenged, "and, we'll believe in Him as well!" Those simple believers fell on their knees before the other village people and, with arms around each other, began to cry out to God in Jesus' Name.....

And the man on the ground stopped howling and writhing and became calm. For a long time the crowd stood dumbstruck, half expecting the man to breathe his last. But soon he was sitting up and clutching his wife and children. Then everyone was weeping and speaking of Jesus and embracing the Christians and asking how they may know Jesus too.

Today that place is known as a Christian village. I believe they have a small church now and a pastor. Many of them are illiterate and they have few resources, but they do know what Jesus can do, and they love Him and serve Him, in spite of government pressure to return to the communist fold.

There's no one like Jesus, and He's the same Jesus in Whitstable as He is in Vietnam!

Ben White
Whitstable, Kent

Footnote:
'Ben White was a missionary in China & SE Asia for many years'

God Spoke To Me Personally in a Supermarket

Well, all I can say is that it's definitely been a journey. Life has it's twists and turns, some my own doing, other times God has stretched me and prompted me to take steps I never thought possible, but the promise through all of that is that He has always been with me, even if I didn't realise He was.

I always had knowledge of God as a child; however I don't believe, until now, that I had a passion to pursue him. I committed my heart to Jesus when I was nine; however, it wasn't until God spoke to me personally in a Supermarket in 2003 that I knew he was chasing after my heart and my life. It was a Sunday morning, in Autumn, at around 11am. Being at University a few short weeks I realised I was actually gaining my independence and being away from home it was a time I could start making my own decisions. So on that particular Sunday morning I decided I would take myself to Tesco, being early on a Sunday, the store was pretty empty. Wandering the cereal aisle, I heard an audible voice, which was direct and authorative 'You should be in church.' Swinging around, I looked to my left and right - no one was there, so just to make sure, I darted round to the aisle either side of the one I was in. No one in those either. So, I stopped in my tracks and listened again. 'You should be in church,' the voice said again. 'Is that you, God?' came my response in my thoughts. 'Yes.' was the reply.

Since then I have always held my attendance at church as high regard, but moreover than that, I have learnt the art, and continue to do so, that it's very important to stop and listen to God. Often times I can find myself talking away to Him, but what He is really after is my heart and although I know he enjoys listening to me, there is something to be said for being quiet before him and just taking time to listen. Sometimes he doesn't speak, because he just loves spending time with me and vice versa, other times he will show me a verse to read in the bible or speak to me directly. Those times are very precious, because they offer direction, clarity and most of all a love that never ceases. It's when I have developed the art of listening to Him that my passion for Him has increased.

Along the journey the fire in my heart for God and His Kingdom being fulfilled on earth, this started as a small fire burn, just as in the natural, has gotten bigger and louder as its momentum has increased. Now I know in my heart, no matter what the circumstance, hard days or good days, dreams fulfilled or dreams unfulfilled, I have the freedom to turn and run to God and what's amazing is that I don't have to run so far as He's with me consistently, in my heart. It's literally a case of just becoming aware of His presence and that Jesus lives within me.

If I can encourage you to do *one thing* is life,
my recommendation is to run to God.

Jo Howlett
A student in Manchester, UK and
Lower Hutt, New Zealand,

A Young Man's Problems

I first heard about Jesus and believed in God when at the age of about 5-7 years old my parents read Bible stories to me. I was amazed at the stories they read, but didn't really understand the relevance that they had to my own life. My parents encouraged me to pray the sinner's prayer, asking God to forgive me of my sins and to accept Jesus as my Lord and Saviour. This I did, but I didn't feel any different after praying those prayers and a relationship with God didn't grow after that. Nonetheless, I considered myself to be a Christian and that is what I proclaimed to those around me in school. My understanding of what it meant to be a Christian at that time was incomplete and I was of the impression that it was about not doing certain things rather than enjoying a life-changing relationship. By the time I had reached 9-11 years of age, my sinful nature was beginning to become more manifest as I got involved in friendships at school that involved destructive behaviour such as vandalism, rebellion against teachers and viewing of pornographic material. My parents took me out of the local primary school and put me in a private Christian school for a couple of years. This was helpful as it broke up an unhealthy friendship. However, I had developed a secret sinful habit that was to grip my life for many years to come. I would sometimes feel that I was permanently separated from God because of that sinful habit.

I was a regular attendee of church meetings as my parents took me along, but I also desired to be there on most occasions. And once I was into my teens, I carried on being part of church life and got involved in a Christian rock band in my late teens. However, I still didn't have a relationship with God and while I was with the band "on tour" I can remember confessing to them that I didn't share their passion for the gospel and what they were doing – there was little enthusiasm for God in my heart.

In my early twenties, the sinful habit I had from the past continued with the viewing of pornographic videos and internet porn. I knew that what I was doing was wrong, but one of the lies that I believed was that each time would be the last time and I would just ask God for forgiveness and carry on. In 1998, I moved away from my parents' home to start a university degree course. It was during that time that I had a very shocking and distressing experience as a result of the sinful habit I had indulged in. I found that each time I woke up in the morning, my mind would be speaking awful things towards God that included sexual words and meanings, but that there was nothing I could do to control it. It was like someone had got into my mind and was playing about with it to distress and attack me. At this time, I was also experiencing the breakdown of my ability to sleep. I had always been a sensitive person and a light sleeper and being in an environment where there was loud music playing until the early hours of the morning, I began to experience some nights with no sleep at all.

By the time I had finished university, my ability to sleep had completely gone and it was now time to start fending for myself by getting a full-time job. About six months later, I secured a job as a computer specialist in a drugs-discovery company in Kent. I was prescribed anti-depressants with a sedative effect to help me cope with my insomnia. I soon found the job to be stressful and with the lack of sleep things were particular difficult. With significant health problems to deal with, I began to take more of an interest in pursuing the things of God. I started attending local church meetings and joined an Alpha course as a way of getting to know people. The people at the church were really helpful and encouraging towards me, but eventually I left and in late 2003 I relocated to Haverhill along with the company I worked for.

The stress in my job intensified after the relocation and I began experiencing huge adrenaline rushes (which I refer to as panic attacks) when I felt fearful in the workplace. These panic attacks were very distressing and left me with a lingering chest pain but the more dangerous effect of them were increases in my blood pressure and heart rate. Another disturbing symptom was redness in my hands. In early 2004, I was finding that during the night I would sometimes wake up with a racing heartbeat. I also experienced episodes during times when I was either waking up or entering into a drug-induced sleep where it felt like my head was being crushed. At the beginning of 2004, I joined a local church as I had a real desire to seek God's help and find friends in my new locality. The church was very welcoming and helpful to me and it wasn't long before I got involved in ministry, playing the keyboard in the worship team and helping with a youth club. However, the job stress continued throughout 2004 and, by the autumn, my blood pressure was so high that my doctor put me on beta-blocker tablets which I have had to stay on ever since. One good thing that did happen at this time was the death of my desire for the sinful habit I had indulged in from a young age. I believe that this was a result of God working in my life, bringing me to true repentance and awareness of self-control.

In early 2005, I was made redundant in my job which was a great relief to me as I had not had the courage or initiative to leave that job. Shortly after that, I took another IT-related job with a small company. But sadly, I experienced many intense panic attacks there and, after six months, I left. It was clear that, with my sensitivities and health problems, IT work and the office environment were not for me.

I didn't really have a clue what I could do to earn a living instead of working in IT and my first job in an alternative field lasted just two days! It was working on a line in a factory and I found the noise alone was enough to put me off (the factory sounds ringing in my ears as I lay in bed overnight). But the Lord soon provided me with something suitable, a job as a cleaner at an insurance company's building in the local town. The job really suited me as I was able to spend large amounts of time on my own and was a great relief from all the stress I had experienced sitting at a computer in an office environment.

So since 2004, my relationship with God was beginning to grow and get stronger and in the autumn of 2006, I had the opportunity to do the one year Foundation for Christian Service course (by Resource Ministries). The idea of the course is to equip believers with a proper foundation for serving in their local churches. I found the course to be inspiring and my hunger for the things of God continued to grow. However, I still had my health problems including lack of sleep and stress. The stress I was experiencing wasn't as bad as when I worked in IT but nonetheless I had been getting chest pains and panic attacks.

In April 2007, the Lord spoke to me in a way that just amazed me. I was attending a talk on Abraham (part of the Foundation course) by a prophet and teacher, Ray Stokes. At the end of the teaching session, Ray was led by the Holy Spirit to prophesy and he was given a prophetic message for every student present at the session. The message the Lord had for me spoke into my situation with accuracy. The Lord said that I had experienced someone pressing on my chest and that my life had been in danger but that He had been very faithful to keep me, protect me and to save me. He said that the hand I had felt pressing on me was the hand of the Spirit of the Lord to come and say "take these things seriously (the things I had been learning on the course), let them go deep into your heart... so that they can be brought forth and accessed and so that God can build upon them in your life." The message also stated that the Lord wants to send me to a people who aren't always that open to the Gospel.

So I was greatly encouraged by that prophecy. This was the first time I had really sensed that God was near, that He cared about me personally and knew my situation deeply. I finished the course in 2007 and I wanted to help in church life in whatever scope or area that I could. God gave me a number of diverse ministry opportunities including building the church website and befriending an alcoholic who wanted to be set free.

Anon

I Never Really Gave God a Second Thought

I'm Andy, I'm 24, and originally from Cambridge, England. I gave my life to Christ in July 2008, at age 20.

As a kid my parents used to take me to church for a while, but it didn't mean anything to either me or them, it was just what you did on a Sunday, and I soon stopped going as I got a bit older. I certainly didn't believe in God or take it seriously, past enjoying the singing and seeing a few of my friends there. I never really gave God a second thought. I was very interested in science at school, and was the sort of person who needed concrete proof for everything.

I considered myself to be a very moral person, and by the world's standards I was – I was well behaved and dedicated at school and my marks were very good. It wasn't until later than I learnt that I couldn't obey even my own moral code, let alone God's, and that his standards were no less than sinless perfection, so that good works could not buy his favour. Instead, at the time, my intellect and high moral standard made me a proud, arrogant and self-righteous person, that looked down on those less intelligent. Had I thought of God at all, I would have considered myself good enough for him.

As a teenager I became an Atheist, and at some times in my life hated God. I had a lot of false conceptions about what Christians were like – that they are intolerant, that the Church is responsible for terrible events in history, that having a faith was only about strict rules and that Christians couldn't have fun. One of the things that first got me thinking about God, was when my girlfriend became a Christian. I found this threatening, and reacted with anger and confusion: I didn't like how this would change our relationship, and was hurt that she could love and value God above me.

I tried to tolerate and respect her faith because of what she meant to me, but saw it as a childish delusion. However through greater knowledge, some of my misconceptions about Christianity and God were broken down. Another large step in my journey came on a friend's birthday, when I asked a Christian friend a few questions about relationships between Christians and non-Christians. We ended up debating for several hours, and my friend managed to breakthrough my stubborn mindset. We agreed that society's morality and laws were set by limited people, and often wrong. She told me about this awe-inspiring God, yet who wants to relate to us as a father would, and that God's rules for living are to keep us from harm like a parent's would, not to limit us, although we may not always understand why a rule has been set. This picture of God as father had real resonance with me, and made a lot of things make sense. She illustrated for me the difference between religion (a set of rules that historically had caused such harm), and faith (a personal relationship with and knowledge of God). This was a million miles from the judgmental religion I had imagined.

It shook me up for a while, as I wasn't used to being vulnerable, to submitting to anything, to the idea that I was not a good and moral person and needed help. However the chat opened a door, and in the following months, I took time to digest the Christian message. Faith didn't seem so odd and alien to me, it made more sense, and so I treated it with more respect. From then on my friends and girlfriend encouraged me to start seeking God and I started exploring my faith, praying, and going to church just to see what the fuss was about. And ever so slowly I felt a response, and felt some glimpses of encouragement. I noticed some prayers answered, and felt some impressions and feelings and suggestions when talking to God. I realised how there were many similarities between the Christian morality, and my own. I found much I could agree with. There was so much of our culture I already found objectionable - how cheap and valueless we view sex and intimacy, the sense of wanting everything given to us immediately without being willing to work for it, the idea that we could pretty much do whatever we wanted and it wouldn't matter.

It was a pretty slow process, and there was no real earth shattering revelation, but I began to see God's influence in my life, how much I'd rebelled against him, and that I had done things wrong that I needed to be forgiven for. There was no real earth-shattering moment where I became a Christian, but I slowly learnt more about who Jesus Christ was, the amazing things he had done for me whilst I was still a sinner, and how I could enjoy forgiveness and a personal relationship with God by accepting him into my heart. I learnt that he had claimed to be the Son of God, and the only way to be reconciled to God, and I came to believe that he was exactly who he claimed to be. I found it completely amazing that Jesus could love me and give his life for me when I still hated and ignored him. He won me with love, when he could have terrified me with his power. I kept pretty quiet about how my faith was growing until a certain guest speaker at church said she hoped she could reach out to those who were not quite comfortable being Christians, and felt that there was at least one person in the room who was yet to publicly declare that they were for Jesus. I certainly fit this category, and although she said there was no pressure if we weren't quite ready, I prayed that God would give her the right word to break through to me, and I believe He did. Before she was halfway done talking, I knew standing up in front of everyone was something I wanted to do, had to do right away, and I publically dedicated my life to Christ that day.

Andy Cuthbert
Haverhill, Suffolk

I Felt a Presence of Someone With me

I lived in East Sussex for many years until I met Diana who I loved and married in 1962. When we were at the Altar, the vicar Rev Phillips saw a bright light above our heads, he gave us a St. Christopher Charm, at the time we did not know why until later.

After our honeymoon, Diana and I went to live with my Grandparents who had a Farm because we didn't have a home to go to at that time, it was at East Grinstead, East Sussex and was close to where I worked at Three Bridges on the Railway.

At nights I had to walk to the Farm from East Grinstead Station in the dark on a late shift, along a country road about 3 miles or so. As I was walking, I felt a presence of someone with me, so I called him Lord and I used to talk to him as I went to the Farm, this lasted for 2 months while I was on late shifts.

From the farm my Uncle Ted told us that the Coal merchant he worked for had a 2 Bedroom House to rent in Eastbourne, so Diana and I applied and got it for 37/6d (£1.87p) per week. We were 'over the moon' with it, at last we had a home. (Maybe the Lord had something to do with that, then).

We had our first son, Graham in December 1963 and when he was a few months old we heard a 'bang' from his bedroom, we rushed up the stairs to his room and found the picture of 'All creatures great and small' had fallen off the wall and landed diagonally across his cot. When we removed the picture and saw Graham he didn't cry at all. The picture size was 2ft 6ins long and 2ft high, the only damage was the glass broken in one corner. The picture was hung directly above his cot and when it fell it didn't hurt our baby, we thought that strange at the time.

Graham was a good baby he would play with his toys and didn't move from where he was in the room. He never got up to mischief and enjoyed playing with his brother, Nigel, who was born in 1965 and his baby brother Alan, born in 1970.

At 8 years old he became very interested in Jesus, so we knew Eileen who belonged to the Salvation Army and lived just up the road from us and Diana asked her if she could tell Graham more about Jesus. Eileen and Graham spent a lot of time together and he began to read books to his brothers.

He would go to church on a Sunday morning and became an Altar Boy, also he joined the Cubs and later the Boy Scouts, in the 11th Eastbourne which he enjoyed. His brother Nigel became a Cub too.

I was ambitious and determined to get on and the Railway helped me after the Control Room at Three bridges as an Electrical Improver. When a Senior Draughtsman saw my sketches he told me to apply for a position as Draughtsman at London Bridge H.O. where I used my talent.
I was promoted from Draughtsman to Technical Officer to Senior Technical Officer within 4 years. I went from Southern Region to Eastern Region , back to Southern Region by 1973, then I resigned in December, 1978 after 20 years on British Rail.

In January 1979 we came to Suffolk in one of the worst winters we ever had. I came to Bury St. Edmunds prior to my family because the house we bought was not built. It was not until May that we finally left Eastbourne and moved into our house.

Within 2 years I was made redundant from Pye Electro Devices at Newmarket where I was Senior Draughtsperson, that was hard for us and I began to think I had made the wrong choice.

After being unemployed for a while in 1981, I managed to get a job as Draughtsman in their office for Wadham

Stringer who made coaches, etc. There I met a woman who nearly wrecked my marriage.

Meanwhile Graham had joined the Scripture Union at his school and met with Mike Reed and from then on he got stronger in the Lord and showed us all the way we should go.

It was Christmas 1981 and January 1982, the worst month of our marriage, which I never want repeated, but thanks to the Lord Jesus I was able to turn around and saw my wife's heart, repented and was baptised in water in February, 1982.

In May 1982, I was made redundant again from Wadham Stringer, so I did odd jobs until September of that year, when I applied to Amot Controls, had an interview at which I was told there were others to be interviewed. I left it to the Lord to sort out.

Two weeks later I received a letter saying I had got 6 months work, starting in September, 1982, so Diana and I were so pleased. In late October, Amots were applying for other Draughtsmen, my Chief Draughtsman said, 'Do not apply, Ken', so I didn't.

One morning, a week later the Lord told me, 'Your Chief Draughtsman will call you into his office at 2.30pm and tell you that you are made permanent from when you started'. Straight away I voiced it to Peter, a Chaplain. 'Son', he said, 'Don't bank on it, Ken'. I said, 'If the Lord said it, I believe it'.

At 2.30pm, the Chief Draughtsman called me into his office and said, 'You are made permanent from when you started'. In November that year my pay went up 10% and in December I received a bonus for Christmas.

From that day I knew the Lord was with me and nobody could tell me different.   *Ken*

                  Bury St. Edmunds, Suffolk

Ken's Wife, Diana's Testimony

I was brought up in the Church of England and went to Sunday school, etc. I met and fell in love with Ken in the sixties. As Ken has said, the Rev Phillips saw a bright light over our heads when he married us and gave us a St. Christopher charm at the Altar.

Nearly two years later we had a baby boy named Graham and when he was a few months old a picture of angels, children and animals fell off the wall and into his cot. When we removed it we saw Graham, his eyes shone like diamonds and he didn't cry at all. It was a large picture and it did not hurt my baby, it was strange.

He would play with his toys in the middle of the room and was very contented and thoroughly enjoyed playing with his younger brothers.

When he was 8 years old, he wanted to know about Jesus and we took him along to a neighbour called Eileen who spent quite a lot of time with him and he started sharing with his brothers. My friends and other neighbours said to me, 'Graham is getting serious. Be careful'.

Then he went to church on Sunday morning as he was a Cub, than in Boy Scouts, also an Altar Boy. When he was about 11 years old, I had a knock on the door. It was the Bishop of Lewes, he said he wanted my son to join the church. I said, 'It's not what you want it's what Graham wants'. All I could think about was mending the holes in the Monk's Robe he was wearing. He left and I never saw him again but a few years later we heard he had got into trouble with young boys, so that obviously wasn't meant.

We moved to Bury St. Edmunds because Ken was fed up travelling on the trains every day and we didn't see him very much. My parents and brother were up here in Bury and the rest of the family lived in Hadleigh, Suffolk. Ken was made redundant from Pye's after 2 years, worked for Wadham Stringer for 15 months, did odd jobs for 3 months, then went to Amots in September.

Graham, Nigel and Alan were settled in their new schools, Graham was an Altar Boy at the Cathedral but one Sunday came home and said he was disgusted about the people in the Cathedral. After the service they would go to Pubs. He said, 'It's not what my Bible says', so he left. Then he joined the Scripture Union in Kegs and met Mike Reed and told us, 'I have found someone at school. I like what he teaches very much'.

I always listened to Graham but found it a job to understand. One day, Alan's hamster died and he was very upset. Graham picked him up and prayed over Hammy, we never seen anything like this before, we all couldn't believe it. The little hamster came alive running round the table and Graham was praising the Lord.

A few years later, things were not right with our marriage. I knew Ken's feelings for me had gone. I had to tell my boys the situation that he had found someone else. I couldn't stop crying, I was in a mess and Graham was praying and talking in a funny language and told me to try to pray, so I did this.

Ken would often go out, he was living with us and helped me with the shopping. I couldn't tell anyone about this. Arguments and heart breaks were horrible. Graham and Nigel went to Pinewood every Friday evening and Sunday morning, always back for dinner. Graham said, 'Do not worry, please mum'. A friend of his came to see and talk to me. She was a born-again Christian and her name was Joy. I said no woman was going to break up my family. A few weeks later, with Joy, I gave myself to the Lord. Joy became a good friend to me and still is. She often sits with me.

Graham went off to pray and fast for us all one weekend, saying 'I'll be back Monday morning'. On Sunday evening I walked out of the house, no handbag, as I couldn't stand any more from Ken. The boys were crying at the bedroom window.

I stood at the bus stop. Where I was going, I did not know. Suddenly a car pulled up, Graham jumped out and Mike said, 'Get your mother back into the house'. Mike and some other ministers came into the house and started to pray for me and the family. I felt so good. They told me that I would have a love that I had never had before. Afterwards, I didn't know what to say, so I offered them a cup of tea.

During this time Ken was in bed. I went upstairs to go to bed and he said, 'Do you feel better now?' My peace was in turmoil and I could have hit him. I didn't know what to say to him.

A few weeks later we were listening to Wendy Craig on TV when the phone rang. Nigel answered and said 'It was Linda, Dad'. I said, 'Who does she think she is ringing up here'? Afterwards Ken said he was going to have a bath. Graham was upstairs, reading his Bible.

He called me and said, 'Dad wants you up here' and I replied, 'No, he doesn't'. 'Come up here, please, Mum'. Ken was dripping wet at the top of the stairs on the landing, crying and he said, 'The Lord has shown me your heart, cut in two, it was bruised and so full of pain'. Ken gave himself to the Lord and repented of what he had done to me and the family.

Graham said we must all go to Pinewood and praise God for what he had done, so we all went off next day, which was a Sunday and met all the people who had been praying for us. They all put their arms around us and were so pleased to meet us. That Sunday afternoon Ken left us and finished with Linda.

On Sunday, 9th February, Ken, Nigel and Alan were all baptised at Pinewood Chapel. The Lord had told me not to be baptised with them at that time, but a few weeks later when every time I opened the Bible, I read about being baptised, I was.

It took about 18 months or more to trust Ken again. He started a new job in early September, 1982 at Amots and was made permanent in October of that year.

I thank the Lord how he changed Ken over a period of time. No more smoking and womanizing as it was before.

Also, I thank the Lord for our family, how He was with Graham at an early age.

After this, Ken could not get enough information about reading the Bible.

Diana
Bury St. Edmunds, Suffolk

240

We All Have The Same God

As soon as I heard that we, the congregation, are welcome to write our testimony which is living proof of what God does in our life, I decided I have to tell my story.

To understand my journey with God I have to start at the beginning. I was born in Warsaw, Poland in 1956, to professional parents (my mother was a paediatrician, my father a lawyer) and it was compulsory for my mother to work (most professionals were murdered by the Nazis), despite that she had two sets of twins. I did not have any aunts or uncles as both my parents were only children. Therefore my family was very small. My mother was Catholic (she was the only one I knew who read the Bible, as the Catholic Church never encouraged it) and my father was Russian Orthodox.

Because my parents were so busy working, our religious education started when we were 8 years old when my parents asked the nuns to prepare us for christening and first communion. My parents encouraged us to go to the Catholic Church, although they themselves never went. Since learning the 10 Commandments I always had a fear of God. When I went to a private Catholic high school I observed the church hierarchy. I was shocked in the way ordinary nuns were treated by the principal nun. When I complained to my mother about the humiliating ways nuns were treated, my mother always used to say "remember that the Catholic Church is the institution which for hundreds of years took, but never gave anything in return. You do not believe in the institution, but in God. There is only one God and you can pray anywhere. All the wars which were waged are not because one God is better than another. We all have the same God."

So when I met my Jewish husband who came from an orthodox, kosher family, I did not think that converting to Judaism was a big deal. After all, Jews believe in God, so I would still be able to pray to God. I thought about Jesus as the son of God, but I do not remember praying to Him. Furthermore my family were so tolerant that they did not see anything wrong either, particularly that my brother had already left the Catholic Church and become a New Born Christian. So in my family of 5 (my brother's twin died at birth) we had 4 different religions. We all went to each other's churches, synagogue etc.

But when I converted, I straight away felt that Jesus exists and is more important than I thought. I also became disillusioned that the Jews recycle their ancient prayers, but do not pray directly to God. Therefore when I went to Poland for a visit I decided to go to the Catholic Church, confess my sins and be part of my old community. However when a priest heard that I converted and got married in a synagogue he refused to give me absolution and told me I cannot belong to the Church. I was shocked. My father could go to the Russian Orthodox Church for confession and take communion in the Catholic Church, but I could not. I had no idea that the Catholic Church is guided by its own laws and the problem did not finish there.

When my two children were born I was more than ever determined to christen them, but another surprise awaited me when I turned to the Polish Catholic Church. I was told that under no circumstances would I be allowed to christen my children unless I divorce my husband. When I refused to destroy my family in the name of God, I was told that I really do not care enough to go back to my Church. I was devastated and very hurt, but I did not give up. Each time I went back to

Poland (4 or 5 times a year) I was trying to find ways that my children could be accepted. After all what have they done to be treated as outcasts?

Meanwhile I decided that my children have to learn about God, so we (my husband and I) took them every Sunday for classes at the synagogue. We also moved to another village and to my complete surprise my next door neighbour was Dianne whom I had met before and she was very kind to take my son to playgroup. Whenever we met outside, Dianne told me that she is a New Born Christian. At the time I did not realise what it means to be a New Born Christian, despite that my brother was one. I could not understand why she was telling me this, and why she is full of love for the Jews. I thought she was a bit mad, as my brother was. But one day she asked me if I would like to study the Bible. I was free in the morning, as my children were at school, so I was very happy to agree.

My mother, along with my brother, gave me a Bible but I had never opened it. I did not think it was important. I knew the 10 Commandments and I tried to live by them. What else could I possibly learn by reading the Bible? However I was intrigued as to why my sister-in-law always talked about it, telling me you can trust God 100% but not human beings, that she does not worry about anything, because as she puts everything in God's hands. (I was sometimes silently annoyed with her because it was me helping her not God, or so I thought) and as to why my mother called the Bible the wisest book ever written. So Dianne started to study the Bible with me and slowly my eyes started to open and I started to understand that each of us has to build our own direct relationship with God, and not through a priest. When Dianne took me to the Alpha Course, I realised that I had wasted 17 years trying to go back to the Polish Catholic Church which is governed by man's laws not God's laws, and for as long as I am married to a Jew, my children and I have no chance of being accepted. It finally dawned on me that I did not know God or Jesus and had no idea about the Holy Spirit. By then I was glad we had been rejected. When my son and daughter finished their Jewish religious education by celebrating their Bar-Mitzvah and Bat-Mitzvah I took them to a Baptist church which was introduced to me by my faithful neighbour Dianne.

Dianne has been my neighbour for the last 13 years, but she totally turned my life around by 180 degrees. By the time my son was 6 years old I already had moved 4 times, so I told my husband that next time I would only move back to Poland. I was unhappy with God that He did not allow me to settle. When our present home got destroyed after only one year of living in it I was devastated. I was angry at developers and the successive governments for allowing the houses to be built with tanks above your heads and paper ceilings. I hated the house and I only bought essential things. I could not imagine living in such a house in my old age. I felt insecure all the time and reacted to any sounds. However I started to pray to God to look after our house. After 9 years, I stopped praying believing that it is long enough and God would look after our house on His own accord. As usually I was not only leaving central heating on when we went away, but Dianne was also checking our house on a daily basis. I was totally convinced that my house is 100% secure! I started to buy things to make the house much nicer for the children.

One year later, our house was destroyed for the second time. I cannot describe how devastated I was. It happened one week before my son's A Level exams. I do not have any family in England and my husband had to concentrate on running his law practice, moving his office and dealing with awkward insurance. It was left to me to save our children's school books and undamaged things. However while we were living in the hotel for two weeks I could not store things there, but it was vital to remove things as soon as possible, before the insurance moves in, as they take away undamaged things and you do not have any access to them. They give you them back after a house is rebuilt, which can be up to one year. Meantime if you replace things which were not damaged, insurance does not reimburse the money you spent. They only pay for damaged things. I called the elder of the Baptist church with a request if any of the congregation would be willing to store things for me until we rent a house. I did not get a positive response. I knew I was on my own. I was unable to think or plan my day. I asked God to do it for me. I asked God to help my son with his studies, as I was unable to revise with him for the coming exams as was our common practice. I put everything in God's hands and prayed every single day as I had never done before. I put total trust in God.

On the day I removed our things from our destroyed house for the insurance and builders to move in, I got a surprise visit from a Polish lawyer. He came to collect £100,000 from me. This money was stolen by my best friend in Poland whom I gave power of attorney. When I learnt about this I started to play the lottery to win the money, just to pay it back. I was petrified as I did not want to go to prison for something I had not done and had no knowledge of. I did not win the money and I had no money to pay it back, particularly that my husband also suffered a financial set back as his long-time client refused to pay him a substantial amount of money for two years worth of work. So I turned to God and put everything into God's hands and I did not take my "friend" to court to recover the stolen money. Instead I prayed to God that he would deliver His justice and I deeply believe that He will. For the last two years I have not heard anything. In the middle of all this upheaval I broke my hand. By then I was grateful to God that it was my left, not right, hand, because I could do most things with one hand.

It took me 54 years to finally learn to pray every day, to put everything in God's hands and trust 100% that He is the only one who can deliver. He is the one who puts on your path people and circumstances which will help you deal with or sort out your problems. In my wildest dreams I never thought I would follow Pastor Adrian Burr to his chapel, but he was the one who helped me in my darkest hours. You get help from the source you least expect, because God is in charge.

Natalia Taylor

4,999 Letters I Never Had to Write

Some people think they don't fit into this world, and as a youngster I thought I was one of them. Unbeknown to me I had been adopted at 6 by my mother's new husband.

When I was around 21 months my mother was full term pregnant with a baby. My mother came upstairs to bring me down after an afternoon nap and on our way downstairs, she tripped, and we fell. She was taken into hospital and gave birth to a little boy – Stephen, with his back broken in two places, and of course dead – what an awful shock for my mother........and me?......well, it was the beginning of a nightmare.

My stepfather blamed me for the death. He had been a prisoner of war for 4 years in Germany, - his nerves were shattered, and his mental health poor, so it was hardly surprising he should think so. My life was a mixture of nerves and sadness and even at a young age I felt more than responsible for this event. I became 'invisible' and lived like that between being welcomed and abandoned for some years. THEN JESUS CAME – I was 14 and somehow life became more bearable. I had lots of interests – music in particular, and my life and soul went into my new found Faith and leisure time. My mother died at an early age of 54, - only 3 weeks after being diagnosed with Cancer, - then she was gone. It was sad, so very sad. 12 more years passed after her death and I had to visit my sister and look after her for a little while. It was during this time that I learned I had a father I never knew. He was an American with the Mighty 8th Air Force, and had met my mother, - planned to marry her, - a wedding cake was made, and a bridal dress bought. Then 'the American' was called out on a raid. He never returned, so was assumed dead. The fact of the matter was that my Aunty wasn't too pleased with him as my mother had become pregnant by him, so she wrote to him and told him off, and not to come near nor by again...... and so he didn't. My mother never saw him again. She was so sad. I was given my real father's ring by my sister. My mother had kept it, and it was found after my mother's death.

She became a Christian before she died.

On knowing about 'this American' I wrote to various places in America, - Centres, Record places, etc, asking if he was known, although I didn't know his full name, - only a nick name. Ridiculous really I suppose, but my mind somehow knew that he could be found, even perhaps in the Records of the American war-dead. The American people wrote me back, - always very kindly and wishing me well and hoping I would find who I was looking for. Then one day, my mother's best friends' picture was in the paper and celebrating her golden wedding. My sister read about it and suggested I rang her and ask my father's name, as she would know. And guess what, - she did, - and gave it to me. A friend then suggested I searched on the internet in the Records of the deceased, but to no avail. Then she made an astounding suggestion – "Well, if he isn't in the Record of the dead, then he must be in the Record of the living!" I was utterly taken aback and thought she must be crazy, but such was her determination to help me to find him, that I agreed to pay for a search with my new found information – and here he was, (among 5,000 others with the same surname!) So we decided to start at the top and write to each one – all 5,000 of them!!!

The first letter was sent, giving only my mother's nick name, or pet name that he knew her by, according to her friend. The first letter I sent came back with its reply, giving all my mother's details, - where they had met, who my grandparents were, etc, etc, and I was able to confirm it all. Here was my real father who acknowledged me and was so pleased to be found – and it was only the FIRST letter that had been written! Incredible! My friend was so pleased for me, - I suggested we made a cup of tea! (not very American!!)

One year later after a lot of correspondence and phone calls I was on my way to visit him in Florida. A wonderful reunion – an amazing likeness, 5 new brothers and sisters and a wonderful Lord Jesus Christ who loved me and gave himself for me and 'Found' me in both physical and spiritual terms. One year later at the 9/11 bombings in the USA , my father was dying with a Brain Cancer – he had been a PR to President Nixon, Reagen and George Bush (Senior) – there he was, The President's Friend – and here I was with an amazing story to tell too. I never saw my father again after that first time, but Jesus had heard my cry to 'belong' – and I did, both to my earthly father and also to my Heavenly Father. My father became a Christian before he died. Amazing. The Lord Jesus knows EVERYTHING, and he wants to show Himself strong to us. I praise Him for His love for me, and I thank Him for His love for YOU.

©LMC

Linda
Pickering, North Yorks

To God be The Glory for the Things He has Done!

What I thought was going to be just another ordinary day turned out to be a day that was going to change my life completely-certainly a day I shall never forget.

The alarm went off very, very early in the morning so that my husband, Graham could get ready for his usual day out with the Hang Gliding Club. A member of the team was going to pick him up en route to the Isle of Sheppey- a closer venue to be tried out than the south coast where they normally went.

I went about my general household tasks when at approximately 3pm I felt a very heavy feeling come over me- I felt something was wrong. A little later the 'phone rang and one of the Team informed me that Graham had had an accident, but not to worry as it did not seem too serious and that he was on his way to Medway Hospital in Chatham.. After some time the 'phone rang again-this time informing me that I should go to the hospital immediately.

I informed Graham's parents who then contacted his brother to take me to the hospital where they would be waiting. On arrival at the hospital we were ushered into the Intensive Care Ward. Never having had such an experience before it came as a total shock to see him lying there with all the tubes and wires attached to his body. The Duty Doctor said he should regain consciousness in a couple of days or so. All I could do was pray and put Graham 'under the Blood of JESUS!' (*A Christian term for claiming the benefits Christ purchased for his followers by His death on the cross to assist a person in need. Ed.).

The accident was announced on the Radio and it so happened that the newly appointed Pastor at the Hadleigh Elim Church heard the news. I was being pestered by the Press/Reporters for information about Graham. There was a knock at my door and I was just about to say, 'No news', thinking it was a reporter when before me stood this young man who only gained entrance to my home because he was wearing a 'JESUS SAVES' badge. The Pastor, who I felt was definitely sent by the Lord came in and joined my mother and I in a comforting prayer time.

Another great shock was to come. The hospital informed me that Graham was showing signs of great distress and would have to be transferred to a nearby Military Hospital as they did not have the necessary X-ray apparatus. They wanted to make sure his brain was free from any blood clots. Prayer was still my only weapon and it was such a relief when my father-in-law rang to say everything was clear and normal. He was then transferred back to Medway Hospital. I had more horrific news to come.

A few days later the Hospital Consultant rang me personally to say that Graham was rapidly deteriorating and in fact he did not hold out much hope and I must be prepared for the worst. The room was spinning around me and I had to sit down but I held on to the fact that the Lord would not fail me- so my reply to him was: 'You might not hold out much hope for him but my God will bring him through'. Praise the Lord.

Graham was in a coma for 10 weeks, during which time the Doctor told him he died. Graham can remember going up to Heaven and seeing his body below- but he was told by an angel that it wasn't his time yet and he must come back to earth. It was a very weird feeling when someone who is held so dear looks at one with no spark of recognition at all. However with non-stop prayer the Lord eventually brought him out of his coma and it was with great joy that we all were able to speak with him and he with us.

It was a great test of faith, but the Lord was with us every step of the way and our gratitude to Him knows no end.

Graham and Gloria Cheshire
Essex.

Footnote:
I am not normally a Radio listener but we had just moved to Yorkshire when I also heard the news of the accident. I was shocked that this highly intelligent, daring young man who had only recently married and had his first child was in this terrible state. I remember falling on my knees and praying that God would restore him to his young wife and family. Later when I met him by chance, he told me he had witnessed the Doctor writing out his death certificate while out of his body and asked him to confirm this when he awoke. He told me the Doctor said, 'For some reason, you came back to us'. God really cares, 'even when a sparrow falls to the ground' and He truly does answer prayer.

Everything is Meant to Happen for a Reason

I became a proper Christian a week before my 30th birthday. I went to church with my friend. I was living in Huntingdon at the time and the Easter story really struck home to me (I had heard it loads of time before but this time it was different). I went home and thought about it and said to the Holy Spirit if you are real you have to show me and if you really want me to be a Christian you will also have to show me. With this I had a massive feeling that I had to go and talk to my friend about being a proper Christian, so I decided to go and see them to ask if I could arrange a time to talk with them the next day, they were out. So I went to work. on my way I said again to the Holy Spirit if you really want me to be a Christian you have to show me my friends. The next thing, from out of no where, I looked round and there was my friend standing in front of me.

I had no choice to but become a Christian. So I went to church, my ex husband was not a Christian, that was difficult because he did not like me going to church etc. Things went wrong between me and my ex husband and we split up. I carried on going to church because I liked going, and I went to bible study. One evening I came home from bible study and did not quite understand what was being discussed. so I decided to go on to a Christian chat room site (I had not been on the chat room site for years) and I asked a question (can't remember what I asked) and someone came and started to discuss the question with me. I thought this person was a female, so I was comfortable enough to chat with the person. After a while, and couple of days, we got friendly and found out this person is a male, I wanted to run. So I stopped talking with this man until one day I needed help with my computer so I plucked up the courage to phone him and ask. We got chatting and every night we chatted a lot of the time through the night. Our friendship started to grow until one day I told him about my feelings towards him we decided to meet up and then our friendship turned into a relationship. And then one day I was having trouble with things in Huntingdon and asked this guy Richard if I could have a break and stay with him for a bit. This was 5 years ago, I have not gone back. I have got married to Rich, this was a year ago. I know we were meant to be together as Rich had not been on the chat site for years either and we both go on at the same time and same day.

I know the Holy Spirit put us together.

Rich has helped me get my confidence back up and I am starting to become a different person. Rich accepts me for who I am, like I accept and love Rich for who he is. He has encouraged me to do a counseling course and I am loving it. I am coming towards the end of my Level 3 and hoping to get onto do Level 4. I feel everyone has the right to be heard and helped out of their dark place so they can see the light again and that's what I want to help people to do.

I feel my life has changed around completely and for the better. I still have a few friends from where I went to church as a teenager, but I have friends also up here as well and I really appreciate all my friends. I feel the friends I have, are given to me by the Holy Spirit. and living up here is where I am meant to be. I believe everything is meant to happen for a reason.

Karen Edwards
Harvington, Worcestershire

I Guess it was Crunch Time for Me

When I was 18 years of age, I had the desire to play the guitar, and during my travels it somehow cropped up in the conversation one day when I was talking to Joan Bruhier. I told her that the only problem is: that I'm left handed, but she said no problem, Trevor Bossley is left handed too & he plays the guitar.

I was introduced to Trevor the following week & he had to make some changes to my instrument. Not only was I there to receive guitar lessons, but Trevor shared with me the Gospel of Christ too. He didn't want any payment after the lesson but I left a little donation each week. During the 1980's my communication skill were quit bad & I found it difficult to talk. Trevor would never run me down like the others and he shared with me that Moses had difficulty in communicating. Trevor would always each week leave me a Chick Track which told a little story about how God had changed people's lives.

I was invited to see a film called "The Cross & the Switch-Blade" with Joan, Trevor, & Chris. I found it quite moving. A few weeks later I was asked if I would like to come along to one of their Meetings. I did & I guess it was crunch time for me. I was challenged by the Lord, then I also knew there were issues in my life that I didn't want to let go of. I did attend other meetings in Haverhill occasionally, but also I was holding back. Then I went through a stage where I just couldn't be bothered if I attended Meetings or not.

In August 1982 the Lord really laid it on me. I just wanted to pour out my heart to Joan, she really shared the Gospel with me and I knew what I had to do. That Saturday I invited Christ to come into my heart & be my personal Saviour. I started attending the Pentecostal Church in Haverhill. The Elders prayed for me to receive the Holy Spirit and I started talking in tongues. David Wilkinson & I played guitars in the Church.

David used to live in the village before moving to Cambridge. We used to have some good times of fellowship & would always break bread together, as well as at church. Throughout the years the Lord has helped me with my speech impediment. I have moved from various churches in my time from the Pentecostal, to the Cambridge Christian Fellowship, to The Christian fellowship in Bishop's Stortford with Mark Hunter. Then on to a Christian Meeting in Takeley, Essex near Stansted Airport, onto The River of Life Christian Fellowship & lastly the Congregational Church in Steeple Bumpstead. God has been and is very Gracious to me, even though at times I'm a brute beast towards Him, but He still lovingly brings me back unto Himself. Amen and Amen.

Andrew Dix
Steeple Bumpstead, Essex

God's Gifts of Children

My wife and I were married in June 1966 and we loved each other very much, and we still do!

In 1968, we were told by the doctor that it was unlikely that we would be able to have children. Two years later, on 15th August 1970, we heard an Appeal at church from the Diocesan Children's Home for more adoptive parents. That same day we wrote a letter asking to be considered.........

With bated breath we watched the post very expectantly and very soon we heard that our application was moving forward. We were visited by the Children's Home social worker who told us we had to ask people who had known each of us for a long time whether they were willing to give us a good reference... and all of these were then followed up by the social worker. More work was obviously done as on 20th November 1970, we both went to the Children's Home, about ninety miles away, and collected our baby boy – God's Gift of a son!

Three years later, we applied again and after about eight months we were again blessed, this time with a daughter and our family was complete – Thank God!

Now, many years on, our two children have given us, between them, seven grand-children – What a wonderful loving God we have, Thank You Lord!

Anon

"I Was Deeply Ashamed of myself But.............."

It's a recorded fact that in AD500, the Eastern Orthodox Church introduced incense as an integral part of the worship of God to mask the smell of unwashed worshippers.

Two thousand years ago an event took place outside the city of Jerusalem which not only divided history into BC and AD, but permanently impacted and changed the lives of millions of people – and I am one of them. The first event was a local issue and dealt with the exterior, whereas the second became global and dealt with the heart condition.

As I'm putting pen to paper, my memory is full of life's situations, some good, some bad and some disastrous – where do I start? I cannot record them all now, except to say that I've done some very stupid things and got myself into lots of scrapes, most of which I surfaced unscathed, or made a slow recovery from still regretting that I ever entertained such thoughts and actions. However, one must not allow these memories to rule our hearts and minds. I've chosen to release them all, even the cherished ones, to the One who promises me true freedom in my heart, the One who keeps no record of my wrongdoings because that's His promise and nature.

Deep within, I recognise that I'm stubborn and not easily persuaded, but I will mention this one situation which convinced me that Someone was there for me when life was caving in, so I thought, as the result of internal and external struggles and I was in utter defeat. Leisure time interests had become a very large area of my life and I had allowed them to become obsessions which were continually driving me on. The enjoyment had all but vanished and inwardly I had become miserable and bereft of fulfilment. The jaws of "must-have" and instant gratification had deeply injured me socially and emotionally, as I went to all lengths to feed these idols of the heart. I had allowed myself to reach an all time low and after telling God my woe, I climbed into bed not expecting to wake up in the morning. I had overdosed and took my chance with the consequences.... No member of my family was aware of what action I had taken – I was deeply ashamed of myself, but went ahead anyway.

Unknown to me, God was working behind the scenes. When I woke up in hospital the next morning, very drowsy, a nurse stood at my bedside speaking to me reassuringly. For some reason I was very concerned that someone had done the buttons up wrongly on my pyjama top and I was becoming frustrated; because however much I tried to solve this problem, I couldn't do it. The nurse took charge, as they do, re-buttoned the jacket and put me at ease. She didn't know me, but had done a shift swap with a colleague and when she came on duty the night before and she read the name CREASY on the ward information board.

She was quite startled, not only because this was her surname, but that it was the more unusual spelling. She must have visited me several times during the night, checking my condition and praying. When I was fully awake, she came and sat on the bedside, took my hand and prayed quietly, but with authority for my complete recovery.

She and I agreed that this meeting of two people with the same surname was a demonstration of God's loving intervention. It was not my time to go.

Peter Creasy
Haverhill, Suffolk

Restore, Encourage, Action, Community and Hope
REACH Community Projects is a Christian social action project based in Haverhill aiming to support local families who are struggling with the effects of poverty. REACH officially began in January 2010 but as you will see really began in October 2005. REACH is an acronym meaning Restore, Encourage, Action, Community and Hope.

It has been and continues to be an incredible journey of faith, uncertainty, excitement and I count it a tremendous privilege to be involved in this work; here is a brief part of my story.

I am married to Angela and have 2 grown up children. I was brought up in Haverhill and worked as a photographer since leaving school. We got married in 1988 and shortly after both of us became Christians.

I was led to serve God fulltime as early as 1991, but this didn't materialise until 2003 when I attended Icthus Christian Fellowship in London for a year's study and training in leadership, discipleship and evangelism. Once I finished this year I was given the task of Outreach & Evangelism at River of Life Community Church (Haverhill) from September 2004.

I had throughout my year at college seen a number of outreach projects ranging from tea & coffee to commuters in Greenwich, a drop-in centre in Soho, to homeless & family projects in Bradford. I knew I wanted to work within my home town of Haverhill but not really sure what I could do. I do recall praying in the February of that year that God would give me insight, or as I wrote in my journal 'keys to the kingdom' in Haverhill, to find a way in. I really wasn't sure what I could do, but the following March (2005) River of Life Community Church received correspondence from Christians Against Poverty (CAP) in Bradford inviting churches to a church leaders day.

We attended in June; fell in love with the work and despite the costs to be involved, we entered into a partnership that began in October with me training as a debt counsellor. I do recall that for us as a church, it was quite a stretch financially, but believing that God would provide and He did so, first with the provision of a little office on the industrial estate – free of charge along with a desk, chair and filing cabinet.

One client I met just before Christmas in 2005, was to become a catalyst in what was to come, but this didn't happen until the following October (2006) when this single mum tried to 'better herself' by getting a full time job. Sadly, the job ended just after Christmas and this meant she had to re-apply for benefits; this took time and she didn't have money to buy food! We did help her, but I remember thinking to myself 'how many more are struggling like this?' Not only that but I was beginning to see the effects that bank charges were having on families, often leaving them with very little of their wages or benefits.

At the CAP Winter Conference I learned of an organisation that helped set up Foodbanks around the country – the Trussell Trust based in Salisbury. I looked into them and visited in April 2007. I wasn't at all surprised to learn that the biggest 2 problems affecting Foodbank clients were 1) Benefit related and 2) debt!! I knew we had to do something, but I didn't know how it would happen. I was already rushed off my feet with the debt work and besides, we had no money and certainly nowhere to store the food!

The next big God moment was about to unfold before my eyes. In May 2007 I went to see a family from Linton, struggling with debt following a time of ill health and the inability to work. I was able to help with the debt, but there was a connection and I invited them to our home to meet my family. It was during this time that there was a bigger connection; this family were related to my wife's family! A friendship began to grow which remains to this day and Ann Merrigan became a central figure in the Foodbank and REACH as it began to develop. It took another year of planning and preparation before we were ready to buy into the Foodbank project followed by a further 6 months to get the project launched to the general public on 23rd October 2008, just as the so called 'credit crunch' began to make the headlines.

As I look back, we bought into the idea (literally 12 lots of £105 on a Standing Order) with £180 in the bank, (a couple from church thought it a good idea and gave us £15 a month towards the work – they still do!!) a bunch of inexperienced (and some very new) Christians and nowhere to store the food! And yet God has continually provided for the work and made it happen. My little 'CAP Office' became the Foodbank warehouse and the warehouse owner let us have the upstairs office too as our CAP & Foodbank office.

Well to bring the story up to date. Lots of things have happened. The warehouse owner gave us even more space to house the ever expanding work. We now run 7 projects, alongside CAP & Foodbank we have Furniture Bank that began in September 2009, the Resource Centre which opened in May 2010, Acts 435 – October 2010, CAP Money – 2011 and Starter Packs in 2012. We have 2 full time employees; me and Ann, Ray (part-time) on the Furniture Bank and around 40+ volunteers. We have helped hundreds of families in debt, handled in excess of 35 tonne of food, more than 1500 items of furniture and seen around 30 people become Christians.

It's been, and continues to be, an amazing experience of God's provision and faithfulness. I'll often say to folks when our backs are against the wall, "God's never let us down in the past, so why should he start now?" Anything we have ever done, in REACH right from the CAP work, we've never had enough money for, but yet felt we should go for it anyway!

Lastly; and let's be really honest here. If I had have applied for my 'current role' in REACH, based on my qualifications and previous experience no one in their right mind would have employed me! I had run a simple 'one man band' photography business based on passion – we just about scraped a living! But one thing I have learned in the Christian life, it's not always about 'worldly qualifications' but about availability and a willingness to go where God wants us to go. Has it been scary? Yes, many times when we're praying for the money to come in, the heart-breaking stories, and the many disappointments. It's been very lonely at times, especially for the first 2-3 years and very hard trying to convince a sceptical set of statutory agencies of our genuine desire to help people and not just 'Christianise' vulnerable people. But on the whole I believe that I'm where God wants me to be at present, and I'm loving it! The challenges and frustrations that go with the work completely pale into insignificance when we see the lives of the people we're trying to help being changed – which we do on a regular basis, I just wouldn't want to be anywhere else!

Henry Wilson
Haverhill, Suffolk

Let's Take This Message to Everyone

I was born in South Africa and I currently live with my wife and family in Colorado Springs, USA. As a child I suffered from dyslexia and at the age of 27 I had never read a whole book. I had many problems but the strange thing was that when I moved from Middleburg to Capetown to get away from them, somehow they followed me. Eventually I found the source of my problem, much to the relief of my family. Now I am the author and co-author of many books and we travel internationally, speaking and talking about the grace of God in classes and meetings and helping others.

As a Christian the way I think and believe is extremely and vitally important to every area of my life! People from different countries and different cultures, like Western, Eastern, and Third World cultures all think differently to each other! E.g. - As an African I know what it is to think "African," and especially what it is to think "South African!" But as a South African living in America, I constantly find myself having to Purposely Focus on thinking "American! I have had to learn what it means to think "American", and sometimes as I travel throughout the USA I find that thinking "American" is not always the same everywhere you go in the USA either! You have "Southern American" thinking that seems to differ vastly from the rest of the United States. But what is important to see is that just as there is "African" thinking, and "American" thinking in this world, likewise in the Church today there are many different schools of thought. There are those who have "Biblical" thinking, and those who have "Word" thinking, or "Old Testament" thinking, and some even have "New Testament" thinking!

As a Christian, I very often talk about the blessings of God and the wonderful things He has done for our family. I am not ashamed of the goodness of God in our lives and love to share this with people around me. But there have been times when I have been told that I live in another world, i.e. not reality! This statement really upset me a while ago when someone very dear to me accused me of the same thing, making me feel that I was a little weird and question some of the statements I had made. After some real soul searching and thought about

my life and how God has led me through the years, I came to the conclusion that:
YES, they are right!!! I DO live in another world!!

Now I absolutely live in a different world, a world where there is hope, love, peace, assurance and goodness in EVERY situation. I live in a world where God (Father, Son and Holy Spirit) are my best friends and care about what happens in my world. It may not always be sunshine and roses because I have issues to deal with in my world too, but the outcome is always to my benefit and the peace I have leaning on God is worth more than anything else. "God always makes everything work for good for those who trust Him" - *Romans 8:28*

On the one hand with all our traditions and manmade reasoning, we (human beings) have separated what we term "God" or church from "real everyday life". We have been taught and had demonstrated that church is spiritual and that this spiritual stuff only happens in certain places, like special buildings or gatherings on Sundays. We are taught that there is certain behaviour that goes along with these times and if we don't conform to that, we are upsetting God and not getting or limiting His favour in our lives. Many times, joy has been removed from these meetings and in some cases joy evaporates when so-called "spiritual" people visit with us in our homes or at our fun times like parties and picnics.

Then, on the other hand we have "real" life that involves things like windsurfing, kite flying, snowboarding, snowmobiles, picnics, fishing, movies, biking, motor cycles, sports or whatever you can think of that is fun times with family and friends. Somehow through the years we have been taught that this life is "outside" church or God or spirituality. There have been times when I have absolutely preferred going away for a weekend rather than being in church because I have more fun outside of church than in church where I often feel I don't measure up to someone else's standards

I have battled to make sense out of this because shouldn't everything that pertains to my life involve God? He is the creator, not me. It's HIS life IN me that gives me passion and love for certain things. Why then would I want to separate myself into compartments? It just doesn't make sense, yet that is what we have tried to do. We separate our lives into certain life and spiritual segments and then we can't understand why we feel so disjointed and unhappy.

I heard a preacher call this full, complete life in God, "The Great Dance" and I love the idea. The illustration he used was of God (Father, Son and Holy Spirit) in a circle, living in absolute harmony and peace, full of happiness and goodness of life. Then they decided to share this wonderful, all encompassing LIFE with other created beings – MAN and creation. Jesus (the Son) was the "gate" by which this sharing of life came to mankind. In the "dance", they opened their arms and said: "Come, share LIFE with us. Enjoy our life. Enjoy your existence. Enjoy being part of a precious family!" What pleasure God took in making this happen!

Long before he laid down earth's foundations, he had us in mind, had settled on us as the focus of his love, to be made whole and holy by his love. Long, long ago he decided to adopt us into his family through Jesus Christ. (What pleasure he took in planning this!) He wanted us to enter into the celebration of his lavish gift-giving by the hand of his beloved Son.
Ephesians 1:4 (MSG)

This was the plan from the foundation of the world. Its not a repair job because someone messed up. God the Father, the Son and the Holy Spirit wanted us to share in THEIR life from the very beginning. And it's easy to take hold of and believe that we are part of this wonderful, amazing family.

Knowing that we belong, that we "fit," gives us an awesome sense of self-worth and feeling of acceptance. Let's take this message to everyone. No one has been left out. No one has been excluded. Telling people how bad they are has never helped anyone. Telling someone good news makes them feel valuable and wanted and guess what? They start to change into the person they are declared to be! News is something that has happened ... not something that needs to be done to make it happen! Good news sets us FREE to feel alive and happy, to enjoy every aspect of life and rest, knowing that we are not under investigation all the time and that God is part of what we are doing all the time.

Arthur Meintjes
Colorado, USA.

I am very PROUD of my God

Son of a pioneer of the early Pentecostal movement in Great Britain who had seen the Welsh Revival, David Hathaway's life is characterised from the very beginning by a desperate, impatient desire to experience personally and demonstrate publicly who the REAL Jesus is. Everyone knows about religion but they don't know who the real Jesus is. Starting his career working in a City of London bank, David has always chosen to live on the edge, in the danger zone, to take amazing risks for God. Miraculously released from a communist prison, healed of cancer twice, almost killed on five occasions, he is still enjoying the unfolding adventure. He says he would rather live in a storm with Jesus than live at peace without Him.

Asked to pastor a church at 18, three months after starting Bible college, he has seen the power of God and miracles of healing from the very beginning of his ministry. After 10 years of UK ministry, in 1961 he organised the first post-war overland expedition to Jerusalem, travelling behind the Iron Curtain . There was so much interest in this that he was virtually forced to set up his own travel company, Crusader Travels. While crossing communist Europe, David saw the desperate spiritual need and God gave him a vision for Russia and the Soviet dominated countries. In 1964 the call was confirmed by a miraculous healing from throat cancer.

David began smuggling Bibles in a secret compartment on his buses – he could take two tonnes of Bibles every time, but in Summer1972, he was stopped at the Czech border with 5000 Bibles for Russia. He was arrested. Tortured and sentenced to five years in prison and another five years for preaching inside the prison!
In answer to prayer, God showed him the exact day of his release. After ten months in prison, God sent the British Prime Minister, Harold Wilson, to bring him out. David told this story around the world before returning to work.

The words of one of his fellow prisoners echoed in his ears, 'David, don't forget us. No one knows, no-one in the West cares'. As a result, he helped work for their release and eventually went into the underground churches, finally openly holding crusades and conferences in the communist countries. In 1988 he held an East-West conference in Karlsruhe, Germany and 600 came from the East. In 1989 he held a second conference, publicly prophesying the fall of the Iron Curtain.

As a direct result of an armed attack in Ukraine on 2nd June 1988, designed to shoot him and stop him evangelising there again, the Eurovision International TV Company was formed, enabling him to reach every home, rather than evangelising in auditoriums and stadiums. He borrowed equipment from the TV station in Lvov, where he had been attacked and went into production. Then after surmounting problems with documents, finally in 1999, top quality, professional TV equipment from Italy was imported legally into the Ukraine. David is now able to show what God is doing among their people, how God is manifesting his power in their country and healing the sick by real-life miracles.

One church in Ukraine was turned out of their theatre building into the streets in temperatures of -25 degrees. As a result, the church grew rapidly and the city authorities said, 'We cannot allow you to preach in the street. This is far too dangerous', and forced the much increased church back into the theatre. That is the way to fill your church. Try it! But it takes faith.

He describes 2003 as the hardest year of his life, being diagnosed with lung cancer in January and miraculously healed in February. When you know you have only a short time to live, you learn how to pray! I would pick up my Bible and God would speak to me, comfort me and I would go back to sleep. I said, 'If you have finished with me just tell me, but if you have a whole new life for me, then I want you to answer and heal me'. I said, 'Lord, I cannot go back into Russia and preach about miracles if I have had my lung taken out'. 'I cannot stand up and boast about the God who can do anything and admit I've had one lung taken out' I don't preach, I boast about my God. He's the greatest, the most powerful.

I am very PROUD of my God!

Footnote:
Adapted from *'The Power of Faith'* by David Hathaway. David has ministered worldwide for over 50 years and written several books. His ministry is available in UK. eurovisiontv.org.uk www.propheticvision.org.uk

It is Awesome to Know He Hears Everything

All told, I had a good life in my early years. Memories of my father are few and vague as he died of tuberculosis in 1948, a result of heavy drinking from his Naval days. It was rumoured that my father was the son of a Cree Indian as his mother had lived for some time in Canada. However, although I was born in Boltonsborough, Somerset, I only knew my family lived in the Old Town in Hastings, Sussex, opposite the bakery. The bakery always felt warm and cosy and I spent a lot of time there as my brother was friendly with the boy who lived there. We were a large family and very short of money. Fortunately, one of my older brothers was a keen fisherman and fish made up a large part of our diet. A 'tallyman' called at our house, bringing an assortment of goods for which we could pay off a little each week. In the evenings we would listen to the radio and there would be wonderful tales of Dick Barton, Special Agent, Journey into Space and Paul Temple. What panic there would be if the light went out when the penny in the meter did not last as long as we hoped. We would turn out our pockets for coins and often run to the off-licence for change. We had usually missed the story when we got back. We used to play games such as Hangman and Hare and Hounds, with small bars of chocolate for the winner and draw, paint or make models. Jan brought home a big, wooden record player and we listened to Johnny Dankworth, Johnny Cash, Glen Miller, Johnny Ray, Joe Loss, Slim Whitman and Hank Williams. We listened to anything from the Hit Parade to mother's classical music and accompanied it on combs covered with Izal toilet paper or anything else which was around. We made our own Easter eggs from dried milk, raw eggs and cocoa powder and always had great fun making a cake and puddings at Christmas before writing the traditional letter to Santa.

We would often hear the sonic boom of the first aircraft which flew over the Channel to break the sound barrier. The noise would make our windows shake. Another familiar sound was the boom of the foghorns at sea, something I now miss together with the smells and sights of the coast.

I was smacked twice, richly deserving it both times. The first occasion was when I was nine and had the whole family and the police out looking for me, only to find me in a field with friends, eating stolen crisps and chocolate and smoking stolen cigarettes. It did little good and later my friend and I decided to walk to London, only to be collected by the police at Tunbridge Wells that night, interrogated for two hours and returned to my mother. I befriended an old lady and I would spin pathetic yarns which got me practically anything I needed, until one day I found her in our living room talking to my mother. I had let slip my address and tried to lie my way out of the situation.

I didn't spend the time in school that I should, playing truant and wandering in the countryside or enjoying my life by the sea. Eventually I left and took to going to pubs to get away from my mother nagging me to get work. Godly things slipped into the background and my brother emigrated to Australia and I have never heard from him since. In 1964 I had a son and mother took on the baby while I took odd jobs for a while.

One day I was waiting to board a bus with my baby when I met an old friend, Ron. He was an elderly man but all I could get out of him was, 'Praise the Lord, I've changed. Hallelujah'. I thought he had 'flipped' but the friend with him told me he had become a Christian and invited us home. I was invited to a meeting in a little village hall in Hurstmonceaux and given a lift there, with several others in an old green Dormobile driven by Alfred, who later became my husband. One night, he dropped the other passengers first, stopped for a moment, kissed me and asked me to marry him. It only took a moment to reply and we were married on Dec. 31st 1965, travelling together to the wedding in an old, green Thames mini bus with me wearing the blue dress his mother made for me.

Alfred worked for a Mission and I became the Mission's cook. In the years following our marriage money was as scarce as it had been when I was growing up, but Christian friends would occasionally give us money or invite us for holidays. One year Social Services gave us vouchers for shoes for our boys, but when we arrived one of our boys was given a pair of girls' shoes and told he ought to be grateful for something to put on his feet. We mumbled, 'Thank you, walked outside and vowed to pray at all times for any future needs we might have. God has never left us wanting. One cold night, two friends visited and said they had brought us a box but were not sure how we would receive the contents. Gladly accepting them, we undid them and found warm clothing, shoes and Wellingtons. Everything fitted and could be used immediately. Another time we had run out of milk when the shops were shut and were greeted by a little girl who asked if we needed milk as they had been on holiday and forgotten to cancel the milk delivery. She brought us six pints. Another time I had to cater for 12 staff and had the exact amount of fish but was told visitors were arriving. I decided to dish up what was in the oven, explaining about the short rations. I handed out whole pieces of fish-and the fish kept coming until everyone was served and I still had portions enough for myself and my husband! Oh, my thanksgiving that day!

In 1989, Alfred produced a map of England and asked, 'Where would you like to go'? The four boys had left home and I put my finger on a town called Macclesfield which I had heard of in a book. Alfred's mouth dropped open. That morning, he had been talking to colleagues in the office who had told him of a 52' narrowboat for sale near Macclesfield. The owner wanted a Christian to buy it and use it to spread the gospel. We missed that boat but the idea was there and we bought another, naming it, 'Friendship'. We had some fun with that boat, learning to live on the Waterways, meeting people, visiting churches and schools and making many friends. We even had curry thrown up the boat walls as another boat passed us at top speed, thinking it hilarious and we were left with a deep yellow wall and a smell of curry for months.

There were sad times, too, such as the night burglars broke in and though it would be fun to set light to the boat. Fortunately for us, and for them, they mistook our industrial washing up liquid for petrol, pouring it everywhere and trying to light it with matches. Had they succeeded, they would have been burnt to death and we thanked God for looking after them and hoping they would realise how narrow an escape they'd had.

Later, both my husband and I had suffered strokes and the boat needed repairs when our son visited and his wife suddenly said, 'Never mind, Dad. I know you will have a home before the end of the year'. Alfred just muttered, 'Okay, Lord, where's the keys'? and held his hand out as if to receive them. I think she felt a little hurt at his reaction. No more was said and they returned to Hastings.

A few weeks later, standing in a strange church, the Pastor said he had a few words for us. He read Jeremiah, chapter 32, verse 41 to the end. The Lord says to you, 'Take the keys'. He held out his hand just as Alfred had done in the boat. We sat open-mouthed, feeling that God had reprimanded us for not trusting Him. It is awesome to know He hears everything we say. We went back to the Council Offices at Congleton where we were told of an empty bungalow and driven to see it. We accepted with grateful hearts and moved in on May 1st. When we looked at the Bible reading for that day, it read, 'And my people shall dwell in a peaceable habitation and in quiet resting places: whoso hearkens unto Me shall dwell safely and shall be quiet from fear of evil'. We still live for Jesus, looking to Him to lead us.

Sylvia Lavender
Staffs.

Footnote:
Sylvia has put this material into a book entitled, 'Fisherman's Daughter', published in 2008.

I Heard The Good News About Jesus

It was said of my father, 'If there were two of them and they could move, Leon would have money on one of them to win', and he was always awaiting his Big Win. So it was that I visited most of the horse and dog racing tracks in the country by coach before I was three. An ex merchant seaman, Dad turned his hand to building and was known to help out any mate who was 'down on his luck' at the local pubs. That didn't leave much for mum and he went bankrupt twice. He started to build us a bungalow with his little daughter as his workmate, (I have surprised a few workmen by offering to mix up their cement for them), but before it was finished he succumbed to pneumonia, then cancer, leaving mum with his debts and our home had to be sold up to clear them. As he had been ill for so long, mum had no widow's pension and no help from the State, so she worked long hours in an amusement arcade in the summer and we depended on 'National Assistance' during the winters. There wasn't much assistance at all and anything in the home other than beds, tables and chairs had to be sold before there was any help whatsoever. Antiques were sold for a pittance to buy food for my sisters when they visited and if I am ever offered another bowl of lamb stew, I shall be ill at the sight of it. But we survived.

Marjorie was ever resourceful and bought a seaside 'shack', letting the three front rooms to an old lady cheaply in return for her caring for me during her working hours, while mum and I (and my sister at weekends) crammed into the back bedroom and kitchen. This was a complete contrast to the spacious, detached home in Finchley where she had been raised. Miss Tilley had many friends and they mainly played cards and held séances to pass the time. Meanwhile I found various dangerous pastimes to keep myself occupied as well as spending hours cycling and watching the local florist. When the London County Council hostel staff were ordered to get rid of their pets, my sister brought the caretaker's terrier down to me and Billy became my constant companion, saving my life on at least two occasions; one of them when a man with a car was clearly trying to kidnap me but didn't like the look of Billy's teeth. God was with me that day!

I excelled at primary school, and learned from other pupils at the age of seven that my dad was dead. I envied them as they walked home laughing with brothers and sisters for company. Public school was different and the clean but scruffy child from a poor background who arrived with a pen, pencil and six coloured pencils was not a welcome addition, however bright and the teachers quickly let me know how inferior my schooling had been. I survived and came out with a clutch of 'O' levels despite the constant nagging of my newly acquired step-father who maintained that girls should start work at 14, like his sisters. 'A' levels were abandoned as my shorthand-typist sister, Estelle Valerie came back to share my small bedroom, after suffering a nervous breakdown in West London. With all the nagging, constant arguments over shortage of money and my sister's radio blaring day and at night in various languages it was just too much and I found a job to help mum with the bills. With my first month's money, I bought our first fridge but my stepfather was still convinced he was supporting the 'spongers'...

There were a few kindly, normal teachers at the school and one gave me a real run-around on the hockey pitch and usually 'thrashed' me at tennis. Curiosity as to why she needed church made me visit a local Baptist church and for the first time I heard the good news about Jesus Christ instead of chanted prayers and the dreaded incense, which always sent me running for fresh air. A few Sundays later, I was sitting alone in the balcony watching and listening and was shocked to hear a semi-audible voice speak to me. There was nobody about but it came again. The morning service ended and I did as instructed and found out how to become a Christian (whatever that was). Having asked Jesus to come into my life and sort out the mess I had made of it, I felt a wonderfully clean, free and light feeling come over me and full of this, I danced my way home to my startled mother and announced what I had done. Her reply was none too encouraging, 'And what good do you think that will do for you. Look what it has done for your sister'. My eldest sister, Pamela Vaudine, had found God in the Billy Graham rallies in London a few years earlier and sent unappreciated 6 page letters filled with Bible texts home at regular intervals to my rather Victorian, upright mum.

Shortly afterwards I met my first love, a young man who had been very strictly brought up and was kind, caring and a first class athlete. Within a couple of weeks we were engaged and saved hard for our future together but his father was having none of that as they had scrimped to keep him at school to 18. Five days before my twenty first birthday he was coming to tell me that his employers had granted us a council flat when his motor bike was hit by an overloaded gas board lorry and he was killed. I sensed something was wrong and arrived at the scene of the accident to be told by the police that he had been taken to hospital but not expected to live. As a passing motorist drove me to the hospital, something which felt like a warm blanket, or a pair of warm arms enveloped me and an amazing peace came over me. I could not grieve as I had a wonderful assurance that he was safe and well with the Saviour he loved and served.

I had taken a temporary job in a bank and didn't wish to pass the scene of the accident each day, so when they offered a travelling job I grabbed it with open arms. It was quite a lonely existence at times, my friends left the area and on a visit home a few years later, I called to see a lady I had met at another church. She was rather busy but told me her son would be pleased to see me. It turned out that he played with a gospel music group and I was invited to see what they got up to. It became quite a regular outing; I was glad of the company and he was happy when I collected his belongings for him. After a year or so he suggested we made the arrangement permanent and when I asked what he meant by that, he said, 'Well, I hoped you might marry me'. I was startled but my mother wasn't as she had noticed he had visited every day for the past two weeks.

Neither of us had money to save but we prayed that if God had a house for us, 'it would walk to us' rather than us wasting time hunting for one. Imagine my surprise when the local architect and surveyor, noted for parking his latest Jaguar almost on the bank doorstep, walked down the road by the bank and asked to see me instead of the manager. I politely asked what we could do for him, thinking his car had broken down and he might need a loan when he blurted out, 'Do you need a bungalow?' 'Where'? 'How much'? 'Why me'? He told me he had been entrusted to sell a bungalow quickly and cheaply as an old lady had been taken into a home. He was driving to the estate agent's when he felt compelled to stop and, on getting out of his car, was propelled by an unseen hand into the bank and could only think of speaking to me. The usually cool Mike was visibly shaking but when I told him my fiancé and I had been praying whether we should buy or rent a property, he breathed a sigh of relief. 'Oh, if God is involved, I can understand it all now. I'm a backslidden Roman Catholic'. We arranged to see the bungalow that afternoon, gave him a £50 deposit, having no clue where the money would come from and rushed back to our parents to ask if we could borrow £10 from each of them. Three weeks later Peter's father announced that he would be giving him £500 from his aunt's estate and asked when he would like it. He was rather taken aback when Peter answered, 'Now' and explained that he needed it for the 10% deposit on a house. We took my manager's advice and got a mortgage but were without money for furniture or re-decoration.

Unusually for me, I had felt an urge to save about 18 months earlier and now regretted that I could not access the money for some while as it was tied up in a bond. I was more than a little perturbed when I heard on the radio that the country's biggest insurer, Vehicle and General Insurance Company had 'crashed' and investors had lost their money. Ouch! Within a day or so there was another announcement, saying that the Bristol & West Building Society, joint issuers of the bond, would be shouldering the debts and all money would be repaid immediately. How great is our God!

We lived in that home for eighteen months and our daughter was born there. Then we moved into a much larger house in Rayleigh, (which had been owned by a potato merchant) with my mother and step-father. Whilst there, another strange thing happened. I had gone to buy a sack of potatoes for our family at the local market but when I went to order them, I found myself following an irresistible urge to buy twenty sacks. I loaded them into our motor caravan and when my poor, hard-working husband came home I had the task of explaining to him why I had no housekeeping left and he couldn't park his car in the garage; there were twenty sacks of potatoes stacked in there! He really thought I had lost it but a month or so later he was happily offering his family and friends cheap potatoes as the price soared to undreamed of heights. We supplied everybody and the last quarter of a bag went in the veggie plot for next year's crop.

His job at Basildon was unstable and a second redundancy loomed. No other job was forthcoming, my parents, who had shared the expenses moved out and the bills were higher than we could afford. People would ask me to do small paid jobs and for eighteen months the bills were paid to the last penny. We wondered why we could not sell and then a thought occurred, there was one place where we would not want to move...Pickering! We knew if we went there we would be drawn into a lot of commitments that we didn't want. Peter decided the issue by saying, 'I saw a little chemical plant down a lane. If God wants us there, they will be advertising for someone with my skills and there will be a job in that plant. I'll ask Chris to call in next time he is passing'. Two days later, the 'phone rang, 'How soon can you come up here for an Interview, Peter?' They sound interested. Peter was just off with a group of Boys Brigade lads for a holiday in Devon and wouldn't be back for 10 days, so Chris forwarded the information. 'Please come up on the Monday morning when you return for an interview'. Now Peter was shocked. He went for the interview and after being accepted, asked how many had applied. He was even more taken aback when the boss produced a very thick wedge of applications from his drawer and flicked through them revealing some very well qualified applicants. On his return from Yorkshire he found that the house he had been trying to sell for two years had sold, so we looked for a house in Yorkshire, knowing we would never afford to move south again.

The house we looked at was taken off the market and we needed to find another in a hurry but in his spare time, Peter had been running a church and Boys' Brigade and we took wedding photos for a local company most weekends. There were about two days in the entire summer when we were free. Then the telephone rang and mum said, 'Don't know if you are interested but have you seen the local paper?. There is a trip to Pickering to visit the North York Moors Railway'. It was a massive co-incidence but more was to come. The trip was on one of the two days we had free. The Merrymaker was leaving from Shoeburyness, using goods routes to cross London (so we didn't even have to change to the tube), straight up the main line to Malton station via York and finishing the final eight miles by coach, leaving 6 hours for sightseeing and train trips (or in our case, house hunting). The whole return journey in one day! The fare to Fenchurch Street alone was normally £3 but the whole return journey to Yorkshire and back cost either four or six pounds. We couldn't believe the price...but it was correct. I made the journey and bought the estate show house for our family while Peter minded our two children, and this time the purchase didn't fall through. The mums, who knew they would miss us terribly, were suitably impressed. Obviously, God wants you up there for some reason. You had better go!

Yvonne Creasy
Haverhill, Suffolk

Footnote:
This is just a sample of the interest God took in the lives of two young people and His provision for our needs. He still provides for our needs and those of our family. We have raised four children when we couldn't have afforded to keep even one by ourselves and have now cleared our mortgage. That is another story. I have written this down to encourage other people to look to God to provide for your needs.

The Compiler's Worries........Solved!

I woke up in the night and the thought of this book came into my mind. What have I done saying I would compile a book of Testimonies? The easiest part of the book is getting the Testimonies, and that was hard enough until the "word" got spread around that I needed Testimonies.

No, the hardest part is yet to come. I now have the big fat book I was told to produce, but how on earth am I going to sell it?

What could I do? The only thing I could do was to pray!!

The answer came to me a couple of days later, in church before the morning service:
"Just as Jesus said, 'I am the vine and you are the branches.' The book is the stem and the people who gave their testimonies are the roots and the sales of the book will come through the roots!"

Problem solved, Thank You Jesus!

Christopher Stirling
Steeple Bumpstead, Essex

Recant or...........die!

Perhaps the greatest privilege I enjoyed in my travelling ministry was the opportunity to meet some great saints who had suffered for their faith. The story of Josef Tson of Romania is one I will never forget.........

I first met Josef in England in the 1960's. He was minister of a large Baptist Church in the country and, as such, was a thorn in the side of the Communist government. They allowed him to come to England to study for a degree at Oxford. That may sound odd to you, but the authorities hoped he would never return. They got their man wrong! His heart (not to mention his wife and daughter) were still in Romania. So, in spite of many friends here warning him he was returning to die, he went back armed with a Ph.D degree.

After some time, the authorities decided they wanted to 'break' him as an example to other believers, whose numbers were growing, even in the face of bitter persecution. He was taken to the infamous Gherla prison – which Joan and I have seen from the outside. Josef never told me what they did to him, but I learned from others that he was beaten senseless, electric-shocked, deprived of food and sleep, plus other inhuman brutalities. We do animals a disservice when we describe people who do things like this as 'animals,' don't we? But, Josef remained firm in his faith.

Finally, the day came when out of shear frustration his tormentors said to him, 'Tson, if you don't recant tomorrow, we are going to kill you.'

That night they allowed his wife one final visit. She saw her husband Josef, hardly able to move, in awful agony, eyes blackened and face bruised. He told her what they had said to him and said he could no longer withstand. He was going to give-in.

She looked him in the eye and said, 'Josef, I would rather be known as the widow of a courageous martyr, than the wife of a coward' and she left him. Josef told me how shocked he was by her amazing words. But, they did the trick.

Next morning, he was dragged from his cell into the torture chamber and they again gave him the ultimatum. Josef replied through battered lips and broken teeth, 'No matter what you do to me, you cannot win. If you kill me I will go straight to heaven to be with Jesus. If you keep me in prison I will be an example to all my Romanian brothers and sisters, and others around the world. If you release me I will continue to preach the Gospel. And if you send me into exile, I will work tirelessly for the downfall of Communism.'

The authorities decided the safest thing to do was to exile him, so they sent him to America. From there he broadcast regularly into his country on Radio Free Europe. He translated many good Christian books into Romanian and they were smuggled into the country. He had secret contacts with underground dissident groups. And when Communism fell, Josef was one of the first exiles to return to his homeland.

So you see why the memory of knowing this dear man and his family mean so much to me!

Ben White
(retired missionary)
Whitstable, Kent

What must I do to have this?

I took as group of believers to Tibet one very cold October. The town we were staying in had the second most important monastery in Tibetan Buddhism. There were thousands of monks, young and old, milling around the town. One followed us after we had visited the market and then had been in the Temple to pray God's blessing on the Tibetan people. He wanted to practice his limited English and was very friendly, so we took him back to our hostel.

He sat in front of the fire in our room and drank tea with us. He was 55 years old and had been a monk since he was a boy. Many Tibetan men become monks for a period of their lives – up to 40% at any one time, I believe. It enhances their 'karma' and gives the family status. A few become scholars and 'holy men', like our friend.

I had a Singapore Chinese girl as my interpreter, so, in a mixture of Chinese and English we shared the Gospel with him. Two things struck him most forcibly in contrast to his own religion. We spoke of our personal knowledge of God and His love for us. He said he longed to know God in a personal way and we explained how we may enjoy this through faith in God's Son, Jesus. Then, of course, we told him how, through Jesus' death for us, we may experience the forgiveness of all our sins and be reconciled to God.

He was wide eyed! He'd never heard anything like this, and admitted he was bowed-down with the burden of his sin and guilt. 'What must I do to have this?' he asked us. When we told him it was a free gift from God and we can receive it by simple faith and confession, he wanted it, more eagerly than almost anyone I've known.

God's beautiful presence filled that room as we prayed with this dear Tibetan and led him in receiving Jesus as his personal Saviour and Friend. And afterwards, his dark face glowed, he wanted to hug all of us! Before we parted, we prayed for him to be filled with the Holy Spirit and Jesus would keep him and lead him into God's truth and freedom.

That was the highlight of that trip, and what a challenge it was to think that truths we take almost for granted should bring such joy and release to this elderly Tibetan monk.

Ben White
(retired missionary)
Whitstable, Kent

One of the Greatest 'Living Martyrs' of China

Most of us will have some knowledge of the turbulent history of China since the Second World War. As Christians, we may also know something of the persecution of fellow-believers, and how, in spite of their sufferings, the Church has grown faster than anywhere else on Earth. It's a thrilling story!

During my years of travelling in China I learned much of this story from those who had lived through it. Let me tell you about one of the greatest 'living martyrs' of China...... Lam Hin Go is known to the western world as Samuel Lamb. His church is in the southern city of Gangzhou (formerly Canton) is probably the best known in all China. Billy Graham, the astronaut Jim Irwin and many other leading Christian figures have preached there. And yet, the authorities continue to this day to oppose him and his church of several thousand believers.

Samuel was born in 1924 to poor Christian parents. At an early age he suffered diphtheria and was given only a 5% chance of survival. He did pull through, but all his life he has had bad health. Living to 87 and suffering as he has done, is nothing but miraculous, and he attributes it all to God. His parents were able to send him to Hong Kong (80 miles away) for his education, and he studied English and Theology. He became a pastor and served in various places before settling in Guangzhou. He was there during the Japanese occupation and the Second World War, faithfully serving his flock in spite of great hardship. He once wrote ' A Christian who has not suffered is like a child without training.'

When the Communist revolution swept the land in 1949 he remained at his post, also marrying a beautiful Chinese girl in 1951. The new government set up their own church authority – The Three-Self Patriotic Movement – through which they hoped to control Christianity (viewed by them as a tool of western 'imperialist' governments). But, Samuel, refused to join it and continued to lead his own Baptist church. And that's why he became a target of the authorities.

His first arrest came in 1955 and lasted for 18 months, much of which he spent in solitary confinement, with intense interrogation and brutality. But, after his release he continued as before, setting an example of quiet trust and joy to fellow-believers. Naturally, the authorities were incensed and he was re-arrested in January 1959, being sent far away to a slave-labour camp. In 1963 he was transferred to a coal mine in northern China, enduring extreme cold and hardship. He received few letters and even fewer visits from his family, but he remained trusting and joyful. His life was a powerful witness to other prisoners and even guards were impressed. He had a phenomenal memory and knew much of the New Testament by heart, which he would recite to sustain himself. In June 1978 he was finally released. He had never been formally charged, tried, sentenced, or granted an appeal, yet he never became bitter or angry, even when he arrived home to find that his dear wife had died a year before his release. Though he is still harassed and opposed by the authorities, his church continues to grow. In his unique English he said to me, 'More persecution, more growing!' What a man! And, what a God!

Ben White
(retired missionary)
Whitstable, Kent

Higher Education in China

In my days in China I often travelled alone because it was safer for the friends I was going to meet. Spending days on trains as the only westerner was never a problem. Chinese travellers were always friendly and it gave me unique opportunities to enjoy God and 'soak up' the culture. On one such occasion I arrived in a northern city and met my Chinese interpreter and an European businessman, as arranged. 'Prepare to travel light', they said, 'but be sure to take warm underclothes.' I thought I was there to teach secret Christian believers, so imagine how intrigued I was when they said, 'we're going mountain climbing'!

We left the city late that night by train and snatched a few hours sleep before getting off in the early hours in a small town. Finding a café open for early workers we sipped piping hot green tea and ate savoury dumplings until we were signalled by two Chinese and herded into the back of a windowless van. After several hours of driving over bumpy roads, we got out in a very isolated place. To our right was a vast flat plain, but to the left was a range of mountains stretching to the horizon.

We drank water and ate some chocolate, before starting up the slopes. Gradually the incline became steeper and the track narrower until we needed our hands to aid our climb. The European was an experienced alpine climber and bounded on ahead of me and 3 rather unfit Chinese. Reaching a height equivalent to Snowden we found a wide plateau and a better track. Imagine my surprise when we rounded a bend and were greeted by a crowd of smiling, cheering young people. Behind them was a series of small caves, some of them with boarded fronts for better protection from the elements.

I learned this was a secret Bible school for training evangelists to go to the Moslem peoples of the Middle-East. The students spent a year in this place before moving on to gain further experiences in secret churches throughout China. Most were young teens from rural areas and quite poorly dressed (our local charity shop wouldn't sell their clothes) but they were so joyful and free that it left me breathless with wonder.

The caves were allocated to girl or boy-students; there was a kitchen and a refectory; and one for 'essentials' (where you had to sing, so others would know it was occupied). The food was very simple, hygiene minimal and the nights frosty. But the 'atmosphere' was warm and relaxed and they were so hungry for teaching from God's word that they sat for hours on little stools hanging on my words. Their Bibles were tattered from constant use and they had notebooks in which they wrote everything with stubby pencils or cheap biros.

What days they were! Although I left feeling tired, dirty and longing for a McDonald's, I still treasure the memories and feel sad that I was able to visit them only twice.

Please do pray for the secret believers of China. It is estimated there are 100 million of them, and they still face persecution or prison if they are discovered.

A Traveller's Serendipity

Haven't you found that some of life's most fruitful and enjoyable things happen by chance? That has certainly been my experience and some years ago it happened while I was on my travels for the Lord. I kissed Joan goodbye at Heathrow, committed to several weeks in Asia but not sure what I might be asked to do. Partway through the trip I was in Vietnam teaching secret church leaders(Vietnam is still a communist country and religion is strictly monitored). The western lady who arranged my time there asked me one day if I'd like to go to Cambodia to do some more teaching.

Cambodia has one of the saddest histories in modern times. For centuries she was exploited by a succession of foreign powers and then the Vietnam War left her impoverished and at the mercy of the Marxist Khmer Rouge in 1975. Perhaps you remember the name Pol Pot? Most wealthy, influential and educated people were killed (20% of the population), and the country was turned into a vast labour camp, (perhaps you've seen the film 'The Killing Fields'). 90% of Buddhist monks and almost all Christians perished in the drive to eradicate religion in the nation. A small number fled to the refugee camps in Thailand and God blessed and multiplied them there.

Pol Pot's regime fell in 1978/9., but there was a bloody civil war for the next decade. I asked my university graduate taxi-driver if he had memories of the bad times. 'There isn't a family in Cambodia who didn't lose someone,' he replied. 'This is still a very sad country.' Today the monarchy has been restored and there is democratic government, but with massive corruption and creaming of the immense amounts of international aid provided.

During the nineties, Christians returned and began to rebuild their work for the Lord. The pastor I stayed with was among the first to restart in Phnom Penh, the capital, and he asked me to train some young church leaders he was mentoring. After a couple of days he remarked, 'tomorrow is a free day; would you like to see my orphanage?' Of course, I agreed.

I expected to go just down the road! We left at 7am and drove over gradually worsening roads for 5 hours. We passed many flagged minefields, so stopping for a comfort break was a challenge. Then, in the middle of the jungle, we came upon a mud clearing with rickety huts around and were greeted by a crowd of shouting, excited youngsters. I was overwhelmed.

His gracious wife and a few volunteers ran the 'orphanage' for abandoned children and those whose parents had died from AIDS. They received no government assistance and no international aid, yet they soldiered on with the most amazing positive and cheerful spirit. It was very humbling to see. And then when the children sang familiar songs and choruses (some in English), their little faces beaming, I felt a pressure in my heart and knew I'd be back, and that I had to do something to help them. Almost as soon as I arrived home extra money started to come in. I rarely asked for money, but, somehow, just talking about 'Hope for Orphans' in Cambodia moved people to give.

The first thing was to build a fence – their animals were regularly stolen and sometimes children were abducted for the sex trade. A gathering of ministers I shared with, provided for that without me asking. And so it went on – a clean, pumped, water supply; permanent, brick buildings, hygienic toilets and washing facilities; and, of course, food supplies........

When I became ill and no longer able to travel, a friend in Reading felt moved to take over and he has done so much better than I, raising hundreds of thousands in the last few years. What a blessing to Joan and I this project has been. And it all started with a 'serendipity'!

Ben White
(retired missionary)
Whitstable, Kent

After My Husband Died, I was Naturally Grieving....

...and one day God spoke to me and said, "I gave you your husband for exactly the same number of years as I gave you my son" And it was exactly right!

Rene Willett
Steeple Bumpstead, Essex

God Has Given Us Special Work To Do

When I was very young my mum asked me if I would like to ask Jesus to forgive the wrong things I had done and to from then on give me power to live for Him. I prayed and my Mum gave me a special verse in the Bible which she underlined for me. It was John chapter three verse 16 "For God so loved the world that He gave His only begotten Son, that whosoever believeth in Him should not perish but have everlasting life."

When I was about 12 I really wanted God to be more involved in every part of my life. I wanted His help in choosing the right career and the right husband who would be faithful. God did both for me, and then also provided very special work for us to do travelling all over this country going into schools and helping churches with Bible Club programmes, helping children to see what a great book the Bible is and how each one of us can have a personal every day relationship with the living God.

God has been so faithful - for 20 years now we have been doing this, never asking for money, and God has provided everything we have needed.

Joy Blunt

Freedom in a Country That is not Free!

Independence movements revere it. Teenagers cry out for it. University students campaign for it. Pop stars sing about it. Artists idolize it. Philosophers write about it. Civil Rights movements champion it. Religions – or at least some of them -aspire to it. As people we cry out for freedom.

I live in a country that is not free so I know a bit about the freedom that everyone craves.

As a small boy living in Germany I remember seeing the wall that enclosed the people in the un-free east - with its watch towers and barbed wire and jagged broken glass. I understood then what a privilege it was to live in the free world.

After that I came to a newly "free" Zimbabwe. Africa is a continent that naturally evokes freedom. When I looked into the sky above the endless open savannah of light and space and saw the bateleur eagle soaring on the wind I saw freedom. Without effort it angled its wings to fly upon the air. It appeared so effortless and so beautiful. The eagle owns nothing that it needs to constantly protect. It is afraid of nothing that may come to injure it or deprive it of its freedom. It is dependant on nobody to continue to enjoy its freedom. It is not being coerced by anything or anyone. It is not taunted. It is not threatened. It is up there as a symbol of soaring freedom for us all.

In the world though, through our short lives, there are always those that wish to try to steal our freedom and bond us into fear and slavery. Power crazed despots intent on having absolute power, coerce others to conform to their will. I came to live in Zimbabwe at a time when unknown thousands of civilians were being murdered by the new regime of "freedom." Dictators are always insecure people, people that are missing the vital ingredient of knowing that they are loved unconditionally. They are deceived in thinking that absolute power and wealth and their own selfish whims will buy them freedom. I have met President Mugabe twice and I know that he is a man who is not free.
When our house was burnt down and everything we ever had was destroyed by President Mugabe's thugs, a friend who had also lost everything on his farm said to me "Freeth, you don't know it yet but you are free!"

It was a hard thing to say – and not something I would have taken to heart from someone who hadn't lost everything himself. As the weeks went by it dawned on me that in some way he was right. We became free from the fear of thugs coming around to beat us or take more things from us or from the police coming to put us in jail for being in our home. Coercion, threats, taunting and the ever present grip of fear in the pit of the stomach because we were living in a country that was not free, gradually dissipated. We had been freed from them when we finally lost everything on the farm.

When I freely chose the only one who could truly set me free I was set free. He was the same one who had started his ministry with the promise of freedom for the prisoners. Of all the things that have ever happened to me this was the most amazing. My chest was so full of joy at the freedom that the indwelling of the Holy Spirit brought, that it felt like it was going to burst outwards. My sternum literally felt like it could not contain the joy that was inside of me. I felt that it must split open – maybe that when it did, I should be able to fly like the bateleur eagle! Being set free carries that kind of joy along with it – and it is there for evermore to draw upon and soar upwards with.

In 2008 I was captured and abducted from the farm and severely tortured by government thugs at one of their torture camps in the bush. My father-in-law and mother-in-law were tortured with me and they broke many of our bones. It was very cold, and through the dark hours of the night we were periodically beaten for the crime of still being on the farm and for taking President Mugabe to court for seizing our homes and livelihoods.

It was not the first time I had been beaten by Mugabe's men. It is difficult to experience such injustice all around one in a country so devoid of freedom - and not allow bitterness to creep into one's heart.

"Love your enemies" Jesus said. Of all the things he ever commanded that has to be the most difficult of all - when your enemies are doing terrible things to you and to the ones that you know and love.

I was tied up on the ground, lying in the dust, broken and bleeding. My ribs were broken from their boots, my skull was fractured from their rifle butts, my whole body was a mass of welts and bruises from their sjamboks - and I knew that there was a strong chance that we would die.

As I was lying there an amazing thing happened. That thing that Jesus said in His sermon on the Mount came into my heart. "Love your enemies!"

The words of Jesus have a life and a force of their own when they come with the power of the Holy Spirit. It was as though the bonds that were holding me captive were suddenly let loose and I was free. There was no hatred or bitterness in my heart for these people that were doing these awful things to us. It was not natural. It was supernatural and it was undoubtedly of God. The "I" that holds onto things had gone. I only felt compassion for these lost souls who would be consigned to Hell if they did not choose the freedom that Jesus bought at such a price.
Spontaneously, without even thinking, I reached out with my tied up hands to the nearest pair of legs. "May the Lord Jesus bless you" I said, touching them. Then the next pair "may the Lord Jesus bless you!" And then again! And again!

It was not long afterwards that we were carried to the car and driven on a long and bumpy journey into town. They undid our bonds and we were left lying by the side of the road between two churches - free.

"If the son sets you free, you will be free indeed!"

I remain free – fighting for freedom for the people of Zimbabwe in various ways. No bond or barbed wire fence or torture camp or prison wall can truly ever bind a man or woman who has been set free by the name of Jesus! We "soar on wings like eagles..." [Isaiah 40:31] as we put our hope in Him. Such hope can never be snuffed out and die. It will always live – forever and ever - whatever the future brings in the difficult days that lie ahead in this land.

Ben Freeth
Mike Campbell Foundation

Footnote:
The aim of the Mike Campbell Foundation is to bring the restoration of Justice, the Rule of Law and Human Rights back into Zimbabwe, so that business and investment can come back to the country and the people can be free. When you have no law and the police are on the side of evil – the people suffer in such a terrible way. We have witnessed this time and time again.

www.mikecampbellfoundation.com

God Brought me off Drugs into Healing and Freedom

I was living in a flat in Norwich. Since the age of 18, I had been addicted to Heroin, Methadone and Diazepam for 10 years and crack cocaine for a year. I would steal, beg on the streets and sell drugs to feed my habit. Drugs were my life, and getting money for drugs was all I would think about.

Eventually I did come to the end of my tether with it all. I was very ill due to not eating properly and my life was in such a mess. I would get out of my head on heroin so much that I would pass out, and then when I woke up I would take more and pass out again. This would go on for days, even weeks. When I took crack cocaine it would often leave me with not enough money to get any more Heroin, so I would then suffer really bad withdrawals. It felt like I had the flu four times over. I vomited often, I had diarrhoea, cold sweats, stomach cramps, sneezing fits, leg cramps and headaches due to dehydration. I had no energy to get up and couldn't walk very far if I did. When I was well I would still often not have much energy because of not eating, and my circulation got really bad. My legs got very cold and numb and my lungs would hurt so much, because of all the heroin I was inhaling. One day I was lying on my sofa feeling like I just wanted to give up. I really wanted to get off the heroin and crack, but I had tried so many times and failed.

I thought about God and how he had revealed himself to me when I was 16 and I took a look at my life and realised what a mess it had all turned out to be. I said sorry to God for falling away and for how my life had turned out and then I felt my life begin to slowly drift away. I let go of my life and handed it to God and said to Him to take me to wherever He wants me to go. I was thinking that it wouldn't be heaven, because I had sinned so badly in my life. But I didn't know God really, I didn't know that He was a God of grace and that when I said sorry and handed my life over to Him at that moment He responded with compassion. I fell asleep, and when I awoke some time the next day I was amazed that I was still alive. I had the energy to get onto my knees and cry out to God to help me. Somehow I could see that God knew I couldn't get off the drugs by myself, but God was going to help me and I was in agreement. After this happened I contacted some people I knew at a church I used to attend now and again and I told them that I wanted to go to a rehab.

They were amazing. Some of them helped me get to an interview with Teen Challenge in Wales. While I was waiting to hear from them, a lovely couple from church took both my dogs and me into their home. They had been praying for me every day and God faithfully gave me the breakthrough I needed to be willing to step into the freedom He died for me to have.

I was finally given a date I could to go into the new women's Teen Challenge that was opening in London. It happened to be my birthday that day and I felt that that was a sign from God that I was definitely meant to be there.

I was put on to Subutex, which was an opiate blocker and helped with the heroin withdrawals, which were then cut down until I came off it completely. The staff there prayed for us all to get through the withdrawal symptoms and I found that it was much easier to come off the heroin than when I had tried before.

I was in for a bit of a shock though when I came off the drugs. My emotions came back with a vengeance. I found it so difficult to control them. I had so much hurt and anger inside. Also I hated being controlled and I found myself rebelling against almost every rule there was at this rehab. Thankfully, the staff there were patient and continued praying for me. We all got straight into a routine of chores while we were there, which was hard for all of us as we had all come out of a lifestyle of doing what we wanted, when we wanted. But keeping busy certainly helped to keep our minds off drugs. We also learnt to read the bible every morning, worship and pray, and someone would also come into the rehab to teach us to study the bible. The problem for me was I had prayed the sinner's prayer while I was there, but I hadn't really surrendered my life completely over to Jesus, so everything that we did was just religion for me and not a relationship with God. I was often told that God loved me, but I had no idea what that meant.

I was there on and off for a year. The last time I left, the staff prayed for me that if I took any drugs again I would be sick. I did go straight out and buy some drugs, and I was very sick indeed. Amazingly I didn't want to touch drugs again after that, but I didn't know where to go from there.

Eventually, after speaking to one of the rehab staff on the phone, I decided to ask my parents if I could stay with them for a short while in Suffolk. Understandably they weren't too sure about it, as they weren't sure if I would go back to the drugs again, but they did agree to me staying.

I came to a crossroads in my life when I arrived at my parents' home. I could see that I had come a long way, from the drugs lifestyle to being free from addiction, and I didn't want to return to that lifestyle. I was also aware that if I did I would most likely die. I had come so close to overdosing when I was on drugs before with all the heroin I had been using.

There was one problem though, I didn't want to go back on the drugs, but I had no idea how to live without them. I believed that God would help me, and I realised that the only way I was going to be able to live this life without drugs was to totally surrender my life to God and live for Him. I joined a Church in Haverhill, Suffolk and I decided to give everything to Jesus and allow Him to heal me of all the hurt and baggage I had carried around for so long. I used every bit of my time, reading the word and allowing the Holy Spirit to teach me. I would also worship and pray often. As I focused on Jesus, gradually and with a lot of tears God began to heal my hurt. I found that the reason I had so much pain was because I was abused as a child. My parents never knew. I had told no-one. I was also verbally abused every day of my high school years, which turned me into such an angry person. One of the ways I tried to cope as a teenager was drinking alcohol, which just made the anger worse. I became so angry and resentful towards society that I would lash out and get into trouble with the police a lot. I ended up in prison at the age of 17. I tried to cope with my pain in there by cutting myself, or not coping by attempting suicide. I also dabbled in the occult during my teens in an attempt to find meaning to my life and to gain some kind of control. This just made things worse and opened myself up to the demonic.

While I was at my Mum and Dad's after I came out of rehab, and I was seeking God and living for Him, I found that spiritually things became more and more difficult the closer I got to God. Some days it was like walking through treacle. I didn't understand it at first and thought it was just something that all Christians go through, until God showed me that I had demons. I prayed and prayed that God would set me free and I looked on the internet for a church in the UK that would cast these demons out. I found a website of a ministry that focuses on setting the captives free and I sent them an email explaining my situation. They sent me a reply saying that there was a new church in Cambridge that should be able to help. One Saturday evening while I was praying, God spoke to me very clearly that He didn't want me to go to my usual church the next day, but to go to the church in Cambridge instead. The next morning I went to Cambridge to find this church and after a few hours searching I eventually found it and walked into the meeting that was just about to finish.

The Pastor said, "If anyone wants healing or deliverance, come to the evening meeting". So I did.

At the evening meeting we all worshipped for an hour or two and then they asked people to come forward for prayer. I went forward and explained that I needed deliverance. The pastor, his wife and another leader laid hands on me and the demons began to manifest. Suddenly a mighty roar came out of my mouth. The Pastor bound it in the name of Jesus, I then felt a horrible choking sensation around my throat and I couldn't breath. The Pastor said, "Spirit of Anti-Christ come out," and then I screeched and fell on the floor. After a minute, I sat up and was in shock for a while. Then I realised that I was free from the majority of the oppression I had been feeling. I wasn't 100% free yet though. One of the leaders there said to me that God had told her that I was going to be completely set free.

About a month later I was invited to go to a Christian meeting in Sudbury where someone was sharing their testimony of being into the occult and drugs. After the meeting I went forward for prayer and he immediately picked up that I needed deliverance. He cast out the spirit of witchcraft and the spirit of death and prayed for me to be filled with the Holy Spirit. I sat there, again feeling in shock, and I went home. That night I suddenly realised that I was finally free from ALL the demonic oppression!! Praise God! And a while later I also realised that the majority of the emotional pain I had had was also gone!

The reason I ended up with demons was because of dabbling in the occult, and also the drugs opened me up to things too. Often you will find that people on drugs will have problems with the demonic. It's nothing to fear though. We have been given the authority over demons and they have to flee in the name of Jesus! The reason many people end up on drugs and alcohol is because of the emotional pain of the past. Many people who are in similar situations as I was might think there is no hope. Perhaps you know of someone who is on drugs or alcohol and it seems like it's impossible for them to be set free. Perhaps they don't seem to want to be set free or they have given up trying. Well, the prayers of a righteous man avails much. Prayer and declaring scripture over them is what will shift things in the spirit realm and it will open up a way for them to be set free. You *will* see the fruit, so don't give up. All things are possible with God.

Since then I have remained in the church in Cambridge and my journey with Jesus continues. I am so thankful to all the people along the way who have prayed for me and encouraged me. I don't think I could have got through it all without you. I am about to start going out onto the streets with the church outreach team soon to help others who are homeless and/or on drugs. I want to love and encourage those who are hurting, and see God bind up their hearts and set them free, just as He has set me free.

I am still susceptible to addiction to things, but I know God has given me the strength to stay free. A few years ago I would drink small amounts of alcohol occasionally, but over time it developed into drinking far too much, too often, so I decided to go teetotal. Now I don't drink at all and I feel much better for it.

I am still having problems with my addiction to nicotine, but I have stopped smoking and am using an e-cig and nicotine chewing gum. I am praying that God will give me the grace to come off it completely like He did with the drugs and alcohol. Getting free from the nicotine will be just that last little bit of addiction to overcome. God says I can do all things through Christ who gives me strength. I know I will succeed.

Victoria

From Down-and-Out Alcoholic to Missionary

As a young boy growing up on a council estate in Warrington, I didn't show much interest in school work and only excelled in sport. Although I won the Lancashire schoolboy's boxing championships in 1960 I showed much more promise as a footballer. I left school and played semi-professional football for many local teams around the Cheshire area and also had trials at Manchester City. I worked in my father's small business, married Jennifer and had three children, the future looked rosy!

But over a period of eight years I went from social drinker to an alcoholic, ending up drinking on public park benches, It is hard to believe that I gave up all the good things I had, for a life in police cells, mental hospitals, halfway houses, drug and alcohol rehabilitation centre's and eventually prison and the inevitable divorce. My wife divorced me in 1977 while I was in Strangeways prison, Manchester.

For the last fifteen years of my thirty year drinking career I tried every possible avenue to stop drinking. I tried every method available to me, counselling, drug's, Christian half way houses, the church, Alcoholics Anonymous for ten years, rehabs and more, but all were to no avail. In 1991 at the age of 46 I found myself in

Winwick mental hospital in Warrington yet again. It was while a patient at this mental hospital that I finally decided to look at the last option available to me............ Jesus Christ.

For many years I had a long term medical certificate with my illness described as alcoholism but my eyes were opened when I picked up a Bible in this mental hospital. As I read it I could find no mention of 'alcoholism' [relating to an illness] or 'alcoholic' [relating to the person] I did however find the words 'drunkard' and 'sinner', and it became clear to me that my problem was sin and the only way to change was to acknowledge and confess that sin to God. As soon as I did this, I received a new nature through God's Holy Spirit and this miraculously took the desire for alcohol away.

From that day on, all I wanted to do was to serve the one who had given me that wonderful elusive peace. I went to a missionary orientated Bible School in Birmingham with the aim of becoming a missionary and after graduating made many trips abroad on short-term missions.

The call to long term mission in Ghana came IN 2000 after a four month stint in America working at a Christian drug rehab in downtown Atlanta. I was asked to go to Ghana to help develop a project for World missions in the predominant Muslim city of Tamale in the Northern Region.

After about one year working on the project I noticed the appalling lack of Christian books in the North and felt that God was prompting me to provide a Christian Book Ministry Centre for the Christian people of that area in Ghana . I contacted a Christian book supplier in the UK and the first 20 ft container of books was sent to me in

Tamale. After a lot of hard work, the Centre was completed in Tamale and Christians there rejoiced that their prayers of many years had been answered. Malak Christian Book Ministry was born. Before this, Christians had to make a round trip of nearly 1,000 miles to Accra to obtain Christian books. Since then another five containers have been sent to Tamale each containing approximately 100,000 Christian books/bibles. To cap it all I married Akua and we have a young son, Sean who is now 8. It was an amazing transformation — from down-and-out alcoholic to successful missionary and family man.

On Friday, 15th May, 2009, there was an explosion at the Centre and Mark Box, a missionary from Florida, USA was killed. Mark and his wife Kim, along with their children Chandler and Sam, were living at the Centre while Akua, Sean and I were in England involved in deputation work. Mark and his family were members of the Mandarin Baptist Church, Jacksonville, Florida and were supported by the Christian Light Foundation.
It was around this time that I met a blind lady name Euphenia Sala Alhassan who told me she had not read anything for seven years since leaving the Braille school for the blind at Wa the capital town in the Upper West region of Ghana. After a phone call to Peter Jackson, a blind author and pianist, I was put into contact with 'Braille publishers, Torch Trust for the Blind in Market Harborough, Leicestershire.

I went to visit Madam Euphenia Sala Alhassan with the books Torch Trust gave me at her poverty stricken home in the centre of Tamale. The joy on her face as she read the word of God in Braille in perfect English gave me the greatest experience in my twelve years of ministry in Ghana. Her face lit up as she beamed "I have not read anything in Braille since leaving blind school seven years ago and now I am not only reading Braille but the Word of God in Braille as well. She told me that she had been brought up in a Muslim home and became a Christian and was baptised when studying at the residential blind school in WA. Turning her back on her Muslim family's faith was not without a cost and resulted in her being disowned by the family, so that she now lives with a member of her church.

My wife and I had several options of how we would use the new building constructed on our compound in 2012, but decided after prayer and the way our circumstances were engineered to commit it to the Lord as a Resource Centre for the blind people of Northern Ghana. Sala's testimony inspired me to use the building not only as a Braille library but hopefully to get computers and other things from the UK to help improve blind peoples' lives in Tamale. Having come to that decision we received emails of encouragement and offers of help from Peter Jackson the blind author and pianist and Janet Stafford International leader of Torch Trust for the Blind. Lutheran Braille Workers [L.B.W.] probably the biggest Christian Braille publishers in the world who operate in many different states in the U.S.A. have sent enough books and Bibles for us to open our Resource Centre. We opened on 7th May 2013 and are excited about this new venture for Malak Christian Books.

Jesus met my need and gave me peace through His Holy Spirit and with it a new nature. I simply wanted to follow the only person who could meet that need and serve Him in mission.

John Cartledge
Tamale, Ghana

Footnote:
For more information about John and his work, please see www.malakchristianbooks.org

My Message of Forgiveness

Hi My Name Is Gail Ostle, I am 51 Year's old, I Live In Rugeley, and I Have Two Beautiful Grown Up Daughters [Kayleigh and Katrina] also Six Amazing Grand-Children. I Attend The Victory Christian Centre in Rugeley, where I am a Missionary, and a Mission's Rep. I Gave My Live To The Lord 12 years ago, and started a wonderful healing journey. This is only one of the many testimonies I have given.

The Lord has sent me to Malawi, Rwanda and India several times with this message of FORGIVENESS. My Hope is, as you read this true life story, it will speak to your heart and set you free from the past hurts and give you hope that there is light at the end of the tunnel, God bless you all.

And so the story begins back in 1984, when I lived with my parents, I am the youngest of 8, and even at 23 year's old, I was still classed as the baby of the family. I consider I had a good up-bringing. My parents loved us all, and I was spoiled by them, and by my brother's and sisters. I was working in photography, at the time, I loved make-up and nice clothes, I always tried to look my best. I was known for always being happy and funny.

I left my job, after 7 years, only to walk on the wild side of life, at disco's and pub's. Hence that's were I met a young lad, who was from a different walk of life, we dated, and I believed we both loved each other, even though he would do petty crimes, like burglary, smashing telephone boxes, verbal abuse to the policemen, fighting, always drink related crime. Hence he was more in prison, than on the outside.

By now I realised I was pregnant! My parents were very supportive, they liked this man, but did not like the things he did. I thought now I was about to have our child, thing's would be different. However it got worse, I became the victim of his abuse. He would thump me in the face, or spit on me, once he kicked me that hard, he left his foot print on my leg for days. After the drink wore off, he would cry and say he would never do it again.

I gave birth to a beautiful baby girl, weighing only 5 pounds. He was once again "in side" and wasn't present at her birth. I was given a flat, and my parent's helped me to move in. On his release, he came to stay with us, every fortnight he would go off to cash his dole-money, but not return as he had promised, but would come back late that night in drink, no money left, and very drunk. I decided this was not the life for me and our child, and I told him our relationship was over, and that we could come to some arrangement for him to see his daughter.

That night in the early hours of the morning, I was awakened by a loud noise!! On my way to investigate, I just remember putting my hands up to my face, and saying "please don't," the next thing I knew was that I could hear my daughter crying and I could feel her next to me, but I couldn't see her, I couldn't breathe. He was crying too. He had placed me on the bed, and put my daughter at one side of me, and he was lying the other side. I was numb, and found it hard to speak, I asked him to get me help, as I thought I was dying. Then all I know is that I was at a neighbour's house outside ringing their bell and I was taken to hospital immediately.

After two weeks I remember hearing voices, but they seemed to be in the distance, and a bright light shining on my face. I was still numb and paralysed by it all. I just lay there, the doctor said I was now allowed to have a bath, then he would come and talk to me, I had to ask the nurse what day it was, and how long had I been in there, nothing made any sense. I thought this is a dream, and I will wake up in a minute. There was a mirror in the bath room, I knew something was wrong with my face, but I had no idea what I would see in that mirror. But to my horror, the reflection staring back was not mine, or at least how I used to look, only weeks before. The whole of my being cried out, this is not me, my face was marred beyond recognition!! My right eye, so the doctor explained, had been kicked so much, that it had come out of its socket, and was now resting on top of my cheek, I had a fractured cheek bone, and a trapped nerve to my upper jaw. I had lost two teeth, and the rest were all loose, in time they could tighten up themselves, and my right ear drum was damaged.

I came out of hospital, and tried to piece my life together. I saw a specialist who was prepared to do surgery on my face, and as I awaited the appointment, the father of my child, who assaulted me that night, was imprisoned for 5 years. It took 2 years before I had 2 skin grafts to put my eye back in place. The surgery was a success. As time went by, the scars on the outside healed, but on the inside the scars of what he did festered, I hated this man. I plotted revenge, what I'd do if ever I saw him again. I was tormented by fear, hatred, anger, bitterness, no confidence, no trust, I became a man -hater, I felt rejected. I was a broken woman, I thought of taking my own life many times, but I could not bear the thought of leaving my precious daughter, bad enough for her not having a daddy, let alone losing her mummy too, I pressed on.

My sister told me about Jesus, she was a born again Christian, and was going to church regularly. She gave me a prayer and I said it, and I started going to church. My daughter and I gave our lives to the Lord on the same day, what an amazing day! From then on Jesus took me on a healing journey. He started revealing the issues in my heart. You see the Lord wanted me to be free from the past, so that I could be all that He wanted me to be. I realised I needed to FORGIVE HIM, because forgiveness is a KEY, that un-locks MY FREEDOM, although he was in prison. I too was in a prison on the outside, like a bird in a cage, trapped, clipped wings, and couldn't fly.

I chose with all of my heart that day, to forgive him for everything he had ever done to me and my family. The results were incredible, I felt as if a big heavy, black sack of heavy weights had been lifted off my back, and I was so LIGHT. I TRULY WAS FLYING, SOARING LIKE AN EAGLE, I have seen and spoken to this man, many times, I have told him I forgive him, and I have asked him to forgive me and we go our different ways, as I have moved on in life.

I have been totally healed, and maintain a great future ahead of me, and it's all thanks to Jesus who came and gave my heart a home. and it is my prayer every day that he too will receive Jesus as his Lord and receive Jesus 's un-conditional love, then he will be free too. But the choice belongs to the who so ever, Jesus loves you too. God bless.

Gail Ostle,
Rugeley, Staffs

I Never Lost Sight of God

I was raised a Christian with early memories of Sunday School, then choir girl, then altar girl. I loved church and the peace I felt there. Jesus was in my heart.

Then life came in the way, my teens were spent studying and making plans. I made new friends who took me down paths of alternative faiths and beliefs. But I never lost sight of God.

Then in my adulthood I reached an emotional crisis and I knew in my heart that God and Jesus were the only ones big enough and strong enough to carry me through. So I opened up to Him, I prayed to Jesus, He gave me strength I needed, I healed and I grew. I lived because He gave me that power.

My path led me to the Congregational Church where I found my family and my home, it was surrounded by them that I entered the waters of Baptism in 2010, being reborn to my Saviour.

Jesus is with me everyday, He's there when I worry from something like a parking space, to being prepared for an interview. I feel His Spirit guiding me and strengthening me each day I am here. I talk to Him, I pray and I listen. He truly is my Rock.

Amanda Mather
Steeple Bumpstead, Essex

Then God Himself Spoke to me

I was born and brought up in a Sikh religion. My parents and family were very proud of out religion and culture, they brought me up to believe that we were a very high caste Jat Sikh and we were to be proud and religious. In the way that we went to the temple, and believed only in the gurus as they were the only way to show us about God and religious duties.

All this was fine I thought, but I never knew of felt God's presence or had any real joy or peace in my heart or life.

I am 44 years old now, but when I was 26 I met a young man called Vic that I was going to get engaged and then married to (he was also from a Sikh religion). Soon after we had met he told me that he had accepted Jesus and had become a Christian, he started going to church.

I was very, very angry with him - I could not understand why he had done this, I knew that my family would go mad - and not allow us to marry. My family had always taught me that Christians were the lowest of the low caste, and we were to have nothing to do with them. So therefore I was very anti-Christ and hated Jesus and all Christianity with a vengeance.

I tried to explain and argue with Vic that Jesus was a God of the English people and that we had our own Gods and religion and we didn't need all this Jesus rubbish. However, Vic would never argue back with me which I found surprisingly unusual - he just seemed to have a peace, this made me more angry and anti-Christ and I felt I hate Jesus and Christianity more that ever.

After a few weeks, Vic told me he would not be able to meet me and go out on Thursday evening's anymore (this was the evening we usually met to go out) this was because he was joining a cell group that evening, and this was where 10/12 Christians would meet in someone's home to pray and talk about the bible. Well I was even more angry than ever, I thought to myself 'these mental Christians are brainwashing Vic, I will ask him if I can go with him one evening and see what they are doing and how they are brainwashing him, and then I can brainwash him back to Sikhism'.

So I asked to go with him and he was very happy about this. So I went along on a few Thursdays and I used to sit in the group with them and watch them very carefully. I thought ' they are only talking about their Jesus and singing songs, we can do this for the gurus, so I wanted to argue with Vic when we came out of the meeting, but somehow I couldn't seem to argue with him, I was just very quiet.

Anyway, one Thursday evening I went along with Vic again, they were all sitting in a group and the topic they were talking about was 'what makes a man or woman hunger for God' and I remember as they finished discussing this they had all closed their eyes to pray.

I remember, I lowered my eyes slightly and I was sitting on a chair with my legs crossed, I opened my heart and said in my mind 'I know there is only one God, and you're the one that created heaven and earth and you're the one that created me' then as I was just looking down I said in my mind and heart 'but who are you'? as soon as I said that my legs and feet just moved and started shaking. (what I did not realise was that the Holy Spirit, which I had never heard of, started powerfully filling me right from my feet to the top of my head, I just couldn't stop the shaking and I began to cry, I could not stop the crying - tears were just flooding down my face and I just kept sensing love upon love upon love, it was like waves upon waves of love just hitting me again and again.

This love I can't describe, it far, far above any human love - far above the love of husband/wife or of a mother and child, it just goes far above that - never ever had I felt love like this before. Anyway, I asked Vic to please take me home - I just wanted to get away and be on my own with this love.

So Vic dropped me home and I went running to my bedroom and closed the door, I sat on my bed and the shaking was still there - I couldn't understand or stop this love upon love, I didn't want it to stop!

Then sitting there on my bed I said I didn't know what to call him but I just knew that this was God, so I said 'God why do you love me so much? What have I done to deserve this love? God spoke to me in an audible voice, I had never heard anything like it before - and he said 'Ruby, I love you - I love you so much - just like I love the whole world, any colour, any race, any person, that is why I gave my only son, so that you and any one else who believes in Him can have this relationship with me'.

So I said 'God, who is your son? Bearing in mind that some people and Vic had been telling me that Jesus was the son of God, but I never listened or was interested or believed.

Then God himself spoke to me right there in my bedroom sitting on my bed he said 'my son Jesus - look how He died that terrible horrendous death on the cross for you' and as I looked it was like scales fell from my eyes and I saw a vision - a vision of a man hanging on a cross, he was bleeding, disfigured, unrecognisable and an absolutely horrible sight. His face was so disfigured, he had been spat on and beaten, battered and bruised. As I saw this vision God spoke again and said to me' Ruby, look at Him, my son- my beloved son Jesus - He did this for you, so that you could have this relationship with me, so that one day when you die on this earth, you will go on to live forever, because Jesus is now RISEN AND LIVES, and you will live forever also'.

Then God said to me, 'You see Ruby, I am a Holy God and I cannot look upon sin and man is a sinner, therefore Jesus became your sacrifice as a sinner to die in your place, He was without sin but became sin for you, He took your penalty and died for you, therefore only Jesus is the way, the truth and the life and no-one can come to me except through Him'.

You can imagine then - I just fell off my bed on to my knees and I said 'Jesus, you're my saviour, you're my God, thank you, thank you Jesus so much, and I was crying, I could not believe and comprehend this amazing love of God!

Ever since then God has completely changed my life inside out. I give Him all the honour and glory. He himself showed me that you can never come to God through any religion, it is about relationship! Because He is the true and living God. Since then I have seen many, many miracles, God has lead me to pray for many sick people and see them healed, from many incurable diseases and illnesses.

Only Jesus can open the eyed of the blind, open the ears of the deaf and raise even the dead to life.

Ruby Chott
Barkingside, Essex

Grace

Ever since giving my life to Jesus I have hungered to know more of Him and understand spiritual things. At the beginning of my journey of learning one word in particular would always catch my attention and yet I never really understood it; GRACE. Many people talked about it and I intellectually understood it but yet I wanted to experience the depths of its reality.

I attended a Christian meeting of several thousand people. A female preacher stood on the platform and began to preach. Instantly I became critical of her because I thought that women were not supposed to teach! She spoke for an hour on the Spirit of God etching plans and purposes within the spirit realm. I was captivated by her message and yet my old religious ideas still judged her for preaching.

She finished her message and left the stage. A man then took the platform in order to close the service. Suddenly the woman came running back on the platform, took the microphone and started shouting, "this is a miracle meeting!" She waved her hands frantically as if she was throwing something onto the people. I felt embarrassed for her. I judged her even more harshly.

As I sat at the back of the massive auditorium I watched as the congregation began to get lively and excited. I watched with critical eyes. Then suddenly I felt something come over me. A wave of emotion that was not in anyway conjured up. I refused to enter into the anarchy that was unfolding before me. However God had another plan. Whether my eyes were open or not, I cannot tell for the things that I had seen were so real.

This is my vision:

I could see an auditorium filled with the presence of God. The air was so thick with anointing that it was tangible. Thousands of people gathered together; they were all pressing in hard to try to get to the front. I could hear a man preaching with fervency the truths of Jesus. As I pushed my way through the crowd I could see people under the power of God. No one prayed for them, no one even touching them. Bodies were restored, demons cast out, the sick and lame healed and many people calling upon God for salvation.

I pushed on through the mass amount of people until I was several metres away from the young man preaching. He was running back and forwards from one side of the stage to the other. People were trembling and shaking and falling to their knees worshiping the Lord Jesus. The Spirit of God was moving mightily upon the people and upon the preacher. Just before I could see the identity of the preacher, I saw an old man who had no eyes standing at the edge of the platform. Within seconds of watching him I witnessed two brand new sparkling eyes appear in his head! The miraculous was flowing so easily!

As I turned to the preacher he walked toward me. My eyes could not believe what I saw; it was me! I broke down weeping in my vision and also in the seat I was sitting. I asked the Lord why He would allow me to do such things? His response was, "This is My grace." I wept all the rest of that night. As I walked home I could not stop crying; as I lay in my bed the tears kept coming.

At that time in my life when God showed me this vision I was still addicted to many bad habits. I was a new

Christian who wanted more of God but yet my flesh still wanted the world and its pleasures. I would continually condemn myself for smoking, drinking and partying. Because of the bad habits I counted myself unusable to God. However, God does not look at the here and now the way we do; He sees the finished work of who we are. God gave me a glimpse of who I would be and as a result it helped me change who I was. Today I am free from every addiction because God accepted me even while I was a sinning Christian!

Ever since God revealed His grace to me, I have walked boldly through many difficult circumstances knowing that God has a plan for me in spite of me! And not only that, but I now gladly listen to women preachers!

Anthony Consiglio

God's Presence in my Home Means ......

Just over a year ago my husband became seriously ill. After three weeks in hospital he was making good progress and was due to come home, when he had a heart attack and died. As committed Christians, I knew without any doubt that he was in heaven with his Saviour, Jesus.

The suddenness of his death was a tremendous shock, and after 46 years of marriage I still miss him so much and had no real idea of how painful grief could be, BUT God's peace, which passes all understanding has remained with me every moment. God's presence in my home means every time I unlock my door I have never once felt I was entering an empty house because Jesus is already there waiting to welcome me home.

As the time approached for the first anniversary of Kerry's 'going home' I had to face up to a very difficult situation and make difficult decisions because of his sudden death, yet as I went through that time God was with me in a very powerful way enabling me to do everything with calmness instead of anxiety, with peace instead of stress. I floated through those weeks on a bed of prayer, the loving support of family and friends, and most of all the sure knowledge that God was with me.

As I look back over the past 13 months I continue to be amazed at God's goodness to me, at the way He cares for me in all the little things as well as the big things.

I am so privileged to have Jesus living with me so I am never alone. He is my Lord and Saviour, my best friend and constant companion.

To anyone reading this, who has not asked Jesus into their heart, Jesus loves you very much and wants you to accept Him as Lord and Saviour.

He has given me:
> Strength for today
> Bright hope for tomorrow
> Blessings all mine
> With 10,000 beside.

Penny Cook
Balsham, Cambs

God Has a Sense of Humour

This is a testimony from me about my daughter Alena. I have prayed for my daughter since the day she was born, I did not marry a believer so found it hard when it came to getting the children blessed, my husband did not want to know.

I woke one morning three years ago to the Lord telling me to go and speak to my daughter about him, she was now 30 years old and living with her boyfriend and has three children, she did not want to get married as it was only a piece of paper, and was not worth the hassle. I was so excited as my daughter did not want anything to do with Jesus, if she got in to my car and I had a gospel tape playing she would take it out and throw it on to the back seat, saying 'Mother honestly, you do listen to some rubbish'. She would switch off as soon as I mentioned God, which hurt me but I learned to just pray for her and leave it with the Lord.

My son had given his life to the Lord two years earlier and she would mock him something shocking, she would say things like, 'he is only doing this to please you' of course he wasn't as I had seen the things my daughter hadn't in him, the way God was working in him.

Anyway, I left my house in a very high spirit to be obedient to God and talk about him to my daughter, when I pulled up outside her house I noticed her friend's car outside, I thought 'oh great Lord, how can I go in there now and talk about you, her friend is there'. But I felt the Lord tell me to go in there anyway and talk about Him.

I didn't beat about the bush, my daughter's friend and

her husband were sitting at the dining table chatting over a cup of tea, I walked in and said I know you all think I am mad but the Lord has told me to come and speak with you today about Him. My daughter immediately said 'oh mum, not that again' but her friend said she wanted to hear what I had to say. So I told them all about how Jesus had died for them and how he loved them, I let the Lord lead me as I didn't know how to go about it. After about an hour and my daughter taking the mickey out of me behind my back, I asked her friend if she would like to meet with a friend of mine who had come from a Sikh family and found the Lord. My daughter's friend was very interested and I said that I would arrange a meet at their house with my friends so that they could hear her testimony, I then said to my daughter would you like to come, she said she didn't think she could make it, so I left it with the Lord.

The day came to take my friends round to my daughter's friends house to meet, I rang my daughter during the day from work and asked her if she would come, she told me that she had a terrible headache so would not be coming. I told her I would pray for her headache and if it goes would she come, she said she would but didn't think the headache would go as it was really bad. I prayed all day while at work, as I left work I called her to see if she would come, she said her headache had got worse so wouldn't. I told her I would call in on the way home to see her and carried on praying on the way home, as I pulled up at her house she said that amazingly her headache had literally just left her so she would come after all as she was curious.

When we got to her friend's house, my friend told them her testimony and after she had finished, my daughter's friend gave her life to the Lord they prayed over her and my daughter said that she wanted to go home. I took her home and asked her what she thought, she said that she found it interesting and thought that there was something in it as she had felt a peace about her as my friend was talking. I then asked her to come with me to their house meeting two days later, she said if her friend goes then she will to support her.

On the Thursday I picked them both up and went to my house meeting, we got in there and introduced them to the group, there was about 14 people there so was quite packed in. We started to worship the Lord and a young girl who was a regular at the group got filled with the Holy Spirit and started to shake. My daughter saw this and nudged her friend to say look at that and started to laugh, then all of a sudden my daughter's legs started to shake and she couldn't control them, her friend was trying to hold them steady as they were seated, my niece who came to the group and was watching them walked over and said to my daughter, 'see God has a sense of humour'. My daughter gave her life to the Lord that night and on the way home in the car they had my gospel music blaring and were crying with joy, they said that they had never felt love like they had experienced that night.

I gave them both a bible and told them to read John 1, the next day they said that things had changed and they saw life differently, almost like they were seeing God's creation for the first time. My daughter would look to the sky and say what a great painter God was as it all looked so beautiful.

My daughter has come a long way and my friends often remind her by telling her they didn't like what they saw in her and that they felt the hardness of her heart when they first met, now they absolutely love her. My daughter has gone on to work in mental health as this is where she feels God wants her, she would never have considered that before as she just did not care.

My daughter got married to her boyfriend last year and said that she felt she had to do it as it was one less sin that she was now living in.

I see so much of what God is doing in our lives, it never ceases to amaze me of his glory and grace.

Colleen Pearson
Ilford, Essex

Cast all your Cares upon Him

God is good! As a recent member of the 'Next Door' drop-in centre team, I still have much to learn. But I love my job and I'm keen to do better.

In 2003, I met Mark in Basildon, Essex, where I was living at the time. Our friendship grew and we fell in love. We knew that we were right for each other and hoped to become engaged later in the year. But something happened to change our plans dramatically. I became afflicted with a severe mental illness, which resulted in a hospital stay of three and a half years.

At the time my Christian faith was severely shaken. I felt unable to pray or read the Bible. It seemed as if God was a million miles away. However nothing could be further from the truth. The Lord was with me all the time.

The following year, while I was still a patient at Basildon Hospital, we mutually agreed to become engaged. Mark encouraged me to read the Bible again by giving me a list of Bible readings for every day of the week. The reading for Wednesdays was, *'Cast all your cares upon Him (Jesus) because He cares for you'*. 1 Peter Chap 5, verse 7 King James Version.

The road to recovery was long and hard. But I've come a long way since then. I am very thankful for the number of people who prayed for me-all over the country.
By the way, Mark and I will be celebrating our 5th Wedding Anniversary next year! (2014).

Ann Davis
Horseheath, Cambs

He is Always There to Guide me

I had just finished a morning helping toddlers with their activities when one of the mums asked me if I'd like to go to church with her the following Sunday. I said I would think about this and we conversed for a short while. Before leaving me, she gave me a tract which she suggested I read when I had time.

It was the early 1980's and I had been working as an assistant playgroup leader since my own two boys were at school. I thought about my conversation that morning and wondered how I'd managed to drift away from church.
As a child I was sent to Sunday school and of my own choice, I attended church services morning and evening too. I loved it, and I thought I was a Christian.

Then I left home and went to teacher training college and occasionally did go along to church. When I left, I started teaching and then got married. We had two children and later a third. We didn't go to church –

although our backgrounds would suggest that we would – (my first husband had been keen to become a Methodist local preacher in his early twenties). I forgot all about Jesus and led a life where bringing up children got mixed up with a life of parties and having fun.

That day, with a tract in my hand, I went home. After lunch, I went and sat on my bed. I read the tract – it said that to become a Christian if you believed in the Lord Jesus and asked God to forgive your sins then you would be saved and go to be with Him in heaven. I'd never heard this message before, although I am sure the vicar at the church I attended would have been preaching it. Just wasn't my time.

I seriously thought about my life, where was I going? What about all the things I had done wrong? If I wanted to become a Christian, I'd have to change and do what God wanted me to do. Did I want to change?

I thought about it. After a few days, I went up to my bedroom and prayed the prayer on the tract. 'Dear Lord Jesus, I am deeply sorry for all my past sins and I want you to come into my life and save me'. God was as good as His Word and He forgave my past sins. I asked that He would help me to live my life as He would want me to.
Then I rang the mum who had given me the tract and said I would see her at church on the Sunday. She was thrilled!

I went to church – it was Easter Sunday. I listened to the preacher and found that once you were saved, you need to be baptised. At Pentecost, I along with one or two others and I was baptised by full immersion!

Since then, I have with God's help tried to live my life as He would want me to. I know that He is always there to guide me and watch over me.

Jean Lane,
Lincolnshire.

Surely I am with you always, to the very end of the age
Matthew 28:20

I always attended church throughout my childhood and teenage years. Looking back, I know I believed in God and, if asked, would have described myself as a Christian. However, I never read the Bible for myself and only prayed when I was in trouble! It always struck me that when I did pray, God answered in surprising ways.
In my late twenties, a new Minister arrived at our Methodist Church. Both he and his wife were Spirit filled. Together their ministry was dynamic and his preaching always relevant and powerful. Through his preaching I began to realise that something was missing in my life. At the same time, I began to cross paths with others who described themselves as 'Christian', yet who had a quality that I lacked. These people were really like lights that shone! They had a joy, warmth and an assurance about them that I had not personally experienced. This combination of hearing God's word preached clearly and personal encounters with people who were born of the Spirit began to have a growing impact on me.

In December 1990 I received a simple testimony book, written about a young man called David Cullimore. It set out in straightforward terms how he came to faith in Jesus. Most importantly, the book made it clear that David had made a personal commitment of his life to

Jesus. I realised that this was something I had never consciously done before. I believed but had never given my life to Jesus. On New Year's Day 1991, I went to bed at night and before sleeping prayed a simple, childlike prayer. But this prayer was from the heart. For all its simplicity, it was sincere and really from the heart. I told God that I wanted Him to be Lord of my life. I asked Him to take control of my life, helping me through the year to come and every year that lay ahead. Waking up the next morning, I can only describe that I felt different and knew that Jesus had heard and answered my prayer. My Spiritual awakening was profound, yet gentle. No flashing lights or anything unusual, but the Spirit of God came to me even as I slept. The manner of God's intervention in my life was very gentle and yet the change I experienced was undeniable. Previously, I could never have stood to publicly speak about my faith, now there was nothing stopping me. I realised that I had no fear of death (quite the opposite). I had a real assurance that all my past sins were forgiven and experienced real joy. Most of all, I had an appetite to read the Bible like never before and the words made sense, coming alive to me.

In 1992/93 I spent a year at Cliff Bible College, which was like being in a spiritual greenhouse! In 1994 I began preaching and two years later met my wife to be. We had longed for children right from the beginning, but tests soon indicated that medically speaking this looked highly unlikely. We never gave up praying and asking God for the gift of a child, and never gave up hope. After eight years of waiting for God's appointed time (and by now both in our forties), we were blessed with the safe arrival of a beautiful baby girl. We had no medical intervention. We chose rather to pray and rely on the faithfulness of Jesus.

There is so much more I could say. So many changes we have gone through, trials experienced and amazing blessings received. The verse I began with (Matthew 28:20) was printed on a bookmarker my Grandmother had given to me as a child. I had always kept this and still have it to this day. Like all of God's words to us, I know the promise of them to be true.

Nigel Bishop
Haverhill, Suffolk

He Gave me a Future and the Strength to Fulfil It

My name is Anne Marie, I am from Normandy, France and I am currently in UK.

I had Fibromyalgia. I had pain all over my body, was in constant fatigue, I had short memory problems, I could not eat more than once a day, for if my body was too tired, it would not accept food. I was told that it was a rare and quite new illness in France. There was no cure and no disability support, no future at all.

One day I said to God, "You have a year to heal me or kill me..."

God took a year to bring me to UK where He healed me, cared for me and restored me,
I went to a bible college. I went every single morning for four years and got better day by day. I also worked 28 to 30 hours in a rest home every single week.

God not only got me healed, but he gave me a future and the strength to fulfil it.

I am shortly returning to France, where I shall hope to tell people what God has done for me.

Anne-marie Duclos,
Normandy, France.

Footnote:
The college Anne-marie attended is the Charis College, Walsall, UK founded by Andrew Wommack, who described himself until 1968 as a self-righteous hypocrite and modern day Pharisee. "God's love consumed me", he says, and as a result he understood that he had been trying to earn God's love by good works and religious performance. He left college and was drafted into the US Army in Vietnam, on the front line, as a chaplain's assistant before becoming a Bible teacher in USA.

Andrew teaches that Christians, by the authority of Christ and the empowerment of the Holy Spirit, can miraculously heal and raise people from the dead; and he claims on his website that his younger son, Peter, was raised from the dead by the power of God on March 4, 2001. "My own son was raised up. He'd been dead for almost five hours, and had already turned black. His toe was tagged and he was lying on a slab in the hospital morgue. I've personally seen three people raised from the dead".

In 1989, during Hurricane Hugo, he received a commission to bring the message of God's Grace and Faith to the UK and as a result he opened the Walsall college, which by full time and correspondence courses equips people to bring God's supernatural ministry of healing and salvation to needy people. Anne-marie's healing is just one example of the ministry of this college.

I Became Closer and Found Jesus

Ever since I was a little girl at the age of four, I had believed in God and how He made Jesus to save our sins and He had done so many miraculous things.

I managed to grasp the story's and understand God's morals. But after 4 years of church, I heard someone call out to me, telling to move to a different church and help me to understand Jesus and become close to Him.

A few months later I did, it made me feel like I have a special relationship with Him, so special that words cannot explains how amazing it feels. To have a friend as sweet and understanding as Jesus has changed me.

It changed the way I looked at things, the way I feel about myself and He has comforted me and helped me when I am at my weakest. He makes me feel so unique and beautiful and He always reminds me that everyone is different and there is no need to bring myself down.

I am now a full Christian and I have a true passion for God and Jesus. I never was Christened when I was a child so I decided to be Christened at the age of ten (14th March 2010) and was baptised in the same year (10th of October 2010), ever since I was baptised I had felt like I had been reborn, it was a wonderful journey to truly bind myself to God and I do not regret it one bit!

I am thirteen now and I am about to start my GCSE's in September, I feel very uncertain about this because I slowly have been drifting further apart to Jesus. And I'm afraid that I won't ever be able to hear His voice again. But ever since last week I feel that I can feel Jesus in my heart reassuring me that everything will be fine. I prayed to Him the other day to help me with my parent's divorce, as it is a very hard time for me, and the amazing power of Jesus is that He made me feel better. This is how I became closer and found Jesus

Jasmine Sutton
Steeple Bumpstead, Essex

This is Something That Changed my Life

One day I was doing some baking in the kitchen with my brother and two sisters. We were making apricot cookies, (apricots are my favourite food) and we went into the living room to play a game to wait while they were cooking. They were meant to be cooked for ten minutes, and well, you can guess what happened. After half an hour we suddenly remembered and all rushed into the kitchen, and guess what? They were fine, ready to come out. They tasted fine too. This was my first miracle I had ever witnessed. I hope this does the same to you as it did to me.

Joshie West
aged 7

I Was Able to Bless and Encourage Others

Wildfire was happening again, this weekend, in fact today. To be more precise, in a matter of hours I would either be on a bus to Cambridge, with a rucksack, or I would be sitting at home with my family probably watching a movie. I cast my mind about a month back and recalled, with fondness, my first trip to a Wildfire event.

331

Wildfire is a Christian event organized by YWAM (Youth With A Mission), a Wildfire weekend was aimed at youth and families. You spend two nights there, arriving on Friday for prayer and worship, doing outreach on Saturday mostly, then more worship on Sunday at the church that you stay at.

The first time I had an opportunity to go, was in March 2013. It was the Thursday before we were to leave and despite the deadline for applications having passed, there was still a chance of catching a lift with our friend, Connie.

This month we were staying in Stafford, just north of Birmingham. We decided to pray, as one does when one finds oneself in a difficult dilemma. I, my brother Josh and my sister Jess went up to our room. "Let's pray to see what we ourselves should do, then share what God has said." We did. It seemed we should both go, but the decision was still hazy. "Now let's pray that God will tell us what the other person should do." said Jess. So we asked God what should happen. This time we heard Him more clearly, saying that yes, we should both go. God prepared the way for us from there right down to there being enough room in the boot of Connie's car for our luggage.

So there I was, in May now, wondering what I should do. Mum, Dad, Josh and Rach (my other sister) were definitely not going. Jess had her final two exams then her dissertation to write, before finishing her degree at Uni, so was slightly pre-occupied. It was up to me if I should go or not. It was difficult. When you have no job, £15 plus bus fare is quite a lot to spend all at once and it would be my first bus journey alone, there and back. We had also planned to spend part of the weekend together as a family. Besides, it was Dad's Birthday on

Sunday.

I decided to pray again, with Josh, in a similar way to last time. Unfortunately our spiritual ears were not finely tuned enough. By this point I was a little distressed and worried, so I decided to phone Grandma. Now, my Grandma is amazing, so sensible, encouraging and has such a positive outlook on life, which was just what I needed at that moment. I explained the situation to her and she replied with:
"I'm sure you'll have a wonderful time, you'll love it," she said, "You know what, I'm quite excited for you, Joely, I think it would be really good for you to do this on your own, just go for it!" Following this I spoke with Jess who looked at bus times with me. Within an hour or so I was on the bus to what would be a fun-filled, God-packed weekend away.

All it took was some encouraging words from family and friends and I felt that much better. Through them encouraging me I was able to bless and encourage others by my presence at Wildfire, Christian and non-Christian alike. So go encourage someone, if you're not already part of one, you may start a chain reaction.

Joel West
aged 15

In His Heart a Man Plans His Course, but The LORD Determines His Steps.
(Proverbs 16:9)

My life was well planned. Nursing career, meet Mr. Right, marry, start a large family, leave nursing, motherhood, grandmother-hood, and finally old age enjoying my extended family!

333

I'd become a Christian in 1980, and never dreamt 5 years later I would be invited on to the church staff of Holy Trinity Brompton to start a street ministry in Earl's Court, London, a ministry responding to AIDS, prostitution, drug addiction, alcoholism and homelessness. This totally new career change resulted from Jesus revealing how judgemental my attitude was towards people whose lifestyles were totally unfamiliar to my own. Rather grumpily I asked the Holy Spirit to change my heart, and within a few weeks the blinkers had been removed from my eyes, I began to see vulnerable people everywhere and longed to tell them about Jesus.

5 years later I was surprised again when I was invited to join the Chaplaincy team at HMP Holloway, the largest UK women's prison in London. Responding (albeit reluctantly) out of obedience to a prophetic word given to me - part of which said I would 'be a key unto many, whom themselves could no longer be free' - I still questioned the Lord as to why I was doing 'prison ministry'. Nevertheless, I visited the prison weekly, my heart breaking as I heard some of the stories from the people I met.

5 years later, I was asked to lead a team to introduce Alpha to HMP Exeter - never dreaming that visit was to be the start of Alpha for Prisons - today in 75% of the UK prisons - and in 68 nations worldwide.

Since 1995 I have had the privilege of visiting over 50% of the UK prisons to speak on Alpha or lead 3 day missions - including many to HMP Highpoint. *(in Suffolk – the nearest jail to Steeple Bumpstead!).*

The work has grown enormously and today the William Wilberforce Trust is the charity that governs all the

Social Transformation ministry at Holy Trinity, Brompton.

Responding again to some specific prophetic words, I now travel internationally to help train and equip prison Chaplains and volunteers to run Alpha for Prisons and to encourage and equip churches everywhere that we have a responsibility to care for ex offenders.

The biggest surprise came whilst doing some Prison Global Alpha Training in May 2011 in Gulu, northern Uganda. The area Bishop, Johnson Gakumba, had been the prison Chaplain of the huge men's prison in the capital, Kampala. I had met him in 2006 whilst speaking at an Alpha conference in Kampala and we had visited Lusira prison where he worked. He had seen how effective the Alpha course had been in introducing Christianity to the prisoners and was keen to train local church leaders and prison volunteers in his new Diocese in the north.

With nothing to indicate what he was about to say, on the second day of the training he said he would like to ordain me! Six months later I became the first European woman to be ordained in the northern Diocese, being given the title: 'Chaplain to the Worldwide Prisons'.

If I had been insistent in following what I thought was the best plan for my life, I would have missed out on the enormous privilege of introducing the Gospel to 100's of prisoners living with little hope of a future.

Today, many ex offenders are some of my greatest friends! I thank God for leading me to work in this amazing ministry, and continue to pray the Holy Spirit will encourage many more people to be sent out in to

His harvest field all around the world. There is still much work to do!

If you would like further information please visit the William Wilberforce Trust website: http:www.williamwilberforcetrust.org/

where you will find information on
• Prison Ministry Conference - November 8th 2013 - at Holy Trinity, Brompton.
• Prisons and Caring for Ex Offenders
• Alpha for Forces
• Cross Light Debt Advice
• Employability, Enterprise and Re-Use
• Addiction, Depression and Eating Disorders
• Drop in and Night Shelter
• Building Community for Single Parents and for Older People
• Counter trafficking
• Hospitality
• Kensington and Chelsea Food bank
• The Money Course
• Adoption, Fostering and Respite Care

Reverend Emmy Wilson
Holy Trinity Brompton | Brompton Road | London | SW7 1JA

"Thanks Be to God for His Inexpressible Gift."
2 Corinthians 9:15

Who would have thought it? Who ME? What? Almighty God who created the heavens and the earth and has the universe to run? Are you SERIOUS? He loves ME? Well, that is the greatest miracle of all.

There's another like it. It was Good Friday, and I was 16. The family was getting ready to go to chapel for the morning service. We had a youth club choir in those days, and I was trying, with chin on chest, to get down to the bottom bass lines in the hymns. The choir was behind the minister in the pulpit (not the best place to be when listening to a preacher). He told us about how Jesus died for us all – each one – that our sins might be forgiven and we could become children of God. The Gospel seed must have floated over his head and into my heart, because during the singing of the final hymn (When I survey the wondrous Cross), I knew Jesus had died for ME. He demanded my life, my soul, my all; and He had it that morning. From that moment on my life changed. I'm not sure from what, because I didn't know where it might have gone. I only knew that now I was going with Him.

The New Birth is the greatest of all miracles. Just a minute. Haven't I said that already? Yes – it's the same miracle – His Love and His Death and His Life poured out for me.

There's more! The Lord God made me what I am, and one Thursday evening in our youth club soon after that Good Friday, during the Epilogue our elderly minister was leading, and talking about living a holy life, my heart was filled to bursting with an overwhelming love for everybody! (What in the youth club? That was a miracle!) I realized that this God who showed Himself to me in Jesus is so wonderful and generous that He keeps on giving and giving. HIMSELF.

There's more! I sensed the call of God to preach the Gospel and enter the Ministry of the Methodist Church. Who me? I felt like Moses – "I can't speak; ask somebody else – like my brother Aaron here.   He's always talking").

So, I thought, I'm too shy?   I've led a sheltered life. I've been nowhere or met many people.   I can't do it.   BUT I DID, because He wouldn't take No for an answer, try as I might.   So, here I am, after forty years in the Ministry and nearly twenty in retirement – AND STILL PREACHING.   It's a miracle, that's what I call it.   And it gets better all the time.   Who, now, will ever shut me up?

There's more!! Many have been born again through the years.   What a mighty privilege that is! How the heart rejoices in seeing another soul saved from hell, just by believing in Jesus the Saviour and Lord.

There's more!!!   Heaven at last!   An eternal life with Jesus and the Father in the fellowship of the Spirit, living for His glory – that alone!

IT'S A MIRACLE.

RichardDavison
Darlington

God Is At Work Today

Today the Gospel Campaign here in Nairobi, Kenya came to a climax as **220,000 packed Uhuru Park to absolute capacity.** In fact, the venue was so full that unfortunately, many people were unable to get in. Those that were there however received a mighty blessing – including our whole team. What **a privilege it is to preach the Gospel** under any circumstances, but how much more to people who are **hungry, open and receptive**. Many thousands received Christ tonight and

338

many more were supernaturally healed. In fact I even heard that miracles were taking place during the preaching!

We heard the testimony of a woman who had HIV AIDS. After the prayer for those with HIV yesterday, she went for a blood test today and brought the diagnosis from the lab to the meeting tonight, I read it with my own eyes, **"HIV NEGATIVE!"**

One precious "mamma" was blind and **received her sight** tonight. She was overcome with emotion as she gave her testimony and we were all rejoicing with her.

A beautiful young lady had paralysis on her right side because of a stroke, but tonight she was **totally healed and praised the Lord** that now she can walk gracefully like she used to.

Another woman testified that she had breast cancer. Last night as the meeting was closing I told the people, "If you have not yet received your miracle, don't worry about it – many of you will be healed on your way home tonight." She said that as she was walking home, suddenly she felt a cold sensation come over her breast and she remembered what I had said. **She checked herself out and realized that everything was normal – she was healed!**

This week has been a very special week for all of us. I was so happy that my wife and my parents were also here with us along with a large group of guests from literally around the world. We are all rejoicing this week at what the Lord has done.

Evangelists Daniel Kolenda and Reinhard Bonnke
Christ for all Nations team

Footnote:

Reinhard Bonnke was born in Konigsburg, Germany. The son of a pastor, Reinhard gave his life to the Lord at age nine, and heard the call to the African mission field before he was even a teenager. After attending Bible College in Wales, and his ordination in Germany he pastored a church and then went on to start missionary work in Africa. It was there, in the small mountain kingdom of Lesotho, that God placed upon his heart the vision of an entire continent, from Cape Town to Cairo and from Dakar to Djibouti that needed to be reached and to hear the proclamation of the signs-following Gospel.

He began holding meetings in a tent that accommodated just 800 people, but, larger and larger tents had to be purchased, until finally, in 1984, he commissioned the world's largest mobile structure — a tent capable of seating 34,000 people! Soon, attendance exceeded this capacity and he began open-air Gospel Campaigns with an initial gathering of over 150,000 people per service! Since then, he has held city-wide meetings reaching as many as 1,600,000 people in single meeting using towering sound systems. It has now been some thirty-five years since Reinhard Bonnke founded Christ for all Nations (CfaN), which currently has offices in the United States, Canada, Germany, United Kingdom, Nigeria, South Africa, Singapore, Australia, and Hong Kong. He has now been joined by his grandson, Daniel.

7th May 2013 in Lagos, Nigeria

Last night, in my open air Miracle Explosion in Lagos, Nigeria a father brought his little daughter and told how she was deaf and mute from birth. He then proceeded to tell how after I prayed, he spoke her name and for the first time ever she turned and looked at him. We tested it and she could hear perfectly and repeated all she heard with me standing behind her to make sure she was not lip reading. Many others told how they too had been instantly healed. A young woman brought her twenty-four year old sister who was also born deaf and mute who instantly heard and spoke for the first time last night.

Tonight a man came forward along with his neighbour and his daughter telling how he was blind and how his neighbour had come to his home earlier today telling of all the miracles she had witnessed the previous night and inviting them to the service. His weeping seventeen year old daughter then told how her father was totally blind, but was instantly healed as I prayed. He demonstrated it to the excited crowd by touching my nose. Another man tonight was carried to the services, having been left paralyzed by a stroke several years ago. He testified that after I prayed he stood and walked for the first time since the stroke. Another woman who had previously not been able to walk, danced to demonstrate to the excited crowd how she had been healed. Witnessing the miracles, thousands are attending, the numbers are increasing every night with vast numbers flocking forward at the close of the service to receive Christ. Jesus truly is the same today!

8th May 2013 in Lagos, God Created a new Navel!

Nigeria Tonight's Lagos, Nigeria crusade service was the most amazing of all. God worked creative miracles in front of people's eyes. A woman came with a stomach bloated from fibroids which she described as making her look "8 months pregnant." She had been to many hospitals but they had no cure. She had attended both previous nights and went home last night and cried, "Lord, why am I not healed. Am I too big a sinner?" Then the first word of knowledge was for fibroids and her enlarged stomach instantly disappeared.

Next a teenage girl came forward and admitted she did not believe in miracles because she had a hole in her stomach instead of a navel, so that her intestines could be seen. The hospital had told her there was nothing they could do and because of the high risk of infection, she probably would not live long. She heard a voice that she believed was Jesus saying if she went to the crusade she would be healed. She told her sisters and they mocked her and did not believe, but they came anyway. I put my hand over the hole and said: "Lord weld it," and she was instantly healed. When I took my hand away, she had a perfectly formed naval as witnessed by all of the crowd. She and her two sisters fell to the ground weeping, her sister asked Jesus to forgive her for mocking what He had said. They screamed and sobbed like babies as they inspected the new navel where formerly the hole had been.

A man brought his 22 year old sister forward who had been totally insane since 2002. She ate from gutters and trash bins and was totally uncontrollable. He had taken her to hospitals and churches but nothing had helped. Then someone on the street handed him a brochure about my crusade. When he got home he put it on the table. The girl grabbed it and for the whole week wouldn't let go of it. So he brought her tonight, when I held a mass deliverance from bondages service. Instantly she was totally delivered and testified how she was set free and now in her right mind. She smiled as she told everyone her name was 'happiness' and now she was happy and free.

Dr Peter Gammons
formerly of Ramsey
Hunts
UK
www.petergammons.org. and www.pgmi.org

Old Jane – New Jane

I can remember being in Church one Sunday and our Pastor saying he sensed there was someone in Church that day who needed to have a talk with him. Further down our row, I heard someone agree!(or maybe it was God agreeing in my mind) . When I left Church that morning I remember saying that it was me who needed to see him. We talked over several things and after that I started to read the Bible and to learn from the books about the Bible that my husband had. Every day I felt more secure and at an Evening service we had in our church, our pastor spoke of the Cross and I could see myself standing before the Cross, all my past life with all its troubles and wrong doings on the left side and all the wonderful things to come on the right. At that point, I felt that I could be released from whatever had been holding me back and that I could now move forward. I knew that I wanted to be set free and that I had to ask God to do this for me. I knew too that I wanted to ask God into my life.

Two days later, I awoke in the early hours and heard these wonderful words:

"You will never be alone,
I will never leave you,
Don't worry about a thing,

343

I will always be there for you,
From now, this moment,
for ever and ever,
EVER and EVER
and EVER."

For the next few weeks it was like a roller coaster, and I had doubts about the wonderful words I had heard. I asked God what I should do about it and I sensed he wanted me to write the words in my Bible. I did this and I soon felt able to pray again.

A few weeks later, I was woken during the early hours with more wonderful words from God
"Walk with me, Walk with me" You can guess what my answer was!

Since then, I have become a much calmer, happier person and I know that God will always look after me, love me and guide me. I am now a new creation and I feel that "Old Jane" has become "New Jane".

"New Jane" felt different to "Old Jane". More patient when things went wrong, A lot more happier and more confident and peaceful and not worrying so much about what people said. I found I had more time in my life although I didn't now seem to have to rush about to get everything done. Also just wanting to learn more about Jesus and just having to go to Church whenever, whatever was on. My Husband told everyone he had a new wife! People who didn't know the Lord commented on how I had changed and seemed so much happier and content.

After an evening service, I could not sleep and sensed that I should think back over the Message. After tossing and turning, I decided a cup of tea might help me to think back over the previous evening's Service. As soon as I turned on the tap to fill the kettle, I had the picture of the Believer's Baptism come into my mind, which had been shown earlier at Church. I had the tea, and feeling peaceful, slept until morning. During the next day I really felt I had to find out more about Believer's Baptism, and within a short time, I knew this is what I should be doing, AND SOON! My husband and I were baptized, by total immersion, soon after.

I wouldn't want to think of a day when Jesus wasn't in my life, He has made me a new creation and I certainly wouldn't want to go back to the old way. I can tell Him all my troubles and He will always be there to lift me up and encourage me. How wonderful to think He is in my heart and therefore part of me. When I come to Him in times of stress He comforts me and gets me back on the right path again. How wonderful to know His forgiveness and that we can forgive people and choose not to remember all the old hurts.

Knowing Jesus gives me the reason to get up in the morning. I know He is always there with me, through the bad times when everything seems to go wrong – sometimes I have to seek to find Him and forget about *my* problems and then I feel His precious love for me. When I read the Bible, or just sitting quietly in Church, I feel such joy, and thanks to the Lord for saving me that it wells up and I either start crying or laughing or sometimes both. I find too, I really want to learn more about Jesus. Sometimes I think following Jesus is rather like following a piece of string, knowing that you must not loose sight of the end of it, not even for a moment, and to always keep it there in front of you. After all, Jesus knows what is best for us, even if we do not always see it for ourselves.

THANK GOD FOR SAVING ME and changing me from "Old Jane" into "New Jane"

Jane Stirling

How God's Love Helped me to Forgive my Mum

All my life, until my mother died, I had this dread when we went out to see people, or friends came over to us, that my Mother would tell the story with much laughter of the time I was taken as a baby only a few months old to a friend's house and left in my Parent's car asleep. When they returned to the car to check on me, they found me on the floor with the carrycot on top of me. I must add this was a long time ago now and long before the days of babies being in their own seats or strapped in. I was o.k. apart from yelling my head off and being rather cross. Of course I do not remember this happening but every time the story was told, even from a young age, I would feel upset and unloved. As the years went by and especially after my mother's death, I would keep remembering the story and after a few years I couldn't think of my Mum without remembering what she had done when I was small and this lead to any mention of Mum bringing tears to my eyes. I think this explains why I still won't go on the underground or a lift, I am afraid I will not be able to get out.

A few years ago, prompted by our Pastor during a service, I plucked up courage to speak about it, and to discuss it with him at a later time. My husband and I spent many late nights and wet hankies and I would unburden my innermost thoughts about my mum and dad as we went through the situation as it was and how it was affecting me and discovering that part of the problem was I had no idea why she thought it so

346

amusing to tell this story, and how unloved it made me feel, even when grown up.

I knew I must forgive Mum, and after a very tearful few minutes, managed to say out loud what I was feeling in my heart. – Just how much it had hurt me that she had left me alone in the car and also that I chose to forgive her and chose "not to remember" this anymore when I thought or spoke of Mum. I felt very empty but peaceful and I remember thinking "what comes next?" I felt sort of numb for the rest of the day, but the next day I started to remember some of the good times we had as a family, and I realised that the hurt was gradually disappearing and was being replaced with feeling of warmth and love towards her and I knew I could talk about her again without the hurt of the past creeping in. Little things started to come to mind of the happy times we had, the things we laughed about and I realised God was showing me just how much she had loved, and cared for me as a child. A few days after this, when I felt unwell and my husband was out for the evening, I longed for her to just walk in the room with a cup of tea. I knew that God has been working in this situation and He has replaced the hurt memories with the good and happy thoughts. I can see now that I chose to forgive her, - no-one said I had to. Over the years since, I have remembered so many wonderful memories of the times we had together and know that I was loved and wanted, and I can talk about her with love and I know that I could only have reached this point by asking God to help me, and I thank Him everyday for His grace to me and I have happy memories of my mum back in my life again.

Jane Stirling
Steeple Bumpstead, Essex

My Life Was Changed As I Read Psalm 40

At the age of 15 I got involved with drugs. First of all it was cannabis, then 'party drugs' but when I was 17 I was hooked on 'crack' cocaine and heroin. By the time I was 21 I had spent time in Glen Parva, Leicestershire and Dorchester prisons.

The turning point in my life came when my mother rang the prison and I had a visit from the prison chaplain who informed me that a good friend had committed suicide. I was devastated.

The Chaplain left me a Gideon New Testament and a Testimony book which I eventually read. My life was changed as I read Psalm 40:
'I waited patiently for the Lord; He turned to me and heard my cry.
He lifted me out of the slimy pit, out of the mud and mire;
He put my feet upon a Rock and gave me a firm place to stand
He put a new song in my mouth, a hymn of praise to our God.
Many will see and fear and put their trust in the Lord.'

After my release, I found a new life. I attended Bible College, finishing there in 2008. I started working with young people in the church, helping them to avoid the mistakes I made in my life. I got married.

Finally, a way opened for me to become one of the pastors of Victory Church, Cwmbran. We have an outreach to prisoners called Victory Outreach UK and over 80 of those prisoners who have found God are in our church, which numbers around 400 and is still growing. The church is only three years old and meets in an unimpressive factory building.

We are experiencing an unusual move of God at present and are holding meetings four nights a week with our 450 seater church full and overflowing. On a Saturday night have our overflow hall full as well, with as many as 700 people hearing God's word and witnessing His works. I have written an account of what is happening here.

Clyde Thomas
Victory Church
Cwmbran

A New Move of God in Wales! Summer, 2013

On the 10th April 2013, our mid-week "Encounter" meeting was in full flow, there were probably about 70 people in attendance and the layout of the auditorium had been changed that very day to make better use of the space. Pastor Richard Taylor preached a message from the book of Esther with the pulpit on the floor, because the stage was at the other end of the room!

As he preached, expectancy seemed to flood into the room, faith levels were high, and people were invited to bring their enemy (sickness, sin, marital, debt problems etc) into the presence of the King. Within moments people filled the front area and prayer was offered.

Paul has been a part of Victory Church for approximately 18 months and had only attended the meeting that night after his wife had persuaded him to go. He felt tired and has since said to me, 'I nearly stayed home'. After sitting in the meeting, his wife encouraged him 'this could be your night, go and get prayer'. He pushed himself in his wheelchair to the front where Pastor Richard was praying.

Paul had been wheelchair bound for ten years before that nightmare ended on 10th April 2013. He received prayer and Pastor Richard declared the word strength over his legs and prayed fervently. Standing right next to him, I watched Paul's legs strengthen, they began to shake violently and within moments, he leapt to his feet, picked up his chair (above his head) and ran around the church!

The place went absolutely bonkers! Our eyes were on sticks at what we had just witnessed. I've witnessed healing before, and prayed for sick people and seen them healed, but this was another level. Paul was instantly healed, his leg grew approximately 2cms and he could not only walk, but he could run! He had picked a very heavy wheelchair up (that I can barely lift) and ran with it above his head. No one who witnessed what Jesus had done that night can deny that this indeed was the Book of Acts in action today.

The praise that erupted that night was incredible. For a space of time – I can't qualify exactly how long – everyone was just completely lost in praise and adoration. God was here. God was in the room. We weren't just saying it, we weren't just believing it. He was actually here, His presence was manifest thickly.

The very next morning, I was driving to church when the Lord spoke to my heart. The words 'I have entered in and I am the King of Glory' rang in my heart. The barriers had been broken and His presence was thick and manifest throughout the building. Pastor Andrew had stayed at the church throughout the night, praying and seeking God. When I arrived, he was already praying for everyone who entered the building. One after another, people were receiving a fresh encounter with Jesus and lay prostrate on the floor, unable to stand because of His presence. It was an incredible sight.

God is not limited to our programmes and agendas, He is bigger than our events and meetings, in fact I think that often God is repulsed by our dependence on these things! What we have witnessed, and are continuing to witness here in Cwmbran, is a sovereign move of God. Meetings are never closed, and we expect God to meet with people at anytime of the day or night.

Within days, news spread fast of this outpouring and it seemed to go viral. Now, nearly one month on, it's building up pace, increasingly people are returning with a bus load of people after visiting early on to check out what was going on. It's humbling to see ministers from all sorts of churches coming and receiving something fresh from God! Many have reported dramatic changes in their own settings! One such church based in Horsham, has reported that their men's prayer meeting jumped from 3 people to 20 this week and an unsaved gentleman was saved during the prayer meeting!

Unsaved souls are finding Christ in vast numbers, and whole families are being transformed. Many families and individuals in Victory Church have seen their loved ones saved as a result of this outpouring.

There are 8 A4 pages worth of miracles so far and that only includes what we have had direct report from the individuals on. We ask people to have their healings medically verified before writing in. Many miracles have taken place in the foyer, on the car park, or in the meetings, but God is certainly not constrained. We are hosting the Holy Spirit, Jesus is at the wheel and the Father's love is reaching many.

Young people are finding freedom in Christ and connecting with God enthusiastically. Largely un-churched, unsaved young people have been transformed after encountering the Holy Spirit, many have got up off the floor saying, 'I need Jesus!' Many of these young people are already sharing their new found faith with friends and relatives and seeing the power of the gospel at work in their world!

Jesus is at work and we give Him all the glory for what He has done!
> The Welsh Outpouring continues!

Clyde Thomas
Cwmbran
office@vouk.org.uk

Footnote:
This is one of about 3 major moves of God in Wales at present. The Cwmbran pastor Richard Taylor, also an ex-prisoner preached at Horsham, Sussex and 200 people were unable to get into a large church there. A church in Whitby, North Yorkshire has also been experiencing an unusual presence of God for some while now and has been holding extra weekday meetings to accommodate visitors. God is responding to the call of His people to come and move in our UK. Just before this book went to the printer in mid-June, we heard that : "We are so excited at what God is doing. Initially, many people were reluctant to accept that God had broken through, but 65 days on, it is undeniable that God is moving sovereignly. We have now seen 642 Salvations and have 15 pages of healing testimonies!

Visitors have continued to pour in from across the globe and we are grateful to God for the opportunity of hosting His presence is such a way. We as a church, as people have been dramatically impacted and found ourselves drawn much deeper with Him.

People ask, "is what's happening a revival?" Our response, thus far, is that what we are seeing here in Wales is an Outpouring of God's Spirit.

On Wednesday night we had the privilege of baptising another thirty people all who have come to faith during the Outpouring! We praise God for this, He is building His Church.

Last night we had people asking, "can I share what God has done with tears in their eyes...." One lady shared how she had an abortion and had been promiscuous in her teens, she had lived in shame for several years, now at 24 she felt so dirty. She testified that she was set free from all shame last night. Her heart was put back together.

Another young girl, Lucy, who we have spoken about in previous posts, shared her story of how God delivered her from serious self harming. Now glowing, she described how three weeks ago she came forward and surrendered her life and all of herself. She felt God lift it all from her, she hasn't self harmed since.
Then there was April, who shared how her daughter who had serious, incurable eye problems was prayed for a few weeks ago, yesterday she was at the hospital and the doctor was stunned, 'there couldn't have been anything wrong with her eyesight!' But there was, and the incurable condition was on her records. The doctor was speechless. April got to church last night and

bumped into the very nurse that she had been with at the hospital that day!

There has not been one single night where people have not surrendered their lives to Christ! We give God all the glory!"

From: http://www.victorychurch.co.uk/category/news

And finally.......................

My hope is that you have been inspired while reading these Testimonies, which were written by ordinary people telling of God's extra-ordinary work in their lives today.

If you would like to see your own Christian Testimony in a possible new Book of Testimonies, please send them, preferably by email, to: Christopher Stirling, address details on page 4.

All Glory be to the Father,
and to the Son and to the Holy Spirit,
As it was in the beginning,
is now and
ever shall be,
Amen.